ZEN AND COMPARATIVE STUDIES

Zen and Comparative Studies

Part Two of a Two-Volume Sequel to *Zen and Western Thought*

Masao Abe

Edited by
Steven Heine

UNIVERSITY OF HAWAI'I PRESS
HONOLULU

Published in North America by
University of Hawai'i Press
2840 Kolowalu Street
Honolulu, Hawai'i 96822

First published in the United Kingdom by
Macmillan Press Ltd
Houndmills
Basingstoke, Hampshire, RG21 6XS
England

Printed in Great Britain

Library of Congress Cataloging-in-Publication Data
Abe, Masao, 1915–
Zen and comparative studies : part two of a two-volume sequel to
Zen and Western thought / Masao Abe ; edited by Steven Heine.
p. cm.
Includes index.
ISBN 0–8248–1831–8 (alk. paper). — ISBN 0–8248–1832–6 (pbk. :
alk. paper)
1. Zen Buddhism—Doctrines.   2. Philosophy, Comparative.
3. Buddhism and philosophy.   I. Heine, Steven, 1950–   .   II. Abe,
Masao, 1915–   Zen and Western thought.   III. Title.
BQ9268.7.A33   1996
294.3'42—dc20   96–7546
                                                        CIP

Contents

PART FOUR   ZEN AND JAPANESE CULTURE

Foreword

Steven Heine

This is the second volume of a two-volume sequel to the award-winning *Zen and Western Thought* (1985) by Masao Abe, the leading exponent of Japanese Buddhism in the West since the death of D. T. Suzuki and one of the major contemporary representatives of the Kyoto School of Japanese philosophy founded by Nishida Kitarō. At the time of the publication of the original volume, Abe had for twenty years been lecturing at numerous American universities, including Chicago, Columbia, Princeton, Hawaii, and Claremont, and publishing in a variety of English-language journals of Buddhist studies and comparative religions, including *Buddhist–Christian Studies, The Eastern Buddhist, International Philosophical Quarterly, Japanese Religions, Journal of Chinese Philosophy, Numen, Philosophy East and West,* and *Scottish Journal of Religious Studies,* among many other scholarly outlets.

The central purpose underlying the collection of essays in *Zen and Western Thought,* edited by William R. LaFleur, is a clarification of the authentic spirit of Zen in light of the history of Buddhist thought and through critical comparisons with Western philosophy and religion. The book is divided into four parts: Zen and Its Elucidation; Zen, Buddhism, and Western Thought; Three Problems in Buddhism; and Religion in the Present and the Future. In each part, Abe draws on the Mahāyāna doctrine of emptiness (*śūnyatā*) as expressed in a uniquely spontaneous, paradoxical fashion by classical Zen masters such as Lin-chi, Chao-chou, and Dōgen as well as his own mentor Hisamatsu Shin'ichi. Abe refutes several common misconceptions, including the views that Zen represents an anti-intellectualism or nihilism, and he contrasts the Zen approach to emptiness with the notions of Western philosophers which seem quite similar, such as Nietzsche's creative nihilism, Whitehead's process philosophy, and Tillich's 'courage to be' in the face of non-being. Through a comparative methodology, Abe constructs Zen philosophy as a spiritual foundation for humanity facing a critical turning point in history. He carefully explains that the notion of emptiness is not merely a form of negation in contrast to affirmation but a 'double negation' that negates and thereby surpasses the polarity between affirmation and negation.

Emptiness thus serves as a basis for a radical realism and a compassionate way of life which can function as a new dynamic and flexible cosmology for the global age.

After the publication of *Zen and Western Thought*, Abe published several volumes, including: his editing of a collection of essays in remembrance of D. T. Suzuki (*D. T. Suzuki: A Zen Life Remembered*, 1986); a translation with Christopher Ives of Nishida's first work (*Kitarō Nishida: An Inquiry into the Good*, 1990); his serving as the main contributor for a collection of essays on interfaith dialogue with eminent Western theologians (*The Emptying God: A Buddhist–Jewish–Christian Conversation*, 1990, edited by Ives and John Cobb); and his collected papers on Dōgen's philosophy of time, Buddha-nature, and the oneness of practice-attainment in comparison with Heidegger and Shinran (*A Study of Dōgen: His Philosophy and Religion*, 1992, edited by Steven Heine). As this is going to press, Abe is scheduled to publish a collection of his lectures in Japanese for the FAS Society, *'Kongen kara no shuppatsu'* (Departure from the Root-source), and a sequel to *The Emptying God* entitled *Divine Emptiness and Historical Fullness: A Buddhist–Jewish–Christian Conversation with Masao Abe* edited by Ives. Also, Donald Mitchell is compiling an anthology, *'Masao Abe: His Life of Dialogue,'* which will be a record of his dialogical activities in Japan and the West for the past four decades.

When Abe and I began planning the sequel to *Zen and Western Thought* at the request of Professor John Hick and Macmillan, we quickly realized that there was simply too much valuable material to contain in a single volume and we decided that it should be divided instead into several volumes. (In addition to the two-volume sequel, Abe is preparing a third volume, *A Study of the Philosophy of the Kyoto School*, edited by James Fredericks, which will contain his explications and interpretations of Nishida and Hisamatsu as well as Tanabe Hajime and Nishitani Keiji.) The first sequel, *Buddhism and Interfaith Dialogue* (1995), highlights Abe's participation in continuing ideological encounter and dialogue with a number of the most prominent Western theologians of the last half of the twentieth century representing a wide range of positions, including existential, mystical, process, kenotic, liberation and feminist theologies. The first and still the most important figure with whom Abe engaged in dialogue was Paul Tillich, the focus of one of the three sections in the volume. The remainder of the volume contains the record of his remarkable exchanges with Thomas Altizer, John Cobb, John Egan, Langdon Gilkey, Paul Knitter, Hans Küng and Marjorie Suchocki.

According to Abe, the forces of modernization, secularization and technologization continue to undermine traditional forms of religiosity while at the same time compelling a vibrant, mutually challenging encounter between Buddhism and Christianity, East and West, in pursuit of a universal and unifying global ideology that is also faithful to the integrity and the innate dissimilarities between the respective traditions.

The current volume returns to the basic structure and methodology of *Zen and Western Thought* in exploring the fundamentals of Zen religious experience, Zen and Western philosophy, current methodological issues in Zen studies, and the relation between Zen and Japanese culture and spirituality. Part One demonstrates the historical and ideological connections between Śākyamuni's basic doctrine of dependent co-origination and the Mahāyāna notion of emptiness, particularly as expressed in the Mādhyamika school and the *Prajñāpāramitā Sūtras,* which serve as the background for the Zen view of *Nirvāṇa* realized in each and every impermanent moment (*setsuna-soku-nehan*). Abe contrasts the Zen experiential approach to emptiness with Western monotheistic notions of an objectifiable, transcendental theology which tend to generate dualities, and he stresses how Zen is based on an intensely subjective realization of Awakening, which overcomes polarities between knowing and speaking, living and dying, being and non-being, good and evil, the momentary and continuity, natural and supernatural and *Nirvāṇa* and *saṃsāra*.

The second part critically explores affinities and divergences with Western thinkers from Plato and Aristotle to Whitehead and Jung, each of whom in his own way tends to privilege being, substance, eternity, and enduring selfhood in contrast to the Zen emphasis on emptiness, insubstantiality, impermanence, and selflessness. Part Three, greatly influenced by Hisamatsu's philosophy of the FAS movement, demonstrates that Zen is neither a museum curiosity nor a disengaged method of contemplation. Rather, Zen, if properly interpreted, offers a viable approach for resolving contemporary social problems by virtue of the Bodhisattva's compassionate sense of commitment and responsibility based on the non-duality of self and world. In a historical era defined by pluralism, the flexibility of Zen's non-sustantive, non-dualistic philosophy can function as a paradigm for a tolerant, open-ended discourse required of all ideologies, whether religious, philosophical, scientific, or secular, seeking to overcome dogmatic, one-sided insistence.

Finally, Part Four examines the development of Zen in the context of Japanese religiosity marked by an interplay and syncretism between Buddhism and Shinto from the time Shōtoku Taishi introduced Buddhism into Japan through the development of the Kyoto School. In particular, Abe shows how Zen's formation in Japan during the Kamakura era in which samurai culture came to be dominant gave rise to a different approach emphasizing both ascetic discipline and aesthetic expression than is found in the Ch'an school in Sung China. It this section, as throughout the book and indeed his entire *oeuvre*, Abe makes a twofold plea for a better understanding of Zen on the part of the West and for an enhanced approach by Zen based on a critical self-reflective stance inspired by its encounter with the West.

ACKNOWLEDGMENTS

The material in this volume was originally written or presented in a variety of journals or at conferences. The following list explains the initial appearance of each chapter:

Chapter 1, 'Zen and Buddhism', appeared in *The Eastern Buddhist*, 26/1 (1993), pp. 26–49, based on a paper delivered as the Charles Gooding Lecture at the Divinity School of the University of Chicago in 1969 and edited with the assistance of W. S. Yokoyama. The author is indebted to Hisamatsu Shin'ichi's essay, 'Zen: Its Meaning for Modern Civilization,' *The Eastern Buddhist*, vol. 1, no. 1 (1965).
Chapter 2, 'The Core of Zen: The Ordinary Mind is Tao', was previously unpublished.
Chapter 3, ' "Life and Death" and "Good and Evil" in Zen', appeared in *Criterion*, 9/1 (1969), pp. 7–11, based on a paper delivered as the Charles Gooding Lecture at the Divinity School of the University of Chicago in 1969.
Chapter 4, 'Emptiness', is from *Our Religions*, ed. Arvind Sharma (San Francisco: HarperSan Francisco, 1993), pp. 114–24.
Chapter 5, 'God, Emptiness, and the True Self', appeared in *The Eastern Buddhist*, 11/2 (1969), pp. 15–30; and in *The Buddha Eye*, ed. Frederick Franck (New York: Crossroad, 1982), pp. 61–74.
Chapter 6, 'The Concept of Self as Reflected in Zen Buddhist Literature', appeared in *Wind Bell*, 22/1 (1988), pp. 3–9.
Chapter 7, 'Education in Zen', appeared in *The Eastern Buddhist*, 9/2

(1976), pp. 64–70, based on a paper delivered at the World Congress on Buddhism and the Modern World held at Dongguk University in Seoul, Korea in September 1976. The author is grateful to Mr and Mrs Peter Schneider for their revision of the manuscript.

Chapter 8, 'Substance, Process, and Emptiness: Aristotle, Whitehead, and Zen', appeared in *Japanese Religions*, 11/2–3 (1980), pp. 3–34.

Chapter 9, 'The Problem of Death in East and West: Immortality, Eternal Life, Unbornness', appeared in *The Eastern Buddhist*, 19/1 (1986), pp. 30–61, trans. David Dilworth, based on a paper originally published in Japanese in the journal *Zengaku kenkyū* (Studies in Zen Buddhism), 51 (1961), pp. 88–112. The author is grateful to Professor Dilworth and to Professor Christopher A. Ives and Professor Paul L. Swanson for their valuable suggestions in the final stages of manuscript preparation.

Chapter 10, *Śūnyatā* as Formless Form: Plato and Mahāyāna Buddhism', appeared in *Avaloka*, 11/1 (1987), pp. 22–9.

Chapter 11, 'The Self in Jung and Zen', *The Eastern Buddhist*, 18/1 (1985), pp. 57–70; and in *Self and Liberation: The Jung/Buddhism Dialogue*, ed. David J. Meckel and Robert L. Moore (New York: Paulist Press, 1992), pp. 128–40.

Chapter 12, 'Time in Buddhism' was previously unpublished.

Chapter 13, 'On the Occasion of Buddha Day 1990: The Future Task of Buddhism', *Pacific World*, 7 (1991), 96–9, based on a lecture at the University of California at Berkeley in May 1990.

Chapter 14, 'Transformation in Buddhism', appeared in *Buddhist–Christian Studies*, 7 (1987), pp. 5–24, based on a paper delivered at the second Buddhist–Christian Theological Encounter at Vancouver School of Theology, March 1985. The author is grateful to Professor Samuel I. Shapiro for his revision and valuable suggestions.

Chapter 15, 'Religious Tolerance and Human Rights: A Buddhist Perspective', appeared in *Religious Liberty and Human Rights in Nations and Religions*, ed. Leonard Swidler (Philadelphia: Ecumenical Press, 1986), pp. 193–211.

Chapter 16, 'Shinto and Buddhism: The Two Major Religions of Japan', appeared in the *Scottish Journal of Religious Studies*, VIII/1 (1987), pp. 53–63.

Chapter 17, 'Zen in Japan', is from *Zen in China, Japan, East Asian Art*, eds H. Brimlar, R. P. Kramus, C. Ouwehand (Berne: Peter Lang, 1984), pp. 47–64.

Chapter 18, 'The Japanese View of Truth', appeared in *Japanese Religions*, 14/3 (1986), pp. 1–6.

We thank the following parties for permission to reprint this material: the editor of *The Eastern Buddhist* for Chapters 1, 5, 7, 9, 11 (also the Nanzan Institute for Chapter 5 and Paulist Press for Chapter 11); the editor of *Criterion* for Chapter 3, HarperSan Francisco for Chapter 4; the editor of *Wind Bell* for Chapter 6; the editor of *Japanese Religions* for Chapters 8 and 18; the editor of *Avaloka* for Chapter 10; the editor of *Pacific World* for Chapter 13; the editor of *Buddhist–Christian Studies* for Chapter 14; Leonard Swidler for Chapter 15; the editor of *Scottish Journal of Religious Studies* for Chapter 16; and Peter Lang Publishers for Chapter 17. (Chapters 2 and 12 were previously unpublished.)

Finally, as in the case of editing *Buddhism and Interfaith Dialogue*, I greatly appreciate the efforts of the editors at Macmillan, and I am especially thankful for the opportunity to assist Masao Abe in the collection and dissemination of his eminently valuable work on Zen Buddhist and comparative studies.

Preface

Not relying on words or letters,
An independent self-transmitting apart from any teaching;
Directly pointing to the human Mind,
Awakening one's Original Nature, thereby actualizing
    Buddhahood.

This expression, attributed to Bodhidharma, captures the fundamental significance of Zen theory and practice in the context of
Buddhist thought and the field of religion in general. Almost all
forms of Buddhism, especially in East Asia, rely on a certain *sūtra* or
scripture as the source of truth. According to this standpoint, that
which has no basis in scriptural authority cannot be called truth.
Thus, almost all forms of Buddhism may be referred to as schools of
'Buddha's word.' By contrast, Zen does not rely on words or letters
and directly points to one's mind as the universal Buddha Mind, and
that is why Zen has sometimes been referred to as the school
of 'Buddha mind.' This implies that Mind is self-transmitting
independent of any particular *sūtra* or doctrinal teaching.

Due to this trans-linguistic, trans-scriptural character, the notion of
'comparative studies' with regard to Zen may seem quite alien.
However, in the modern age, comparative studies is extremely
important in understanding the nature of world philosophy of
religion, and this approach can and must also be applied to an
elucidation of Zen. The traditional Zen standpoint beyond words
should be framed and analyzed in light of cultural history and
comparative philosophy. The title of this collection of essays, which I
wrote over a period of two decades, highlights the sharp contrast and
conflict as well as the areas of compatibility and complementarity
between Zen and comparative studies. In Part One, Fundamentals of
Zen, I elucidate the meaning of Zen as a self-transmission of mind in
its own terms. These essays take up the topics of 'ordinary mind is
Tao,' life and death and good and evil, emptiness, selfhood, and
education. On the other hand, in the essays in Part Two, Zen,
Buddhism, and Western Thought, I situate Zen in a comparative
philosophical context thought discussions of the Aristotelian notion

of Substance, Whitehead's notion of process, and Plato's idea of Form (eidos). Focusing on the problem of death, the article on 'The Problem of Death in the East and West' tries to elucidate the essential characters of Platonism, Christianity and Buddhism, especially Zen, through a systematic comparative approach.

In Part Three, Current Issues in Buddhism, I pick up a number of contemporary topics such as monotheism versus monism, time and self, human rights and religious tolerance from the angle of comparative studies. Finally, Part Four, Zen and Japanese Culture, attempts to clarify the role of Zen in terms of the intellectual history of Japan from ancient literature and Tokugawa Shinto thought to modern philosophy.

Part One
Fundamentals of Zen

1
Zen and Buddhism

INTRODUCTION

'Is Zen a form of Buddhism?' The answer to this question would have to be in both the affirmative and the negative at the same time. In the affirmative because, historically speaking, Zen is conceived as a form of Buddhism founded by Bodhidharma in China in the sixth century. As it developed in China, Korea and Japan, it acquired the trappings of a religious order, with its own temples, rituals, and robes. In this sense, Zen can be called a particular form of Buddhism standing alongside other forms of Buddhism, such as the T'ien-t'ai (Tendai), the Hua-yen (Kegon), the Chen-yen (Shingon) and the Ching-t'u (Jōdo) sects. Further, in terms of its teaching and practice, Zen, in the course of its long history, has come to generate its own particular doctrines and methods comparable to those of the other schools. We may call this form of Zen 'traditional Zen.'

At the same time, the question, 'Is Zen a form of Buddhism?' must be answered in the negative, for Zen, we would assert, is not merely one particular form of Buddhism, but rather, in a fundamental sense, the basic source of all forms of Buddhism. This idea is well expressed in the Zen statement, 'Zen is the integrating storehouse of the Buddha-dharma.' Alluded to here is the all-encompassing dimension of 'Zen itself,' that is, Zen that is at once Buddhism itself. The Zen claim to be the root-source of all forms of Buddhism can be seen in the following classic formulations:

Furyū-mōji 不立文字 not relying on words or letters;
Kyōge-betsuden 教外別伝 an independent transmission apart from the scriptural doctrine or any teaching;
Jikishi-ninshin 直指人心 directly pointing to the human Mind; and
Kenshō-jōbutsu 見性成佛 awakening to one's Original Nature, thereby actualizing one's own Buddhahood.

Since these formulations clarify the Zen position as distinguished from other forms of Buddhism, it is important to elucidate their

3

meaning. However, before we can do so and, most important, before
we can consider why Zen is called the very root-source of all forms of
Buddhism, a review of the nature and development of Buddhism is in
order.

THE NATURE AND DEVELOPMENT OF BUDDHISM

To review the nature of Buddhism it would be helpful to clarify the
similarity and difference between the terms 'Buddha' and 'Christ.'

The affinity between 'Buddha' and 'Christ'

What we today call Buddhism has its origins in the teachings of
Śākyamuni Buddha, who lived in northeastern India between 560
and 480 BC. 'Śākyamuni' means 'the sage from the Śākya tribe.' His
family name was Gautama, his given name, Siddhartha, meaning 'He
whose aim will be accomplished.' After his Enlightenment,
Siddhartha Gautama came to be called the Buddha by his disciples,
meaning 'Enlightened One' or 'Awakened One.' What was it to
which he became awakened? To Dharma – to the law of the universe,
that is, the law of dependent co-origination. The Buddha realized that
everything in the universe is co-arising and co-ceasing; that
everything is interdependent with each other; that nothing exists
independently; that nothing has its own enduring, fixed being. In
other words, the term 'Buddha' indicates one who has awakened to
this Law. Unlike the proper nouns 'Gautama' and 'Siddhartha,' the
term 'Buddha' is a generic term or title, which applies not only to
Siddhartha Gautama, but to anyone who has awakened to the
Dharma, the law of dependent co-origination.

In this sense, the term 'Buddha' shares an affinity to the term
'Christ.' In Christianity, one speaks of 'Jesus Christ.' 'Jesus' is the
given name of the carpenter's son born to Mary at Nazareth at the
beginning of the Christian era. It is the Latinized form of the Hebrew
word for 'Joshua,' meaning 'God will save.' 'Christ,' however, is a
common noun meaning 'the Anointed One,' referring to the Messiah
whose appearance is prophesied in the Old Testament. The term
being such, 'Christ' is applicable not only to Jesus of Nazareth, but
also to anyone deemed qualified to be called 'the Anointed One.' The
Jews, for instance, do not call Jesus of Nazareth 'Christ,' simply
because they do not regard him as *the* Messiah – although many of

them regard him as a prophet. Only those who admit Jesus *as* the Christ are properly to be called Christians. Later, 'Christ' gradually came to be applied as a proper noun, that is, as part of the name of 'Jesus Christ.' Originally, though, the term 'Christ,' like the term 'Buddha,' was not a proper noun, but a generic name or title.

I understand that Paul Tillich has coined the phrase 'Jesus *as* the Christ' to express the essential relationship between Jesus of Nazareth and the Christ as the long-awaited Messiah. Buddhists might well follow Tillich's example to refer to Siddhartha Gautama *as* the Buddha. At any rate, we can detect here a certain parallel between Gautama as the Buddha and Jesus as the Christ.

The disparity between 'Buddha' and 'Christ'

A great disparity exists, however, between the terms 'Buddha' and 'Christ.' In Christianity, the title 'Christ' properly applies only to Jesus of Nazareth. In Buddhism, on the other hand, the title 'Buddha' can legitimately be applied not only to Siddhartha Gautama, but to anyone who attains enlightenment to the Dharma. Thus, in Buddhism, there are many Buddhas – indeed, too many to count. This difference arises for the following reasons: first, in Christianity, 'Christ' is the Messiah, a figure endowed with a divine character, hence it would necessarily be the case that the term is an exclusive one and cannot be ascribed to just anyone. In Buddhism, however, the 'Buddha' refers to one who awakens to the Dharma, an awakening that lies within the realm of possibility of all human beings. Second, in Christianity, Jesus as the Christ is the Son of God, the *only* incarnation of God in the history of the world; consequently, his historical existence is essential as the final revelation of God. Again, Tillich employs the term *final* revelation to refer specifically to Jesus Christ. He recognizes the possibility of preliminary revelation or partial revelation outside of Jesus Christ, but insists that Jesus Christ is the *final* revelation, indicating that he is the *last, genuine and decisive* revelation. In Buddhism, by contrast, Siddhartha Gautama does not hold the exclusive role of being the only Enlightened One to appear in human history. In a sense, Siddhartha's historical existence could be said to be far less essential to the Buddhist religion as the Dharma he realized.

A comparison of relevant Buddhist and Christian sayings may serve to underscore the similarities and differences between the Buddha and Christ. The first set shows their similarities; the second set sets forth their essential difference. The first set is as follows:

GAUTAMA BUDDHA: 'Who sees Dharma, sees me. Who sees me, sees Dharma. Because it is by seeing Dharma that one sees me, it is by seeing me that one sees Dharma.' (*Saṃyutta-nikāya*, 22.87; this is not Gautama's own saying, but a passage from one of the oldest Buddhist scriptures.)

JESUS CHRIST: 'If you had known me, you would have known my Father also; henceforth you know him and have seen him.' (John 14:7); and 'He who has seen me has seen the Father; how can you say, "Show us the Father?" ' (John 14:9)

In this set of sayings we can see a striking affinity between Gautama and Jesus in identifying themselves with the Dharma and God the Father, respectively. Both of them strongly emphasize their identity with Dharma or Father. In the second set of quotations, however, we realize a remarkably different aspect of these identities. The second set reads as follows:

GAUTAMA BUDDHA: 'Regardless of the appearance or non-appearance of the Tathāgata (Śākyamuni Buddha) in this world, the Dharma is always present.' (*Saṃyutta-nikāya*, vol. 12)

JESUS CHRIST: 'I am the Way, and the Truth and the Life. No one comes to the Father, but by me.' (John 14:7)

As this quotation indicates, the identity of Jesus Christ with God the Father is unique to him, realized only by him and not by anyone else. He is the *sole* incarnation of God and the mediator between God and human beings. On the other hand, Gautama Buddha's identity with Dharma is not unique to him, not realized by him alone, but can be realized by anyone. He is not the sole mediator between Dharma and his fellow beings. In marked contrast to the Christian understanding of Jesus Christ who is *the* center of history as well as *the* final revelation of God, Gautama Buddha is neither *the* center of history, nor *the* final revelation, nor *the* final awakening.

The position of the historical Buddha in Buddhism

What position, then, does Siddhartha as the Buddha hold in Buddhism? He may be said to be the *first* person to awaken to the

Dharma and thereby become a Buddha, the first to realize *what* the Dharma is, the first to realize with his total existence the way to realize the Dharma. For these reasons he is called the founder of Buddhism. Essentially, though, anyone can become a Buddha, just as Siddhartha did, if one follows the same path, and in fact, it is incumbent that one do so in so far as one is a Buddhist. In this sense, Buddhism is not only comprised of the teachings of the Buddha, but can rightly be characterized as the 'teaching of becoming a Buddha.' On the other hand, though Christianity contains the teachings of Christ, it can never be called the 'teaching of becoming a Christ.'

This disparity is seen also in the medieval Christian spirituality of *imitatio Christi*, and especially the doctrines of baptism and Eucharist. A Christian becomes one with Christ as Christ is one with the Father through the sacramental union with Christ in baptism and in the Eucharist. The Christ with whom the Christian becomes one represents the only genuine and decisive revelation and stands at the center of history. To become one with the Christ means to *participate* in Him, not to become Christ. Therefore, one does not become one with Christ in the same way that one becomes a Buddha.

The Buddha's disciples clearly assumed they could never stand on a spiritual par with their teacher Śākyamuni. For them it seemed unconscionable even to entertain the notion they would ever experience the complete enlightenment Śākyamuni had. No matter how far they progressed in their ascetic practices, they thought the highest goal attainable was the stage of the Arhat, literally, 'the Worthy.' Though becoming an Arhat was short of becoming a 'Buddha,' this, for them, especially in the Theravāda Buddhist tradition, represented the final stage of spiritual progress. Mahāyāna Buddhism, however, took the Buddha's teaching to heart and developed various ways for one to become a Buddha.

The fact that Siddhartha as the Buddha, Śākyamuni Buddha, is neither the only Buddha, the center of history, nor the final Awakening to the Dharma, was clearly and impressively expressed by Śākyamuni himself. Shortly before his death, seeing the anxious look of those surrounding him on his deathbed, Śākyamuni addressed Ananda, one of his ten great disciples, as follows:

O Ananda, be ye lamps unto yourselves. Rely on yourselves and do not rely on external help. Live the Dharma as a lamp. Seek salvation alone in the Dharma. Look not for assistance to anyone besides yourselves.

Obviously, when he said to his disciples, 'Do not rely on external help,' and 'Look not for assistance to anyone besides yourselves' he was including himself among those he referred to as 'external help' and 'anyone besides yourselves' – this despite the fact that he had been their teacher for many years. Less apparent is the significance of this statement in the context of the other passages – 'Rely on yourselves ... Seek salvation alone in the Dharma' and 'Be ye lamps unto yourselves ... Live the Dharma as a lamp.' In this address Śākyamuni did not claim exclusive identity with the Dharma, identifying it instead with each individual disciple. This would indicate that the identity with the Dharma is not unique to Gautama Buddha, but is common to all people. Further, in the concrete situation of his death, he emphasizes each person's direct identity with the Dharma, characterizing it as an identity that is without external help or mediator.

Jesus not only emphasizes his identity with the Father, but also the possibility of his disciples doing even greater works than he had accomplished. At the same time, he clearly states: 'Believest thou not that I am in the Father, and the Father in me? The words that I say with you I speak not from myself: but the Father abiding in me doeth his works' (John 14:10). This means that the possibility of the disciples' doing the same work as Jesus had done is dependent entirely on their belief in Jesus. Our identity with the Father is exclusively based on the belief in Jesus' identity with the Father. Thus we see a significant difference between Buddhism and Christianity in terms of our identity with the Dharma or the Father. In other words, in Buddhism we have a direct identification with the Dharma without Śākyamuni's mediation, but in Christianity our identity with the Father is mediated by the belief in Jesus' identity with the Father.

Now the next point is this: in Buddhism, despite the identity of a particular individual with the Dharma and despite the identity of even Śākyamuni himself with the Dharma, the Dharma can be said to exist beyond all particular existences. The Dharma exists universally, apart from all human existence. Even Gautama Buddha is not the creator of the Dharma, but only its discoverer. This point he clearly states himself, saying, 'I only found an old path in the woods.' And this is the reason why he says, as quoted before, that 'regardless of the appearance or non-appearance of the Tathāgata (Śākyamuni Buddha) in this world, the Dharma is always present.'

Although the Dharma transcends all individual existences, that of Śākyamuni Buddha included, and is present universally, there is no

Dharma without someone to realize it. In other words, the Dharma is realized as the Dharma in its absolute universality only through a particular realizer. Without such a person no one would know of the existence of the universal Dharma functioning throughout the world. Yet who is qualified to discourse on the Dharma in its absolute universality? Certainly not those who have never realized it. Those who fail to attain their own realization come away with an understanding of the Dharma that is lifeless and empty. Only those who have realized the Dharma with their entire being can truly speak of its absolute universality. Thus, as its first realizer, Śākyamuni was cognizant with *his entire being* of his being a realizer of the Dharma for his own sake as well as for all posterity. This he clearly points to, saying, 'He who sees me, sees the Dharma.'

While Śākyamuni Buddha may be the *first* realizer of Dharma in our era, he is not its *sole* realizer. As a realizer of the Dharma in its total universality, Śākyamuni becomes *a* center, not *the* center, of the Buddhist religion since anyone who realizes the Dharma in effect become one of its centers as a realizer of the Dharma, that is, a Buddha. Hence, the significance of Śākyamuni's historical existence stands on a par with that of all others who realize the Dharma, except that he was the first to do so.

The self-awakening of the Dharma

How can we maintain these two apparently contradictory aspects of the Dharma: that is, its total universality on the one hand, and its dependency upon a particular realizer on the other? The answer lies in the fact that the realization of the Dharma is nothing but *the self-awakening of the Dharma itself.* Your Awakening is, of course, *your own*; it is *your* awakening to the Dharma in its complete universality. But this awakening is possible only by overcoming our self-centeredness, i.e., only through the total negation of ego-self. Our self-centeredness is the fundamental hindrance for the manifestation of the Dharma. Originally, the Dharma is present universally, but due to our self-centeredness it does not manifest itself to us. Therefore, when our self-centeredness is overcome and selflessness is achieved, i.e., *anātman*, or 'no-self', is realized, the Dharma naturally awakens to itself. Accordingly, the self-awakening of the Dharma has the following double sense. First, it is *your* self-awakening of the Dharma in your egoless true Self. Secondly, it is the self-awakening of the *Dharma itself* in and through your whole existence. In other words, a particular individual's self-awakening to the Dharma and the Dharma's self-awakening are not two, but one.

Newton, Christ and the Buddha

In order to elucidate the true meaning of the self-awakening of the Dharma, let us to compare it with Newton's discovery of the universal law of gravity and with the idea of Jesus Christ as the final revelation of God. The universal law of gravity was discovered by Newton in the seventeenth century. Before Newton's discovery, no one knew of the existence of such a law. This fact, however, does not mean no law of gravity existed prior to its discovery. On the contrary, it had been functioning from the beginning of the universe and will function until the end. In other words, the law of gravity exists and functions by itself apart from Newton's discovery. Newton did not create the law but simply discovered that which had always existed universally, by itself. It is, however, also true that apart from Newton's discovery, no one would ever have known of this law. Thus, as in the case of Buddhist Dharma, we encounter two apparently contradictory aspects of the law of gravity, that is, its total universality and self-existence on the one hand, and its dependency upon Newton's discovery on the other. But these two aspects do not result in a contradiction. Instead, they consist of one single reality, that is, the 'discovery of the law of gravity.' For with Newton's discovery, the law of gravity manifested itself in its entirety, hence his discovery and the manifestation of that law are not two but one.

This, however, does not mean that Newton's *entire being* is identical with the law of gravity. Of course, his *physical body* is subject to, and thereby is constantly affected by, the law of gravity, but his mind, heart, consciousness, spirituality and personality are free from that law. In short, Newton's *personal existence* as an individual human self is not identical with the law of gravity, while his physical body is subject to the law. Consequently, unlike Gautama Buddha, *only* by pointing to *his physical body* can Newton say, 'Those who see me see the law of gravity.' This is because the law he discovered is one governing the physical world, the objective world of nature. It is not a universal law governing both the objective and subjective world, as in the case of Buddhist's law of dependent co-origination. In Newton's case, his discovery did not require the *total* negation of his ego-self, that is, the realization of no-self, although it required the negation of the mere subjective view of the world.

In this regard, the self-awakening of the Dharma in Buddhism is more akin to the divine revelation of Jesus as the Christ in Christianity. In some interpretations of Christianity, God exists as a universal Godself, without dependence upon anything else. Yet, without Jesus Christ as the revelation of God and as the incarnation of the Son of God, we cannot see God. This is precisely the reason Jesus says, 'Those who see me see God.' Jesus' flesh manifests itself as the Son of God who has emptied himself without counting himself as God's equal. This means that Jesus' *entire being* is nothing but the revelation of the Will of God. Jesus' historical existence and the revelation of the divine will are not two but one. Unlike Newton's discovery of the law of gravity, this oneness refers not to the law of the objective world but to a deeply subjective religious truth. Again, unlike Newton, the revelation of Jesus as the Christ requires the death of the ego-self to reveal the Will of God. In this regard, there is a great affinity between Gautama's self-awakening of the Dharma and Jesus as the revelation of God. In both cases the total identity between the person and the universal principle is fully realized through the death of ego-self.

As Jesus says, 'I am the Way, the Truth and the Life. No one comes to God but by me.' Jesus is the only person in whom that total identity is realized. Furthermore, the universal principle with which he is totally identical is the personal God whom he calls 'Father.' Gautama Buddha, on the other hand, is not the only person in whom that total identity is realized, but one of many. The universal principle with which he is totally identical is not a personal deity, but an impersonal law, applicable equally to human beings and nature alike. In this respect, Gautama's case is more akin to Newton's discovery than to that of Jesus, although in the former, Gautama as the Buddha is identical subjectively or existentially with the universal law of dependent co-origination through his self-awakening, whereas in the latter, Newton is identical objectively with the universal law of gravity through his scientific discovery.

The two aspects of self-awakening

As I have stated above, in Buddhism the self-awakening of the Dharma has two aspects. First, it is *your* self-awakening of the Dharma in your ego-less true Self. You are the subject of awakening and the Dharma is the object of awakening. Second, it is the self-awakening of the *Dharma itself* in and through your entire being, with the Dharma as the subject of awakening and you as the object through which Dharma awakens to itself.

This explanation, however, tends to be overly analytical and by sifting out these two aspects does not convey the true character of the self-awakening of the Dharma. In reality, these two aspects are completely inseparable from one another and are fused into one single reality of the self-awakening of the Dharma. Strictly speaking, though, even this explanation falls short. In reality, it is *not* that *on the one hand* there is an aspect in which you as the subject awaken to the Dharma as the object and *on the other hand* there is another aspect in which the Dharma as the subject awakens to itself through you as the object, *and that then* these two aspects are united and fused into one single reality of the self-awakening of the Dharma. This type of explanation is an objectification of the self-awakening of the Dharma from outside and thus conceptualizes it. The self-awakening of the Dharma, however, can be properly understood only through a non-objective existential approach. If the self-awakening of the Dharma is grasped from within, that is, existentially, you will realize that this living reality known as the self-awakening of the Dharma is originally and fundamentally single and undifferentiated, completely free from any form of subject–object duality, exists prior to any separation of subject and object. Herein, the whole universe is the stage of the Dharma's self-awakening. It is not that we exist outside of this single reality of the Dharma's self-awakening: we are identical with it. Only when we analyze it from the outside do we resort to such explanations as its having such and such an aspect on the one hand, such and such an aspect on the other, only to conclude that, further, they are inseparably united. We must, however, clearly realize that fundamentally there is one single non-dual reality of self-awakening of the Dharma. 'Your awakening to Dharma' and 'Dharma's self awakening in and through you' are just two different ways of expressing one and the same dynamic reality.

Accordingly the two aspects of self-awakening of the Dharma are not to be divvied up fifty-fifty. The aspect of *your* self-awakening of *Dharma* is one hundred percent complete, just as the aspect of the self-awakening of the Dharma is one hundred percent complete. These two aspects in their fullness are dynamically united without contradiction, because the self as the subject of your awakening of the Dharma is not your ego-centered self but your true Self realized through the realization of no-self, the complete negation of the ego-centered self. Without the realization of no-self as our true Self, it is impossible for us to realize the dynamic reality of the self-awakening of the Dharma.

It was on the basis of this self-awakening of the Dharma that Śākyamuni said without any sense of contradiction, 'Rely on yourselves,' and 'Seek salvation alone in the Dharma.' The statements, 'Be ye lamps unto yourselves' and 'Live the Dharma as a lamp' are complementary and not contradictions. Your self as the ultimate reliance is not the ego-self, but rather, the true Self as the realizer of the Dharma. Just as Śākyamuni's awakening was the self-awakening of the Dharma in the double sense mentioned above, so too is anyone's awakening the self-same self-awakening of the Dharma.

Schisms in the development of Buddhism

This is the basic standpoint of Buddhism, which after his Awakening was clarified by Śākyamuni himself throughout his life and particularly, as mentioned before, as he stood on the threshold of death. His death, however, sent shock waves through all his disciples and followers, for not only had they lost their revered teacher but also had to face the undeniable fact that even Śākyamuni Buddha, the Awakened One, was subject to decay and death just like they themselves. As they pondered the meaning of his death, they gradually began to idealize his existence and personality. This led to the development of elaborate Buddhological systems, with their various doctrinal interpretations of the meaning of Śākyamuni Buddha's historical existence.

In its historical development Buddhism has experienced various schisms, one of the most basic of which is that between Theravāda and Mahāyāna Buddhism. Theravāda means 'those who hold to the Doctrine of the Elders,' indicating the Theravāda's origin in the elder monks of the Buddha's following. Conservative in the orientation of its teaching and practice, it respects the Buddha as the supreme Enlightened One, and strives to maintain the original form of the Buddha's teaching and practice. The goal of the monastic life they lead is Arhatship, which they pursue in their search for *Nirvāṇa* for their own emancipation.

The Mahāyāna, on the other hand, originated in the Mahāsaṃghika, or 'Great Assembly.' More liberal and progressive than the Elders, it included monks and nuns of lesser attainment and even lay practitioners. They insisted that Gautama Buddha's teachings and practice reflected the historical and social situation in which he lived and that he might teach differently in a different historical and social situation. What is important is not necessarily the formal teaching and practice of the Buddha, but the intent with which the Buddha advocated these received forms. Accordingly, among the main concerns for the Mahāyānist were the questions, 'What is the sole purpose of the appearance of Gautama Buddha in this world? What is Śākyamuni Buddha's originally cherished intention for his appearance in this world?' As Edward Conze states, 'A free and unfettered development of the doctrine was thus assured, and innovations, even if intractable in the existing body of scriptures, could be justified as revelations of the real principle of Buddhahood' (*Buddhism: Its Essence and Development*, New York: Harper & Row, 1951, p. 121). Through a free interpretation of what they perceived to be Gautama Buddha's inner intent, Mahāyānists tried to deepen the Buddha's original teachings, to explore their religious depths. One of the developments of the Mahāyāna doctrine was the emphasis of the Bodhisattva ideal. Unlike the Arhat, the Bodhisattva is one who attempts to lead all sentient beings to attain *Nirvāṇa*, believing that one's own awakening can only be ultimately consummated by first helping others to attain awakening. This ideal of Bodhisattva is a fitting model for the Mahāyāna, or 'the Great Vehicle,' with its goal of universal salvation.

In the centuries after the Buddha's demise, Theravāda Buddhism spread to Sri Lanka and other Southeast Asian countries such as Burma, Thailand and Cambodia, where it has maintained considerable conformity. Mahāyāna Buddhism, on the other hand, developed in northern India, and was disseminated to China, Tibet, Korea and Japan. In the course of its centuries-long development it produced many sutras, or holy scriptures. Basing themselves in a particular sutra as their authoritative text, various Mahāyāna schools arose such as the Mādhyamika, Yogācāra, T'ien-t'ai, Hua-yen, Chen-yen, Ch'an (Zen), Pure Land and Nichiren sects. Christianity has also experienced various schisms, resulting in the Roman Catholic, Greek Orthodox, and Protestant Church, the latter further divided into the Church of England, Lutheran, Calvinist, Presbyterian, Methodist, and Congregational Church. The diversity within Mahāyāna Buddhism, however, is greater than that in Christianity, because there is no single authoritative canon like the Christian Bible, and, instead of talking about one absolute God, takes *śūnyatā*, or 'emptiness,' as its ultimate Reality.

KYŌSŌ-HANJAKU

When a new sect was established, particularly in China and to some extent in Japan, there arose the practice of *kyōsō-hanjaku* 教相判釈 , the judgment and interpretation of the various facets of Buddhist teachings. In my own view, *kyōsō-hanjaku* was needed for two reasons, one historical, and the other theological. The historical reason stems from the fact that the so-called Mahāyāna sutras came into existence intermittently over a period of nearly a thousand years. They grew out of different situations calling for different systems of thought, over a broad geographic area. Thus, the Mahāyāna sutras, which are many in number, do not necessarily have an ideological consistency, and in fact show a great deal of variation in their teaching. These Mahāyāna sutras were over time translated into Chinese by various groups of people without any overall agenda. Perplexed by the influx of sutras maintaining divergent positions all under the name of Buddhism, Chinese Buddhists felt a need to judge and classify them in some way, hence the historical rise of the *kyōsō-hanjaku* systems.

The idea of *kyōsō-hanjaku*, however, is also based more essentially on a theological principle. Certain of the great Buddhists and Buddhist scholars who later became founders of new sects had serious religious concerns as to what was the genuine spirit of Buddhism and which sutra most clearly embodied that spirit. From out of such theological concerns developed the *kyōsō-hanjaku*, which importantly applied new standards for evaluating and grading the various sutras. Thus, the *kyōsō-hanjaku* was not merely the systematic classification of the Mahāyāna sutras, but was rather a critical new device to determine what sutra contained the true spirit of Buddhism, the selected work being then used to found a new Buddhist system. In this practice the other facets of Buddha's teaching were not excluded, but were integrated as different stages on the way to the ultimate truth represented by the new school.

The establishment of a new sect of Buddhism in China and in Japan would have been well nigh impossible without some sort of *kyōsō-hanjaku* system. The most typical examples of *kyōsō-hanjaku* in China are the 'Five Periods and Eight Doctrines' (*gojihakkyō* 五時八教) of the T'ien-t'ai sect and the 'Five Doctrines and Ten Tenets' (*gokyō jusshū* 五教十宗) of the Hua-yen sect. In Japan, we may cite the arguments of Kōbō Daishi, the Great Teacher, on the *kenmitsu-nikyō* 顕密二教 (Two Teachings, Exoteric and Esoteric) and the *jūjūshin* 十住心 (Ten Stages of the Mind), and Shinran's *nisō-shijū* 二隻四重 system as other examples. Also, in the early history of Buddhism in India, a distinction was made between so-called Hīnayāna ('Smaller Vehicle') and Mahāyāna which, though it cannot be called *kyōsō-hanjaku* proper, may be said to be an anticipation of it.

What is interesting to note in this connection is that, in some instances, when a new *kyōsō-hanjaku* classification was declared, while it may have opened new theological dimensions by its new interpretation of certain sutras, it resulted in almost all other extant forms of Buddhism being discarded or being regarded as secondary. Notable examples of this sort of *kyōsō-hanjaku* are *Kenkyō* 顕教 (Exoteric Buddhism) versus *Mikkyō* 密教 (Esoteric Buddhism), *Shōdō-mon* 聖道門 (Holy Way teaching) versus *Jōdo-mon* 浄土門 (Pure Land teaching), and, with reservations which have to be explained, but in a sense the clearest and most unique example, *Kyō* 教 (Teaching) versus *Zen* 禅 (Meditation).

In these cases, the whole of Buddhism was divided in half, not by simply classifying the extant forms of Buddhism into two groups, but by taking a stance beyond all existing forms of Buddhism and by disclosing a new religious dimension lying at the heart of Buddhism. This newly discovered aspect of the faith may have only faintly appeared on the surface of Buddhism prior to this. These new paradigms introduced a revolutionary development, creating a new antithesis over against the established forms of Buddhism by radically critiquing their existing foundations. The new positions were of course criticized in turn as heretical by the established Buddhist schools. Nevertheless, the newly forged Buddhism usually insisted that it was the real source of Buddhism, while all other forms were secondary and contrived.

The Chen-yen, or Shingon, sect established the distinction between Exoteric and Esoteric Buddhism, insisting that while Exoteric Buddhism focused on the written teachings of the historical Buddha, Esoteric Buddhism contained the secret and much more profound teaching of Mahāvairocana Buddha, the manifestation of the formless Dharmakāya, which is Truth itself. According to the Chen-yen sect, all other forms of Buddhism was nothing but Exoteric Buddhism, and that Exoteric Buddhism was but an offshoot of the genuine Buddhism of Esoteric Buddhism represented by the Chen-yen sect itself.

Similarly, Pure Land Buddhism set up the contrast between the Holy Way teaching and the Pure Land teaching. This distinction is often referred to as *jiriki-mon* 他力門 (Self-Power Gate) versus *tariki-*

mon 他力門 (Other-Power Gate). Pure Land Buddhism insists that while all Buddhist schools up to now have emphasized Awakening through one's 'self-power,' the present is the age of the Latter Dharma (*mappō*), for which the practice of the Holy Way is no longer suited. Only the Other-Power teaching of Pure Land Buddhism is the proper way for an essentially powerless humankind. It also maintains that the Pure Land teaching was provided from the very beginning by Amida Buddha who foresaw the suffering of people during this age of the Latter Dharma and thus fulfilled his vow of universal salvation in light of this predicament.

Zen also makes a sharp distinction between what they call *Kyō* and Zen. *Kyō*, meaning 'the teaching,' in the present case refers to 'doctrines' and 'scriptures.' Strictly speaking, this distinction made by Zen is not *kyōsō-hanjaku* per se, for rather than 'judging and interpreting various aspects of the Buddha's *teachings*,' Zen resolves to take a stand over against any form of 'teaching' as such.

At any rate, *kyōsō-hanjaku* as practiced by each newly established form of Buddhism critically evaluated the Buddhist scriptures and tended to belittle all the other forms of Buddhism. To be exact, the distinction between Exoteric and Esoteric Buddhism was made by Esoteric Buddhism, that between the Holy Way teaching and the Pure Land teaching was established by the Pure Land school, while the contrast between *Kyō* and Zen was set up by Zen. This means that the characterization of Exoteric Buddhism, the Holy Way Gate, or *Kyō* was put forth not by these groups themselves, but by the newer forms of Buddhism. In other words, the various forms of Buddhism classified by Esoteric Buddhism as Exoteric Buddhism do not necessarily call themselves 'Exoteric Buddhism.' The same is true of those classified as the Holy Way Gate or *Kyō*. In exactly the same way, the earlier distinction between so-called Hīnayāna and Mahāyāna was made by Mahāyāna Buddhism.

Further, as I have noted above, these newly established Buddhist positions respectively constituted an antithesis over against the hitherto existing forms of Buddhism by severe criticism of their spiritual foundations. They usually insisted that their own positions were the real root-source of Buddhism from which all other existing forms of Buddhism came and to which they may be reduced. This sort of revolutionary development was the way in which an entirely new form of Buddhism was established by means of *kyōsō-hanjaku*. One reason why it has been possible for this revolution to occur time and again in the course of Buddhist history is because the ultimate truth of Buddhism, the Dharma, does not represent an all-controlling principle such as the Will of God, but is predicated, rather, by the principle of self-emptying, as expressed by *anātman* (non-ego) or *śūnyatā* (non-substantial emptiness, void).

In summary, Buddhism, particularly Mahāyāna Buddhism, was able to flourish according to the spiritual climate of the time and place into which it was introduced due to its theological basis in the notions of *anātman* and *śūnyatā*. Thus, throughout its long history in India, China, and Japan, Buddhism produced many divergent forms that differed radically from the original form of Buddhism preached by Śākyamuni. Nevertheless, these novel forms were not purged from the Buddhist world, and instead became the spiritual fountainheads from which new energy entered the Buddhist world. One Buddhist scholar has even suggested in this connection that the history of Buddhism may be regarded as a history of heresy, meaning by this that Buddhism has developed itself by constantly daring to embrace paradigms that may border on the heretical, but which ultimately serve to open new spiritual horizons of the Buddhist world.

In the West, where up until recent times the Mahāyāna Buddhism of China and Japan was relatively unknown, people are apt to judge the whole of Buddhism by taking the so-called original form of Buddhism preached by Śākyamuni as the standard. Such a static view fails to appreciate the dynamic development of Buddhism. The history of Buddhism, especially of Mahāyāna, is no less rich and profound than that of Western philosophy and religion, its various developments issuing from the inexhaustible wellsprings of *anātman* or *śūnyatā*. Yet, this 'history of heresy' that Buddhism manifests has evolved without serious bloody inquisitions, religious wars or crusades. In this respect I would like to suggest that it was the application of *kyōsō-hanjaku*, backed up by the notions of *anātman* and *śūnyatā*, that may have made the decisive difference.

KYŌ AND ZEN

To return to the distinction between *Kyō* and Zen, all forms of Buddhism, according to Zen, are ultimately based upon the 'Teaching' delivered by Śākyamuni, that is, the spoken teaching recorded as sutras. Traditionally, the Buddhist sutras were believed to be the records of Śākyamuni's sermons and were considered the source and norm of Buddhism. Nowadays, however, as a result of historical and text-critical studies of the scriptures, it is known that the so-called sutras do not necessarily record the *ipsissima verba* (the precise words) of Śākyamuni. Many of them, particularly those of the Mahāyāna, were composed much later. Until this became known, however, the sutras were generally regarded by Buddhists as the ultimate foundation and authority of Buddhism. Thus, according to the traditional Buddhist view, the final norm of truth was contained in the sutras, and that which had no basis in the sutras could not be called Buddhist truth.

Each Buddhist school has its own particular sutra (or sutras) as the ultimate authority for its teaching: the Hua-yen had the *Avataṃsaka*; the T'ien-t'ai and Nichiren, the *Saddharma-puṇḍarika Sūtra*; and the Pure Land, the Three Pure Land sutras. To show they are Buddhist and to demonstrate the truth of their teaching, each school makes recourse to the respective sutras. Zen, however, takes exception: it has no such authoritative scripture upon which it is based. This does not mean that it is arbitrary and ignores scriptures, but it dares, rather, to be independent of scripture. In other words, Zen seeks to return to the source of the sutras – that is, to that which is prior to the sutras. 'Prior to the sutras' here does not mean prior in a temporal or historical sense. It refers, rather, to the spiritual source 'prior to' what is expressed in the sutras. This source is the self-awakening of Śākyamuni which, in Zen, is often expressed by the term 'Mind.' Being independent of the sutras or scriptures, Zen tries to transmit this Mind of self-awakening from person to person, from generation to generation. This is the meaning of the first two Zen phrases mentioned earlier, 'Not relying on words or letters,' and 'An independent transmission apart from the scriptural doctrine.'

When Zen was founded, it distinguished itself from all other forms of Buddhism based on sutras by calling them *Butsugoshū* 仏語宗 , or 'Buddha-word schools,' while calling itself *Butsushinshū* 仏心宗 , the 'Buddha-mind school.' Zen also called other forms of Buddhism '*Kyō*' or 'Buddhism standing within *Kyō*, or Teaching.' Accordingly, the whole of Buddhism was divided by Zen into either *Kyō* or Zen, the former being 'Buddhism within the scriptural teaching' and the latter 'Buddhism outside the (scriptural) teaching.' Through its criticism of the existing forms of Buddhism, and by taking an antithetical stance towards them, Zen disclosed a 'new' religious foundation lying at the depths of Buddhism, a foundation which had been obscured by the dogmatism and philosophical speculation rampant in the religion up to that time.

Hence, while Zen describes itself as an independent transmission outside the scriptural teaching, 'outside the teaching' does not mean outside Buddhism; rather, it refers to an *inner* source of that which is 'within the teaching.' Seen from the point of view of the sutras, Zen is 'outside the teaching,' but looked at from the religious realization expressed in the sutras, Zen is even more 'inner' than what is ordinarily called 'Buddhism.' Thus, from a Zen perspective, what is usually thought to be 'inside the Teaching' is, in fact, 'outside.' In this way Zen manifests its main concern over entering directly into the inner source or Mind.

Let us now turn to the meaning of 'Mind' as it is understood in Zen Buddhism. The 'Mind' with which Zen is concerned is neither mind in a psychological sense nor consciousness in its ordinary sense. It is, as I have said before, the self-awakening of the Dharma through which one becomes an Awakened One. It is this Mind, lying at the very source of the scriptures, that is being referred to in the citations, 'Directly pointing to the human Mind' and 'Awakening to one's Original Nature, thereby actualizing one's own Buddhahood.' The word 'Nature' in the latter refers to the *true way of human being*. In Buddhism, this is generally called Buddha-nature or Mind-nature, which are simply other terms for Dharma. Zen, however, speaks of it in terms such as 'Self-nature' or 'One's Original Face,' expressions which have far more intimate connotations. This is because, in Zen, Buddha-nature or Dharma is by no means something foreign to one's true Self-nature. For Zen, it is precisely the original nature of human being which is the Buddha-nature; it is precisely this 'human Mind' which is the 'Buddha-mind.' Apart from this 'human Mind' there is nothing which can be truly called 'Buddha' or 'Dharma,' nor do we seek for Buddha or Dharma outside of this 'Mind.'

In spite of Śākyamuni's exhorting his disciples to rely on themselves as a lamp, most of them idealized Śākyamuni as an object of worship or took the teaching of the sutras as the authoritative basis for Buddhism. Yet, in so doing, they relied on something in the past, i.e., on the historical Śākyamuni or the sutras as the record of his reputed teachings. On the basis of past teachings, they searched for ultimate salvation as a future ideal not to be actualized in the present. In contrast to this attitude, Zen emphasizes, 'Directly pointing to the human Mind,' and 'Awakening to one's Original Nature and thereby actualizing one's Buddhahood.' 'Directly' in this phrase does not necessarily mean 'immediately' in a temporal sense, but 'right now' in the absolute present which is beyond past, present and future. Hence Zen insists on entering directly into the source 'prior to the sutras.' Radically criticizing every other form of Buddhism, Zen faithfully returns to the realization of Śākyamuni, that is, to the self-awakening of the Dharma.

Christianity, needless to say, is not comprised merely of the writings in the Bible. What is important for a Christian is the divine Revelation of the living Christ ever present and effective. The Christ experience, which a Christian re-enacts in himself or herself, is the foundation of his or her faith. In this sense, Christianity too is based on something beyond the Bible, something prior to the Bible. However, the Bible is the necessary canon through which a Christian must approach that what is beyond the Bible. In general, Christianity would be classified among the religions Zen calls *Kyō*.

ZEN BEYOND THE SCRIPTURES

The Zen position of transcending the scriptures is seen in the following accounts. Chung-feng Ming-pen (J. Chūhō Minpō, 1263–1323), a Chinese Zen master of the Yuan dynasty, said, 'With the words of Mahāyāna scriptures and discourses, memories exist in the mind. This is what is called gaining understanding by something other than myself. It hinders the way of self-awakening.'

One day the Emperor Wu of the Liang dynasty, a devoted Buddhist follower, requested Fu Ta-shih (497–569), an outstanding lay Zen Buddhist of that day, to discourse on the *Diamond Sūtra*. Fu sat solemnly in the teaching chair, but uttered not a word. The Emperor said, 'I asked you to give a discourse. Why do you not begin to speak?' One of the Emperor's attendants explained, saying, 'Your Majesty, Master Fu has finished discoursing.' What kind of a sermon did this silent Buddhist philosopher deliver? One Zen master, commenting on this story later on, said: 'What an eloquent sermon it was!'

The following story may help underscore the difference between Zen and *Kyō*.

A monk once asked Lin-chi (d. 866), the famous Chinese Zen master of the T'ang dynasty, 'The twelve divisions of the Three Vehicles of the Buddha's teaching reveal the Buddha-nature, do they not?' Lin-chi retorted, 'This weed-patch has never been spaded!' This puzzled the monk who was a lecture-master and who made his living by discoursing on the various scriptures. The twelve divisions of the Three Vehicles of the Buddha's teaching are, in fact, the foundation of the sort of Buddhism Zen calls *Kyō*. Wondering why Zen intentionally took its stance outside the scriptures, the monk had raised a question which was quite understandable to ordinary Buddhists in those days. Elsewhere, Lin-chi even goes so far as to say, 'The twelve divisions of the Three Vehicles of the Buddha's teaching are all toilet paper.' Lin-chi was telling the monk two things: first, that the monk had not yet begun to 'spade the weed patch' of his own mind; and secondly, that he, Lin-chi, had never bothered, since his own awakening, to seek the Buddha-nature in the 'weed patch' of scriptural verbiage. With this implication in his answer, Lin-chi broke through the monk's bondage to the scriptures, to point directly to the 'human Mind.' Studying the scriptures, religious literature and massive commentaries, students of religion are apt to be caught up by the words, only to miss the living truth religion would have us understand. Lin-chi's answer – 'This weed-patch has never been spaded' – was a sharp criticism of the monk's superficial under-standing of merely the words, which also served to liberate the monk from his bondage to the scriptures. To Lin-chi's answer, the monk then replied, 'How could the Buddha deceive us?' For the monk, the twelve divisions were the true and authoritative words of Buddha himself. To call them a 'weed patch,' or worse, 'toilet paper,' was unpardonable. The sacred words preached by the Buddha could not have been in error, hence the monk's retort. Lin-chi then said, 'Where is the Buddha?' The monk, known for his eloquence on scriptural matters, fell silent. Lin-chi, of course, would have rejected the answer that the Buddha lived in India in the sixth century BC.

In a somewhat similar vein, you may recall that Søren Kierkegaard emphasized 'contemporaneity' (*Gleichzeitigkeit*) with Jesus Christ as the necessary condition for faith. In *Philosophical Fragments* he wrote, 'One can be a contemporary (in time) without being contemporary (in spirit)' if one has no faith. The real contemporary is not contemporary by virtue of an external, immediate contemporaneity, but by virtue of an internal, religious contemporaneity through faith. For Kierke-gaard, to encounter Christ one must see him not with the eyes of the body, but through the eyes of faith. As the First Epistle of Peter puts it, 'Without having seen him you love him; though you do not now see him, you believe in him and rejoice with unutterable and exalted joy' (1.8). 'The real contemporary,' wrote Kierkegaard, 'is not an eyewitness in the immediate sense of the word; he is a contemporary as a believer. Through the eyes of faith every non-contemporary (in the immediate sense) becomes a contemporary.'

Zen, likewise, emphasizes contemporaneity with the Buddha, not by virtue of an immediate contemporaneity, but by virtue of an internal contemporaneity. In Christianity, however, the subject of contemporaneity is the Christ, as we see in his words, 'I, when I am lifted up from the earth, will draw all men to myself' (John 12:32). In Zen, on the other hand, the subject of the contemporaneity is none other than the person concerned. Not faith in the Buddha, but the self-awakening of the Dharma is essential to Zen. Wu-men Hui-k'ai, a Chinese Zen master of the Sung dynasty, said, 'If you pass through the gateless barrier of Zen you will not only immediately see Chao-chou (the great Zen master of the past); you will also walk hand in hand with the successive Patriarchs, mingling your eyebrows with theirs, seeing with the same eyes, and hearing with the same ears.' In Zen, to become a contemporary of the Buddha means that one becomes an Awakened One oneself by awakening to the self-same Dharma to which Gautama Buddha and the Patriarchs awakened. For Zen and for original Buddhism, there is no Buddha apart from one's own self-awakening.

When asked by Lin-chi 'Where is Buddha?' the monk, had he really understood the meaning of 'Buddha,' should have pointed to the Buddha-nature actualized in himself, and said, 'Here is Buddha.' As it was, he was struck dumb. But how different was his speechlessness from the silence of Fu Ta-shih before Emperor Wu! While Fu's silence eloquently revealed the Buddha-nature, the monk's speechlessness only exposed the powerlessness of his brand of Buddhism which had relied so heavily on the scriptures.

In his discourses, Lin-chi addressed each person in the audience as 'the one who is, at this moment, right in front of me, solitary, being illuminated, in full awareness, listening to my discourse on the Dharma.' 'If you wish to transcend birth-and-death, going-and-coming, and to be freely unattached, you should recognize the *person* who is listening at this moment to this discourse on the Dharma. *He* is the one who has neither shape nor form, neither root nor trunk, and who, having no abiding place, is full of activity. He responds to all kinds of situations and manifests his activity, and yet comes out of nowhere. Therefore, as soon as you try to search for him he is far away; the nearer you try to approach, the farther he turns away from you. "Mysterious" is his name.'

We should not miss the point that it is our 'True Self' that Lin-chi called 'Person' and 'Mysterious.' To awaken to 'Man' or to the 'True Self' who 'is, at this moment, in full awareness, listening to this discourse on the Dharma,' is nothing but self-awakening through which one becomes an Awakened One, a Buddha. Huang-po, Lin-chi's teacher and an outstanding Zen master of T'ang China, once said, 'Your Mind is Buddha; Buddha is this Mind. Mind and Buddha are not separate or different.' Buddha is not separate even for one instant from our Mind.

Let me quote one more story. The Chinese Zen master Nan-chüan (748–834) was once asked by Pai-chang (720–814), one of his fellow monks, if there was a truth that the sages of old had not preached to people. 'There is,' said Nan-chüan. 'What is this truth?' asked Pai-chang. 'It is not mind,' answered Nan-chüan, 'it is not Buddha; it is not a thing.' To this, Pai-chang replied, 'If so, you have already talked about it.' 'I cannot do any better,' was Nan-chüan's answer. 'What would you say?' 'I am not a great enlightened one. So how do I know what either talking or non-talking is?' answered Pai-chang. 'I don't understand,' said Nan-chüan. 'Alas,' said Pai-chang, 'I have already said too much for you.'

No matter how many words we use when we talk about Zen, we can never reach it. On the contrary, the more we attempt to explain Zen, the further we go astray. Since Zen does not rely on words, we ought to be silent. Yet, even if we remained silent, we would be severely beaten by Te-shan (782–865), another Zen master of T'ang China, who said, 'Though you *can* speak, thirty blows! Though you *can't* speak, thirty blows!' This is to say, mere speechlessness is an empty or dead silence. Zen, however, finds itself in league neither with speech nor with silence, neither with affirmation nor with negation. We can reach Zen only by transcending speech and silence, affirmation and negation. But what is beyond speech and silence, beyond affirmation and negation? – *that* is the question.

2

The Core of Zen: The Ordinary Mind is Tao

What is Zen? To answer this question, words are not always needed or altogether adequate. One may answer the question by lifting one's finger or pounding on a desk with one's fist or just by maintaining perfect silence. These are non-verbal answers to the question, 'What is Zen?' – the true expression of that which ultimately resides beyond words and intellectual analysis.

It is, however, not necessarily impossible to give an answer with words to the question what is Zen. The history of Zen testifies to this fact. There are many such cases in which Zen masters have given verbal answers to questions raised by their disciples. Such verbal answers, however, often tend to be quite abrupt, eccentric or illogical. When asked, 'What is Buddha?' – which is equivalent to 'What is Zen?' – the answer given by Tōzan (Tung-shan, 807–869) was, 'Three pounds of flax!' Jōshū (Chao-chou, 778–897) replied, 'The oak tree in the front garden!' Ummon (Yüa-men, 862–949) said, 'See the eastern mountains moving over the waves!'

These eccentric verbal answers cut off the intellectual reasoning implied in the questioner's wording of his question. As they point to the reality of Zen which is beyond description in words, the verbal answers serve not as a simplified and limiting depiction of the moon, but instead as nothing more than fingers pointing to the moon. Accordingly, if you cling to the verbal answer and try to analyze what the logical connection might be between question and answers, you will certainly miss both the finger and the moon. These verbal answers are not mere fingers, but fingers which serve as 'spring-boards', pushing aside the approach we would ordinarily take at first, and enabling us to leap to the moon itself as the 'Reality'.

In this chapter I would like to take up the Zen kōan called 'Ordinary Mind is Tao,' case nineteen of the *Mumonkan*.

Mumonkan (Ch. *Wu men kuan*) is one of the most important pieces of Zen literature. It was compiled by Mumon Ekai (Wú mén Hui-kai,

1183–1260) in the early thirteenth century, late Sung China. Often translated as *Gateless Gate*, *Mumonkan* is a collection of 48 kōans, Zen questions based on the stories of eminent Zen masters' enlightenment experiences in the past, which are assigned by a master to his disciples to grapple with in order that they might realize their own enlightenment.

> Jōshū [Chao-chou, 778–897] once asked Nansen [Nan-chüan, 748–835] 'What is Tao?'
>   Nansen answered: 'Ordinary mind is Tao.'
>   'Then should we direct ourselves toward it, or not?'
>   'If you try to direct yourself toward it, you go away from it,' answered Nansen.
>   Jōshū continued, 'If we do not try, how can we know that it is Tao?'
>   Nansen replied, 'Tao does not belong to knowing or to not-knowing. Knowing is illusion; not-knowing is blankness. If you really attain to Tao of no-doubt, it is like the great void, so vast and boundless. How, then, can there be right and wrong in the Tao?'
>   At these words, Jōshū was suddenly enlightened.[1]

There are two reasons for taking up this kōan to clarify the core of Zen. One reason is that the subject of this kōan, 'ordinary mind is Tao' is a verbal statement. Unlike the example of verbal answers given earlier, this statement is not eccentric or inaccessible, but is rather amenable to being traced by our intellect. Further, the ensuing dialogue between Jōshū and Nansen is not abrupt or illogical, as is often the case with Zen dialogues, but touches on a crucial matter which modern people must confront.

Such an intellectually accessible dialogue is rather unusual in Zen. This is the reason why Hakuin (1686–1769), an outstanding Zen master of Tokugawa Japan, said in criticism of Nansen, 'I do not like such grandmotherly mildness. He ought to have beaten Jōshū severely without saying anything.' This 'mild' dialogue may in fact appear rather 'un-Zen-like' and may not be as interesting as the eccentric style of many Zen dialogues. It may also lack the dramatic sense of the 'beat-and-shout' exchange in which the master beats the student, and shouts at him, in an attempt to allow the student to break through normal intellectual reasoning in order to awaken to his true nature. Such a 'mild' dialogue, I think, is very helpful, however, in order for us modern people to avoid the pitfalls of common misunderstandings about Zen. The 'beat-and-shout' exchanges or eccentric 'Zen-like' dialogues have created the misunderstanding that Zen is something merely anti-intellectual or enigmatic. This assertion forms one of my reasons for dealing with the present case. Even then, however, we must be careful not to overlook the fact that in dealing with this 'mild' dialogue, it points to the *same* reality of Zen as that of other eccentric or tangential dialogues, or 'beat-and-shout' Zen exchanges.

My second reason for taking up the present case is that the true reality of Zen, here referred to as 'Tao' or the Way, is given as our 'ordinary mind.' One misunderstanding of Zen sometimes seen in the West is manifested in the belief that Zen is something not merely anti-intellectual, but also something mystical, and fantastic, 'floating in the sky,' so to speak. The present kōan clearly crushes such a misunderstanding by indicating that our ordinary mind is the true Reality of Zen, emphasizing the down-to-earth nature of Zen.

Another misunderstanding of Zen is overcome by this kōan. It is somewhat the reverse of the above misunderstanding, that is, rather than seeing Zen as something mystical or fantastic, people sometimes strike upon the immediacy of Zen in terms of doing and acting 'without thinking.' Zen is thus understood as a cheap intuitionism or as an easy spontaneity, 'to eat when hungry, to drink when thirsty,' as the Zen expression may imply. Here the down-to-earth nature of Zen is mistaken for a mere pragmatic way of life without philosophical or ontological foundation. What is meant by the down-to-earth nature of Zen is clearly brought forth in this dialogue between Jōshū and Nansen, however. In other words, what Zen is, as shown in the 'ordinary mind is Tao' case, debars us from regarding Zen as possibly signifying a mere immediacy or an animal-like spontaneity without ontological foundation.

Thus, in sum, the present kōan is helpful in overcoming two possible misunderstandings of Zen: at one extreme, Zen as something mystical, and at the other extreme, Zen as something merely pragmatic.

What then does Nansen mean by 'ordinary mind' when he speaks of Tao? In order to answer this question, we must turn to the text itself:

Jōshū once asked Nansen: 'What is Tao?'
    Nansen answered: 'Ordinary mind is Tao.'

The term 'Tao' (the original Chinese character of which is 道) has a rich and profound meaning in the intellectual history of China and Japan. Literally signifying a Way or a road for man's comings and goings, Tao implies the manner of living, the right path for man to follow, moral law, or even the fundamental principle on which the whole universe and its movement are based. It has been used as a key term in Taoism.[2]

As the modern Japanese Zen Master, Zenkei Shibayama-rōshi comments, it must have been this question 'What is Tao?' that made young Jōshū, an ardent student of Buddhist doctrine, give up his academic studies of Buddhism prompting him to travel all the way from North China to Nansen's monastery in South China. To realize experientially 'What is Tao?' was his most urgent and important task. To this question of Jōshū, Master Nansen quite plainly answered, 'Ordinary mind is Tao.'

The term 'Ordinary mind' (*heijōshin*) may also be translated 'everyday mind,' 'usual mind,' or 'normal mind.' It is the mind working in our everyday life, in our usual daily activities, such as getting up in the morning and going to bed in the evening, drinking tea and eating meals, talking with friends and working in the office. It is not mind in a special, unusual, extraordinary state such as spiritual elevation, or upheaval, ecstasy, trance or religious rapture. Accordingly, 'Ordinary mind is Tao' literally means: 'Everyday mind as it is is the Way.' No one can, however, simply and immediately accept Nansen's instruction and say, 'Yes so it is.' This is because 'from ancient times Tao has been treated by many saints and wise men as a fundamental principle and truth and if it is literally our everyday mind as it is, farmers and fishermen's wives would all know it, and we would not have to wait for saints and wise men to teach us and save us.'[3]

Such being the case, it was perfectly natural that young Jōshū was unable to simply accept the instruction of Nansen. He thus had to ask, 'Then should we direct ourselves toward it or not?' In what direction should we strive in order to open our spiritual eye to the fact that our ordinary mind is Tao?

To this Nansen answered, 'if you try to direct yourself toward it, you go away from it.' This means that your very striving and attempting to attain it already causes you to alienate yourself from Tao. Thus the more you try to direct yourself toward it, the further you go away from it. Nansen clearly rejects the idea that one can attain it by trying.

Jōshū's questions continue without hesitation: 'If we do not try, how can we know it is Tao?' We might say that it is quite reasonable for Jōshū to ask this. Without striving to attain it, without speculating about it, how can we be convinced that ordinary mind is Tao?

He has already given up his studies of Buddhist philosophy and travelled all the way from North to South China to study under the Master Nansen. We hear the bleeding cry of a truth seeker who has been driven to a desperate deadlock. The quest in his mind urges him to break through it even at the cost of his life. Yet no approach is possible. Any Zen man without exception has to experience such an excruciating inner anguish before he eventually attains *satori*.[4]

Finally Nansen gave instruction, saying:

> Tao does not belong to knowing or to not-knowing. Knowing is illusion; not-knowing is blankness. If you really attain to Tao of no-doubt, it is like a great void, so vast and boundless. How, then, can there be right and wrong in the Tao?

This answer implies that Nansen does not agree that one can arrive at Tao by not trying. He seems to reject both trying and not trying to arrive at Tao. In this final instruction of Nansen, we also should not overlook that Tao is said to be beyond both knowing and not-knowing, that not only knowing is negated but also not-knowing. In short, the double negation of knowing and not-knowing is necessary for awakening to Tao. This double negation of knowing and not-knowing is linked with the double rejection of trying and not-trying.

However, why must both knowing and not-knowing be negated? This is because, according to Nansen, knowing is illusion and not-knowing is blankness. What does this mean? We modern people are so familiar with various forms of knowledge, especially scientific knowledge: to know an object does not constitute an illusion but gives us clear and unambiguous objective knowledge of it, and so we can say such objective knowledge represents universal truth. A question must be raised in this connection, however. Does objective knowledge of a thing really represent the reality of that thing? In knowing objectively, there is implied a duality between subject and object, that is, a duality between the subject of knowing and the object of knowing. This means that to know something is to objectify that thing as an object from the point of view of the subject. This also indicates that to know something is to know that thing only in so far as it is objectified by a subject. The schema would be:

$$\text{Subject} \xrightarrow[\text{(objectification)}]{\text{Knowing}} \text{Object}$$

Subject (the knower) — Object (the known)

Scientific knowledge is nothing but the purest form of objective knowledge which is attained by eliminating and excluding the subjective point of view. In this objective knowledge, however, what is known is only the object and the subject remains unknown, that is, the knower remains unknown. The known and the knower are two different entities.

Furthermore, what is known of the object is the reality of that thing not in its totality but only so far as it is objectified. The thing is not known as it is. Accordingly, in knowing something as an object, we cannot know the complete reality, but only the partial and conceptualized reality of the thing in question. Therefore, if we take the objective knowledge of a thing as representing the total and authentic reality of that thing, it is a gross mistake. Indeed, knowing the thing objectively implies concealing the clear reality of the thing. In this sense, the objective knowledge of a thing or of the world, however clear it may be objectively, may be said to be an unreal illusion because it does not reveal the true reality of that thing or the world.

On the other hand, Tao is the authentic Reality in which things and the world reveal themselves in their total presence and in which the known and the knower are not two but one. Thus, with Nansen, we must say that Tao does not belong to knowing because knowing is an illusion. To attain Tao we must negate knowing together with its subject–object duality.

The negation of knowing naturally leads us to 'not-knowing' in which the subject–object duality disappears. There is then 'not-knowing' and thus there is neither subject nor object, neither knower nor known. This, however, leaves us with a sheer blankness. While knowing is an affirmation of each and every thing, not-knowing is the negation of things. In not-knowing, there is only indifference. Tao, however, does not belong to not-knowing because not-knowing is merely a negative side of knowing. Tao is not attained in such an indifferent blankness. The true Tao is really beyond both knowing and not-knowing, beyond both affirmation and negation.

What is it, however, that is beyond both knowing and not-knowing, beyond both affirmation and negation? It is emptiness or *śūnyatā*. This is the reason Nansen says: 'If you really attain to the Tao of no-doubt, it is like the great void, so vast and boundless.' And this Tao which is like the great void is realized nowhere other than in the ordinary mind. This is the meaning of Nansen's first statement, 'Ordinary mind is Tao.'

This ordinary mind, therefore, is not the ordinary mind *prior to* attaining the realization of emptiness, but the ordinary mind *after* or *through* attaining to and being supported by the realization of emptiness. This is the down-to-earth nature of Zen. Zen does not talk about something mystical, supernatural or transcendental. Instead it says, ordinary mind is Tao. However, this does not indicate a superficial affirmation of the everyday mind because Tao as the ordinary mind does not belong to knowing or to not-knowing. By negating both knowing and not-knowing, and only by rejecting both trying and non-trying, may one awaken to the great void so vast and boundless. It is only through the awakening to this great void that the ordinary mind is realized as Tao.

What is most important in this regard is that the great void or emptiness is not a mere emptiness but rather fullness. For, being beyond both knowing and not-knowing, the great Void reveals a higher form of knowing which itself is neither knowing nor not-knowing, but which includes both of them. Indeed, being freed from the duality between knowing and not-knowing, the great void can utilize both of them freely without being shackled by them. This higher form of knowing is knowing in and through not-knowing. It is knowing which itself is not-knowing. It is not-knowing which itself is knowing. This higher form of knowing is nothing but *satori* or enlightenment which is also called in Buddhism *prajñā*, that is wisdom.

In knowing in the ordinary sense, the knower and the known are separated; they are two not one. In not-knowing there are neither the knower nor the known; duality of the knower and the known disappears. However, in that higher form of knowing that is knowing in and through not-knowing, the knower and the known are entirely one and yet their distinction is clear. In other words, the self and others are one and yet the self is really the self and others are really others.

In this connection it may be helpful to quote a well-known discourse given by Chinese Zen Master, Ch'ing-yüan Wei-hsin of the T'ang dynasty. It reads as follows:

> Thirty years ago, before I began the study of Zen, I said, 'Mountains are mountains; waters are waters.' After I got insight into the truth of Zen through the instruction of a good master, I said, 'Mountains are not mountains; waters are not waters.' But now, having attained the abode of final rest [that is enlightenment], I say, 'Mountains are really mountains; waters are really waters.'

The first stage of understanding, that is 'Mountains are mountains; waters are waters' indicates 'knowing' in the above discussed objective sense. The second stage of understanding, that is 'Mountains are not mountains; waters are not waters', signifies 'not-knowing' as the negation of 'knowing.' And the third and final stage of understanding, that is 'Mountains are really mountains; waters are really waters', refers to a higher form of knowing, that is knowing in and through not-knowing. Here in this knowing, everything is clearly realized in its distinctiveness as it truly is, no more, no less, and yet everything is equal and interchangeable in its as-it-is-ness, that is to say, 'Mountains are really mountains; waters are really waters.' And yet, mountains are waters, waters are mountains. Likewise, we can say I am really I; you are really you. And yet I am you; you are me. This interchangeability or interpenetration is possible because the higher form of knowing, that is enlightenment, is realized in and through not-knowing. Everything's distinctiveness and everything's interpenetration go together dynamically because these two aspects are realized in the great void, so vast and boundless. This is the reason I said earlier that the great void or emptiness is not a mere emptiness but rather fullness.

In the realization of the Great Void which is neither knowing nor not-knowing everything is affirmed as it is in its reality, no more, no less. Thus Mumon states in his poem:

> Hundreds of flowers in spring, the moon in autumn,
> A cool breeze in summer, and snow in winter;
> If there is no vain cloud in your mind
> For you it is a good season.

If you are free from knowing and not-knowing, that is if there is no vain cloud in your mind, your everyday mind is Tao. Tao or Truth is not over there, is not something to be realized in the future, but is right here, right now, in our ordinary mind.

As an ancient sage says:

Tao is never away from us even for a moment.
    If it is, it is not Tao.

3

'Life and Death' and 'Good and Evil' in Zen

Although life and death are common to both man and animals, it is only for man, who has self-consciousness, that the 'facts' of life and death become a serious 'problem.' Man worries about 'having to die' rather than about death itself. Life and death are for man not mere natural or value-free phenomena. Life is desirable, and death is repugnant. Thus man consciously and intentionally tries to overcome death by perpetuating life. On the other hand, the problem of good and evil is peculiar to man, for good and evil are matters neither of instinct nor of reflex movement, but of human decision based on free will. Furthermore, the problem of life and death and the problem of good and evil, although essentially different, are inseparable in the depths of human existence. For example, in Buddhism to be born male or female is understood to be an effect of karma, that is, the result of past deeds. In Christianity death is said to be 'the wages of sin.'

Dōgen, a Japanese Zen master of the thirteenth century, said, 'It is a mistake to understand that one passes from life to death.' In our daily life we ordinarily think that we are now alive, and that we will die sometime in the future: we think of ourselves as gradually moving from life to death. Dōgen insisted that this understanding of life and death is mistaken. His approach is expressed in the following question: When we consider the relationship between life and death in this way, *where* are we taking our stand? In life or in death? Or do we make this judgment from another vantage point? When we look upon the relation of life and death as a *process* moving from the former to the latter, our 'existential' posture is *outside* of both. That is, we objectify our death as something in the future, and objectify our present life as well.

An objectified or generalized life, however, is no longer real life. Likewise, an objectified or generalized death is an abstraction. Such a viewpoint offers neither a serious enquiry into the significance of life, nor an existential realization of the anxiety of death. Real life cannot be viewed objectively from the outside. It must be grasped subjectively from within. Once we have taken life subjectively we realize that life and death are not two separate things. We do not find ourselves moving from life to death, but living *and at the same time* dying. This is true regardless of our age. A new-born baby, fresh from his mother's womb, is beginning his death, even as an old man on his deathbed is still living. Without dying there is no living, and without living there is no dying. A rigid separation of life and death is abstract and unreal. It is only a conceptual understanding which objectifies life and death by taking its stand beyond both, in an imaginary place established by thought alone.

Through objectification we cling to life and hate death. We are shackled by the opposition between life and death. Nevertheless, we are always confronted by death through the very fact that we are alive. Life and death are as inseparable as two sides of a sheet of paper. Nor is this an ordinary sheet of paper upon which we may idly gaze. We *are* this sheet of paper with its two sides of life and death. Therefore, *at any moment* of our life we are all life and all death. Our life is not a movement from life towards death, but a continual living-dying, a paradoxical and dynamic oneness of life and death. This is the reason Dōgen says, 'It is a mistake to understand that one passes from life to death.'

In Plato, man is understood as mortal, that is liable to death, and the immortality of the soul is treated as a serious issue. In Christianity, man must die because of his Original Sin. Through faith in the resurrection of Jesus Christ, Christians look forward to eternal life beyond sin and death. In contrast to these views, Buddhism sees man *not* as mortal in Plato's sense, nor as having to die because of sin, but as living-dying in terms of *karma*. Buddhism speaks of this incessant living-dying in terms of *samsāra* and birth – death transmigration. Accordingly, what Buddhism looks for is not the immortality of the soul, nor eternal life in the Kingdom of God, but *Nirvāṇa* in which living-dying itself is completely abolished. For this reason, *Nirvāṇa* is often called *fushō-fushi*, unborn-ness and undying-ness, a liberation from both birth and death. Zen especially emphasizes this kind of liberation. For if we are liberated from the duality of birth and death, or life and death, we can work in this world freed from dualistic tensions.

Kanzan Egen (1277–1360), the founder of Myōshinji Temple in Kyoto, asked a new monk, 'For what purpose did you come here?' 'I have come here because, try as I would, I could not solve the problem of life and death,' replied the monk. 'For me there is no such thing as life and death!' the master replied and drove him away. With this rude treatment Kanzan tried to cut off the roots of the monk's attachment to life and death.

By presupposing mortality or life as their bases, both Platonism and Christianity take the position, severely rejected by Dōgen, that one moves from life to death. In other words, are not the ideas of immortality in Platonism and Eternal Life in Christianity extensions of life beyond death, notions presupposing life as the ground even of death? Yet how is one justified in assuming that 'life' is the basis upon which one overcomes the problem of life and death? How can one overcome death in terms of life while life and death are essentially inseparable? These are the questions which Buddhism as well as Zen cannot help asking of Christianity.

Speaking of God as *Being* itself, Paul Tillich has said that 'Being "embraces" itself and non-being. Being has non-being "within" itself as that which is eternally present and eternally overcome in the process of the divine life.'[1] According to Tillich, this is because, 'Being precedes non-being in ontological validity, as the word "non-being" indicates.'[2] Apparently, being precedes non-being because non-being is the negation of being and not vice versa. On the basis of the ontological priority of being over non-being, life is seen essentially prior to death, and good is essentially prior to evil. This is, I think, the basic understanding of life and death, good and evil, common to both Greek philosophy and Christianity.

In this connection Zen is forced to raise the following questions: How can 'Being' embrace both *itself* and non-being? Is not the *very basis* on which 'Being' embraces itself and non-being, neither being nor non-being, that is, 'Emptiness' in the Buddhist sense? Is not 'Being' in Western philosophy and religion uncritically assumed to be superior to non-being, with the result that 'non-being,' or the negative principle of life, is not taken seriously enough or understood in adequate depth? If so, is not God – that is 'Being' which embraces both itself and non-being – after all, an assumption?

In Buddhism as well as in Zen, death and evil are not overcome by life and good. Life and death, and good and evil, have equal power and depth in human existence. The idea of the superiority of life over death or good over evil is an illusion. We would like to overcome death by life, and *it is no doubt a moral imperative to conquer evil by good*. Nevertheless, however natural these impulses may be, we cannot reach our goal unless we begin from the proper starting point. This starting point is not Being itself which is uncritically presupposed to be superior to the negative principle of human life. We cannot really overcome death by the principle of life and thereby reach eternal life. Again, we cannot really conquer evil by the principle of good and thereby reach the highest good.

If we begin in this way, we shall surely fall into a 'false endlessness' (*schlechte Unendlichkeit*). Clearly realizing that Platonism inevitably entails this self-contradiction inherent in human existence, Christianity, with its doctrine of Original Sin, has gone beyond such an idealism, finding a way of salvation in the Cross of Jesus Christ, i.e., in his death and resurrection. But in Christianity as well, and especially in Tillich, the superiority of being (life and good) over non-being (death and evil) is basically the same as in Platonism. For the Christian, the only way to escape this false endlessness is faith and hope. Tillich emphasized the 'courage to be' in the name of faith. It seems to me, however, that faith as the 'courage to be' is the necessary outcome of a theological position which takes as its starting point the superiority of being over non-being.

Should we not honestly recognize that being and non-being, life and death, good and evil have equal powers and roles in human existence? And should we not therefore try to overcome the contradiction between them? Accordingly, the goal of Zen is not Eternal life as the Supreme Good, but that which is neither life nor death, neither good nor evil, namely, Emptiness or *śūnyatā*. For Zen, Self-Awakening rather than faith is the standpoint we should take. Here I am not concerned with 'What is Zen?' but with 'What is Reality?'

Life and death, good and evil, in Buddhism have equal power and work in opposite directions in the depths of human existence. However, this is not a thoroughgoing dualism such as we find in Manichaeism. There the fundamental principles of light and darkness, good and evil, contend against one another – each dwelling within its respective realm, coeternal and independent. In Buddhism, on the other hand, life and death are a paradoxical oneness in which living and dying are inseparable.

The living-dying in Buddhist teaching is neither process nor continuity. If we *actually*, or *subjectively*, *realize* that we are living and dying *at every moment*, we will attain the paradoxical oneness of living and dying which is true of all our life – *right here* and *right now*. At this point we come to realize that *our living-dying existence itself is death*. It is not death as a counterpart of life, but death in an absolute sense. In

Zen this is called the 'Great Death', through which one attains *Nirvāṇa*, having been 'reborn, after thoroughly dying.' This means that at the very moment you die, the 'Great Death' – 'Great Life' clearly manifests itself. In the *Blue Cliff Record*, one of the most important Zen documents, we find the following kōan: Chao-chou (in Japanese Jōshū), a Chinese Zen master of the T'ang dynasty, asked T'ou-tzu (Tōsu) 'When a man who has experienced the Great Death comes to life again, what then?' In his comment on this kōan, Yüan-wu (Engo) says, 'You must die this Great Death and at that point attain Life.'

In other words, Buddhism, as well as Zen, does not teach dualism. On the contrary, our living-dying must be *subjectively* realized as a whole *at this moment*. In this realization of 'Great Death,' we return to the root of our life-and-death, and there extricate ourselves from living-dying at its very root. This is a discovery of 'Great Life,' the 'New Life,' in which one can live the living-dying life freely without becoming shackled by it. The following verse by Shidō Bunan, a Japanese Zen master of the early Tokugawa era, is a good expression of this New Life in Zen:

> While living, (to) become a dead man
> Thoroughly dead
> Then do as you will,
> All will be all right.

There is an equivalent to this Zen experience in Christianity. Paul says, 'We are always carrying in the body of the death of Jesus, so that the life of Jesus may also be manifested in our bodies.'[3] A new eon begins in Christ; the immortal God tastes death and in so doing destroys it.[4] In baptism the Christian experiences union with Christ, participating in both his death and resurrection not as mere ritual, but as the symbol of this real sharing. For Paul, faith implies dying daily, whereby the 'old man' of sin is crucified and dies, in order that the 'new man' may be raised from the dead by the same power of God that raised Christ.

It is clear that Christianity does not simply re-present the Platonic duality of body and soul. For body and soul, though not always compatible, are both God's creations. Consequently, Christianity teaches not just the immortality of the soul, but the resurrection of the body as *sōma pneumatikon* (i.e., spiritual body). Even in Pauline mysticism there are more important distinctions between man and

God, the creature and the creator, the believer and Jesus Christ as the incarnation of God and center of history. These distinctions imply that there is still a fundamental vertical dualism in Christianity. As I understand it, this vertical duality implied in the divine-human relationship has a positive significance. It is based on the idea of man's original sin, which was a rebellion against the word of God, and the redemption of man by Jesus Christ on the cross. Man's rebellion and God's incarnate work of redemption point to a gap – a duality – between man and God.

Zen's emphasis on 'killing the Buddha, and killing a patriarch,'[5] and on 'Emptiness, no holiness,'[6] points to the necessity of overcoming even a 'vertical dualism.' In my view, the vertical duality in terms of the divine-human relationship as seen in Christianity is inseparably connected to the idea of the superiority of being over against non-being. Tillich's statement, 'Being embraces itself and non-being within itself,' expresses the all-inclusive nature of Being or God. However, this idea of Being is tautological instead of dialectical, and presents a closed circle. How can Being embrace both itself and non-being? Is not this concept of 'Being' as such supported and objectified by 'something' hidden behind the whole scene?

It appears that Tillich was aware that his position revolved in a closed circle when at the end of his book, *The Courage to Be*, he presented his new phrase, 'The God above God.'[7] At this point, the Zen Buddhist is tempted to ask – Why must 'God *above* God' be '*God* above God'? If we are looking for something *above* God, are we really looking for *God*, or for something else? For Zen, that which is above God is not God. It is Emptiness, no holiness, or *śūnyatā*. If that which is *above* God is still *God*, it is not really *above* God.

Emptiness, or *śūnyatā*, realized by 'killing the Buddha' or by transcending even the religious transcendence, opens all closed and circular ways of thinking about being. But if Emptiness 'above God' is found *outside* of oneself it is not really all-inclusive nor is it completely free from tautology. Only when Emptiness is self and self is Emptiness is it all-inclusive in the true sense whereby one avoids the tautology involved in 'being itself.' At this point, the negation of even 'Emptiness' as the object of one's spiritual quest is necessary. What is required is a complete re-conversion from Emptiness as the *end* to Emptiness as one's *ultimate ground*.

To return to the problem of life and death, let us consider the following story. Tao-wu (Dōgo), a Zen master of the late T'ang dynasty, went one day with his disciple Chien-yüan (Zengen) to visit a family in order to mourn for the dead. Chien-yüan was a young monk seeking for truth, and was especially concerned with the problem of life and death. To learn what was in his master's mind, Chien-yüan knocked on the coffin and said, 'Living or dead?' Tao-wu instantly responded, 'Living? I tell you not! Dead? I tell you not!' 'Why not?' asked the disciple. To this the master replied, 'I won't tell! I won't tell!' This was a Zen answer designed to liberate the disciple from the dualism of life and death. Chien-yüan, however, had not yet come to himself. When they were halfway on their homeward walk, he again accosted his master, saying, 'O master, please tell me about it. If you don't I will strike you down.' The master responded, 'As for striking, it is up to you. As for talking, I have nothing to tell you.' Thereupon the disciple struck him. Had Tao-wu at that time proclaimed the immortality of soul or the eternal life to Chien-yüan, the disciple might have been satisfied. But the master had repeated the same negative answer, and Chien-yüan was quietly sent away. Later he went to Shih-Shuang (Sekisō), one of Tao-wu's disciples, and telling him his story, he asked the monk to enlighten him on the matter. Shih-Shuang also said, 'Living? I tell you not! Dead? I tell you not!' 'Why won't you tell me?' demanded Chien-yüan. 'I won't tell! I won't tell!' replied Shih-Shuang. This instantly opened up Chien-yüan's mind.[8]

The conversations Chien-yüan had with Tao-wu and Shih-Shuang were exactly the same. In the first case, however, Chien-yüan was misled by the external meaning of his master's remark. In the second case, he awakened instantly. We do not know how much time elapsed between these two scenes, but during the interval Chien-yüan must have struggled more seriously with the problem of life and death than before. When he visited Shih-Shuang, his dualistic way of thinking had reached its limit. The last defensive barrier was broken through by Shih-Shuang's words, 'I won't tell! I won't tell!' Thereupon the subject–object structure of thinking collapsed, and beyond all dualism his true self awakened.

Chien-yüan awakened to his 'Original Face' through the problem of life and death. Let us consider a case in which one awakens to his True Self through the problem of good and evil. When the sixth patriarch Hui-neng (Enō) was asked by the monk Ming (Myō) what Zen was, he said, 'When your mind is not dwelling on the dualism of good and evil, what is your Original Face?' Struck by these words, Ming immediately awakened.

In Zen, which denies all dualities including the vertical one, there is neither the rule of God nor the idea of creation nor the last judgment. History as well as man's living-dying existence (*saṃsāra*) has no beginning and no end. There is only a beginningless beginning and endless end. This is, however, not a vague notion, but a concept made possible through negation of a vertical duality implied in historical incarnation. Since *saṃsāra* is without beginning or end, history has no center. Accordingly, every point in history is a center. This is the reason, as I stated earlier, that at every moment of our living-dying existence we realize the paradoxical oneness of living and dying in its totality, and thereby we are liberated from it. At the very moment of our existential realization, 'Great Death' and 'Great Life' take place in us. And so there is no process in history. At every moment a profound disjunction is realized. Time and history, *from the point of view of our existential realization*, are the conjunction of actual disjunctions, just as one lives 'Great Life' through 'Great Death' realized at every moment.

The seventeenth-century haiku poet Matsuo Bashō was strongly influenced by Zen. On his deathbed he was asked by his disciples to compose a farewell poem. Traditionally, a poet in such circumstances is thought to put his whole heart and soul into a final poem. Regarding this request, Bashō said, 'I have no particular farewell poem. The poems which I have composed day by day are all my farewell poems.' For Bashō, life was not a process moving from life to death. But every day and at every moment he devoted himself entirely to poetic composition through the Great Death and the New Life. Today does not bring us closer to eternity, but today at this moment, Eternity is completely manifesting itself.

4

Emptiness

THE MEANING OF EMPTINESS

The ultimate reality in Buddhism is not God, or Being, or Substance; it is *Śūnyatā*, which is often translated as 'Emptiness.' Why does Buddhism take 'emptiness' as the ultimate reality? What does Buddhism indicate by the term 'emptiness'? To understand the real meaning of 'emptiness,' one must begin by emptying one's mind of the negative connotations the word has in the English language. In this regard the etymological explanation of the term *Śūnyatā* will be helpful. As Garma C. C. Chang discusses in his book *The Buddhist Teaching of Totality: The Philosophy of Hwa Yen Buddhism*:

> ... Śūnyatā is a combination of the stem *śūnya*, 'void or empty,' and a participle suffix, *tā*, here rendered as 'ness.' *Śūnyatā* is therefore translated as 'Voidness or Emptiness.' It is believed that *śūnya* was originally derived from the root *svi*, 'to swell,' and *śūnya* implies 'relating to the swollen.' As the proverb says, 'A swollen head is an empty head,' so something which looks swollen or inflated outside is usually hollow or empty inside. *Śūnyatā* suggests therefore that although things in the phenomenal world appear to be real and substantial outside, they are actually tenuous and empty within. They are not real but only appear to be real. *Śūnyatā* denotes the absence of any kind of self, or selfhood. All things are empty in that they lack a subsisting entity or self-being (Svabhāva).[1]

This is the connotation of the term *Śūnyatā*. The realization that 'although things in the phenomenal world appear to be real and substantial outside, they are actually tenuous and empty within' was intuitively realized in *Prajñāpāramitā* literature and was logically or philosophically formulated by Nāgārjuna, especially in his important writing, *Mūlamadhyamakakārikā*.[2] The basic purport of *Prajñāpāramitā Sūtra* and *Mūlamadhyamakakārikā* is that if a phenomenal thing is

42

real as *svabhāva* (self-being or self-existent thing), then we cannot understand the world of causality and change in terms of arising and ceasing – which we are, in fact, constantly experiencing. Accordingly, the phenomenal thing does not exist as *svabhāva*. In terms of a self-existing thing, the phenomenal thing is empty.

The Buddhists believe that to be called 'substantial or real' a thing must be able to exist on its own. However, if we look at the universe, we find that everything in it exists only in relation to something else. A son is a son only in relation to the father; and a father similarly in relation to the son. Fatherhood does not exist on its own but only in relation to something else. The Buddhists use the word *svabhāva* to denote existence on its own, that is, non-dependent existence, which alone, according to them, qualifies as true or genuine existence. But if everything in the world depends on something else for being what it is, then nothing in the universe can be said to possess *svabhāva* or genuine self-existence; hence it is empty. For instance, we are familiar with the phenomenon of fire. We also know that fire requires fuel to burn. However, can fire ever exist without fuel? It cannot. And can fuel exist without fire? We may be tempted to say yes, but Buddhism asks us to pause for a moment before we do so. A log of wood cannot qualify as *fuel* if the phenomenon of fire did not exist. A log of wood would then remain merely a log of wood – it is the possibility of using it for fire that makes it into fuel. Hence it possesses no *svabhāva* or self-nature as fuel.

Through these examples of Nāgārjuna, we are led to a definition of *svabhāva*. That is: *Svabhāva* is that which is self-existing because it is not something that is produced dependently by something else. It is an enduring, permanent being without change, birth, and death. *Svabhāva* is a singular being without partition. In short, *svabhāva* in Nāgārjuna's sense is a self-existing, enduring, singular substance. Such a self-existing *svabhāva* is nothing but a substantialization or reification of the concept and does not exist anywhere outside of the realm of thinking and language. In our daily lives the role of language is so great that people easily reify or substantialize the word or concept as if there is an enduring, unchanging reality corresponding to the word or concept. In other words, people often apply the universality and constancy implied in the meaning of a word to the object. Especially those who have entered into the realm of metaphysics constructed through reification of concepts think that the self-existing *svabhāva* is truth, while the realm of fact is merely phenomenal. In the days of Nāgārjuna, various forms of metaphysics of language, such as that of the Abhidharma philosophy, were prevailing. The *Prajñāpāramitā Sūtra* and *Mūlamadhyamakakārikā* were composed to break through such an attachment to metaphysics.

CONCEPT, LANGUAGE, AND REALITY

Let me explain this issue further by citing from our daily experience. People of America are used to calling California the 'West Coast'; thus, they often think that California is an entity called 'the West Coast,' or a substance corresponding to the notion of 'West Coast.' However, although California may be called the West Coast from the viewpoint of Washington, DC, New York, or Boston, West Coast is merely a relative notion, not a self-existing entity. If we look at California from the point of view of Hawaii or Japan, California is not the west coast but the east coast. Again, if we look at California from the point of view of British Columbia, California is not the west coast but the south coast. East and west, south and north – all are relative notions without enduring reality. There is neither absolute east nor absolute west; neither absolute south nor absolute north. Such a notion of absolute east or absolute west is simply a human conceptual construction; it is not real. Rather, it is non-substantial and empty. This is easily understood. Exactly the same understanding can be applied to the notion of right and left, high and low, big and small, and so on. There can be no absolute right, absolute high, or absolute big in reality.

However, when we move to the notions of good and evil, true and false, or beauty and ugliness, the situation is not so simple. Many philosophies and religions talk about the absolute good (for instance, the Supreme Good, or summum bonum) and absolute evil (original sin and eternal punishment). This is because, unlike the notions of east and west, high and low, big and small – which refer to the physical, objective, value-free dimension – the notions of good and evil, true and false, and beauty and ugliness denote the existential, subjective, value-oriented dimension. They are situated not merely in the ontic, or ontological, dimension (a dimension concerning how something *is*) but also in the axiological dimension (a dimension concerning how something *ought* to be). Due to this axiological nature, the notions of good and evil, true and false, and beauty and ugliness inevitably lead us to the notion of absolute good, absolute evil, absolute truth, absolute falsehood, and so forth. Thus people believe, for instance, in the notion of absolute good as the enduring, unchangeable, and universal reality, and they take it to be the ultimate goal of their ethical life. However, Buddhism, particularly Nāgārjuna and his Mādhyamika philosophy, insist that such a notion of absolute good (and similar notions) is not unchangeable or enduring, but non-substantial and empty. This is because in the axiological dimension, the notion of absolute good, for instance, is nothing but a reification or substantialization of the notion of good. To begin with, the very distinction of good and evil is, to Nāgārjuna, nothing but a reification or substantialization of a human concept that is devoid of reality. In short, all value judgments are, after all, unreal human conceptual constructions.

In Nāgārjuna all value judgments arise from *vikalpa*, human thinking, which is a discriminating, bifurcating, and dualistic way of thinking. To him, this *vikalpa* is the source of human suffering because people are attached to it and grasp discriminating and dualistic thoughts as true and real. If we are free from *vikalpa* and awaken to the emptiness of dualistic discrimination, then we are emancipated from suffering through the realization of *Śūnyatā*. In the *Mūlamadhyamakakārikā*, chapter 18, Nāgārjuna states the following:

> On account of the destruction of pain (*kleśa*) of action there is release; for pains of action exist for him who constructs them. These pains result from phenomenal extension (*prapañca*); but this phenomenal extension comes to a stop by emptiness. (18:5)
>
> When the domain of thought has been dissipated, 'that which can be stated' is dissipated. Those things which are unoriginated and not terminated, like *nirvāna*, constitute the Truth (*dharmatā*). (18:7)
>
> 'Not caused by something,' 'peaceful,' 'not elaborated by discursive thought,' 'indeterminate,' 'undifferentiated'; such are the characteristics of true reality (*tattva*). (18:9)[3]

Prapañca, here translated as phenomenal extension and discursive thought, originally indicated diversity or plurality including the complex development of thinking and language. To Nāgārjuna, *prapañca* implies verbal pluralism or fiction of language. *Vikalpa* arises from *prapañca* because human thinking is nothing but a fiction unrelated to reality. The process of human knowledge based on language is a perversion. It is necessary for us to retrogress from attachment to thinking and judgment to the realm of non-discursive intuition. In so doing we face reality prior to language. This is the realm of 'emptiness.' Emptiness indicates the reality of the world in intuition apart from language; therefore, there is emancipation from suffering caused by attachment to discrimination. Accordingly, Emptiness is not only a philosophical notion, it is also a religious and soteriological one.

REIFICATION IN THE RELIGIOUS DIMENSION

Earlier in this chapter we saw the problem of reification and substantialization of human concepts in the ontic, or ontological, dimension and in the axiological dimension as well. Also, it was suggested that we must be liberated from such reification of human concepts through awakening to the non-substantial emptiness of phenomenal things to realize true reality.

Exactly the same issue is involved when we move from the realm of ethics to the realm of religion. In the axiological realm, or the value-oriented realm – such as good and evil, truth and falsehood, beauty and ugliness – the criteria for value judgments are crucial. Therefore, a value judgment and its criteria are easily reified, or substantialized. However, the realm of religion is beyond such value judgment because it is based on the unconditional love of God or the unlimited compassion of Buddha, which are supported by the divine will of God or supreme wisdom. Unlike the realm of ethics (good and evil), the realm of learning (the true and the false), and the realm of aesthetics (the beautiful and the ugly), the realm of religion is free from the reification or substantialization of value judgments. For instance, in Christianity Jesus says, 'I have not come to call respectable people, but outcasts' (Matt. 9:13, *Good News Bible*). In Buddhism, Shinran (1173–1262) emphasized the unconditional compassion of Amida Buddha. He declared, 'Even a good person is saved in the Pure Land. How much more so is an evil person.'[4]

Thus, in both Christianity and Buddhism, value judgment is not only transcended, but it also reversed. However, if we go a step further, we see a significant difference between Christianity and Buddhism in regard to value judgment and the understanding of ultimate reality. In Christianity, although all human-made value judgments (including wisdom in the sense of the Greeks) are transcended by God, God himself is believed to be the 'only wise God' (Rom. 16:27) and the 'judge of all' (Heb. 12:23). Indeed, God, the ultimate reality in Christianity, is believed to be the Supreme Good beyond the duality of good and evil and the source of all value judgments. The will of God is believed to be self-existing. By contrast, in Buddhism the ultimate reality, *Nirvāṇa*, is not the supreme good or the judge of all, but that which is *neither* good *nor* evil. This is because in Buddhism the ultimate reality is to be realized as non-dual by *completely* overcoming all duality.

It is clear that the Christian notion of God is not merely transcendent. In terms of *homoousia*, God is fully immanent and fully transcendent in the incarnation of Jesus Christ. However, this paradoxical identity of immanence and transcendence, the human and the divine (both truly human and truly God), is realized without the clear realization of *neither* immanent *nor* transcendent, *neither* human *nor* divine. The paradoxical identity is realized somewhat objectively without the negation of negation, that is, absolute negation. Hence, although through faith in Jesus Christ a Christian *participates in* the death and resurrection of Jesus Christ, he or she does not become *identical* with God except in some forms of Christian mysticism. In this sense the Christian notion of God is fundamentally transcendent and is not completely free from reification and substantialization. Here I am using the terms reification and substantialization in a special sense. It is definitely clear that the Christian notion of God is not a reification or substantialization of the divine – especially in the Trinitarian notion of God, which is dialectical, reciprocal, and necessarily understood in terms of Father, Son, and Spirit. However, are this Trinitarian God and the human self completely reciprocal; are this Trinitarian God and each and every non-human creature also completely reciprocal?[5]

On the other hand, Buddhism clearly realizes the possibility of reification and substantialization in the religious dimension. In the first place, when Buddhism transcends the axiological dimension, it overcomes all duality completely and attains a non-dualistic position. This means that both ends of duality, for instance good and evil, are equally overcome through the double negation of the two ends – i.e., good and evil. This double negation of both ends of duality does not entail the supreme good, but that which is neither good nor evil. This is the reason why in Buddhism ultimate reality is not God as the supreme good, but Emptiness, which is neither good nor evil.

The preceding is the first important difference between Christianity and Buddhism. This difference derives from the fact that Buddhism *completely* overcomes the duality of value judgment in the axiological dimension through the negation of negation, and thus reaches the religious dimension, which is entirely free from even the notion of absolute good. Christianity, however, transcends value judgment in the axiological dimension, not necessarily through the realization of negation; that is, not through completely overcoming duality itself, but by moving toward the extreme point of good.

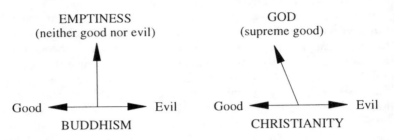

Again, this difference takes place because, in Buddhism, the non-substantiality and emptiness of the notion of good and evil are clearly realized, and reification and substantialization of any sort are carefully rejected, whereas, in Christianity, the non-substantiality and emptiness of the notion of good are not categorically recognized due to Christianity's emphasis on divine justice. And, when the notion of good is absolutized, some reification and substantialization are inevitable. Here we must notice how crucial the realization of non-substantiality and emptiness of the notion of good is, even when it is absolutized, for us to attain ultimate reality by going beyond any possible reification and substantialization.

SELF-EMPTYING OF EMPTINESS

The second important difference between Christianity and Buddhism concerning ultimate reality is as follows. In Buddhism, Emptiness as ultimate reality must be emptied. However important Emptiness may be, if it is represented and we attach ourselves to it as 'emptiness,' it is not true Emptiness. In Nāgārjuna's *Mūlamadhyamakakārikā*, emptiness that is dimly perceived is likened to a snake wrongly grasped, or (magical) knowledge incorrectly applied.[6] Emptiness that is objectified and conceptualized must be emptied. The self-negation, or self-emptying, of Emptiness is essential for the authentic realization of Emptiness. By contrast, in Christianity the *kenosis* (self-emptying) of Christ is emphasized (Phil. 2:5–8), but not necessarily the *kenosis* of God.[7]

Christian theology generally states that the Son of God became a human being without God ceasing to be God. In his book *Does God Exist?* Hans Küng says:

> The distinction of the Son of God from God the Father, his obedience and subordination to the Father, is of course upheld everywhere in the New Testament. The Father is 'greater' than he is and there are things that are known only the Father and not to him. Neither is there any mention anywhere in the New Testament of the incarnation of God himself.[8]

From what has been discussed, it is hoped that the following three points become clear in regard to the Buddhist notion of Emptiness.

1. To attain ultimate reality, Buddhism rejects the reification and substantialization of human-made concepts and emphasizes the importance of realizing the non-substantiality and emptiness of all dualistic notions in the ontic and axiological dimensions.

2. Thus, ultimate reality in Buddhism is not God, Being, or Substance; rather, it is 'Emptiness,' which is freed from any reification and substantialization in the religious dimension.

3. This Emptiness itself must be emptied by rejecting any attachment to emptiness. True Emptiness is not a static state of everything's non-substantiality, but rather a dynamic function of emptying everything, including itself.

When Buddhism declares that everything without exception is empty, these three points are implied.

EMPTINESS AND DEPENDENT CO-ORIGINATION[9]

The notion of Emptiness is not nihilistic. It has a positive and affirmative aspect. What is ultimately negated in the teaching of Emptiness is the Self (Ātman) and any self-substantiated entity (*svabhāva*). Through the negation of the Self and the self-substantiated entity, true reality manifests itself. Although negation is an essential factor of Mādhyamika philosophy, if it is a mere negation, Mādhyamika philosophy would be nihilistic. It is the law of dependent co-origination (*pratītya-samutpāda*) that manifests itself through the negation of Ātman and *svabhāva*, that is, through the realization of the emptiness of everything. In Nāgārjuna, emptiness and dependent co-origination are synonymous. This is why he states in the *Mūlamadhyamakakārikā*, chapter 24,[10] that:

> The 'originating dependently' we call 'emptiness'; this apprehension, i.e. taking into account [all other things], is the understanding of the middle way. (24:18)
> Since there is no *dharma* whatever originating independently, no *dharma* whatever exists which is not empty. (24:19)

Indeed, it is the central task for Mādhyamika philosophy to penetrate into the truth of dependent co-origination.

Dependent co-origination presents the fundamental standpoint of early Buddhism and is its most basic teaching. Historically speaking, the teaching of dependent co-origination has been continually maintained from early Buddhism to Mādhyamika. In this process of development, contrary to the Hīnayāna interpretation of dependent co-origination, which had been stereotyped, Mādhyamika philosophy revived the original dynamic nature of dependent co-origination on the basis of the full realization of Emptiness. Although the teaching of dependent co-origination indicates causality (i.e., a causal relationship from cause to effect), the dependent co-origination as understood by Nāgārjuna does not signify a process from a self-existing cause to a self-existing effect. As he states in *Kārikās* 24:19, 'there is no *dharma* whatever originating independently, no *dharma* whatever exists which is not empty.' Both the dharma called the cause and the dharma called the effect are equally devoid of a self-existent entity. We know that fuel is the cause of fire and fire the effect of fuel. Let us now ask the further question, Which came first, fire or fuel? If we say fire came first, we face the logical absurdity of fire burning without 'fuel.' If we say fuel came first, we face the logical absurdity of identifying a cause without knowing about the effect. If we say they appeared together, then all fuels will have to be simultaneously on fire. In Nāgārjuna, dependent co-origination in the true sense is realized when the self-existent entity of each and every thing is completely negated and realized to be empty.

In the first chapter of the *Mūlamadhyamikakārikā*, which may be entitled 'An Analysis of Conditioning Causes (*pratyaya*),'[11] Nāgārjuna states:

> Never are any existing things found to originate from themselves, from something else, from both, or from no cause. (1:1)

However, this statement does not deny 'originating.' Fire does empirically 'originate' in fuel. Rather, it denies the existence of any self-substantiated entity. In other words, that statement simply indicates the function of originating dependently without any independent entity. Thus we come to know that in Nāgārjuna, the realization of Emptiness is inseparably connected with the law of dependent co-origination.

THE TWO TRUTHS THEORY

In Mādhyamika philosophy, this identity of emptiness and dependent co-origination is always linked with the two truths theory.[12] You might respond to what has been said above with bafflement and complain that all this philosophizing runs counter to your daily experience of life. No amount of theory can refute the fact that you actually use fuel and fire to barbecue. It is the nature of the fire to cook (however, can it cook itself?), and you enjoy your steak, despite all this talk about both fuel and fire being empty.

The Buddhists do not deny that our everyday ideas of things such as fire and fuel possess practical efficacy. All they say is that they cannot stand philosophical scrutiny. We see the sun rise every morning. The astronomer sees it rise too, but the astronomer knows that this experience will not bear scientific scrutiny because the sun is a fixed star. It cannot rise. It only appears to rise because of the rotation of the earth. Thus we are operating at two levels: From the pragmatic viewpoint, we see the sun rise and also say the sun rises, but from an astronomical viewpoint we deny that this happens.

The Buddhists similarly speak of two levels of truth: the conventional and the ultimate. Conventionally, the sun rises; really, it does not. Conventionally, objects exist; really, they are empty.

Dependent co-origination, before or without the realization of Emptiness, indicates the worldly, conventional truth of birth and death transmigration – that is, the realm of *saṃsāra*. Speaking from the standpoint of ultimate truth, this realm of transmigration, or *saṃsāra*, is the realm of suffering based on ignorance. However, in our everyday life, the notion of dependent co-origination, as understood in terms of causality and transmigration, is useful and true conventionally. Speaking from the worldly, or conventional, standpoint, *saṃsāra* is not merely unreal but includes conventional truth. But the process of *saṃsāra* (however conventionally true it may be) is rooted in fundamental ignorance and full of suffering, because the causal relationship is understood there without the realization of Emptiness. Thus, it is necessary to overcome ignorance in order to awaken to wisdom; it is essential to be emancipated from transmigration to attain *Nirvāṇa* – a blissful freedom from birth and death.

This is why Buddhism emphasizes not abiding in *saṃsāra*, or being attached to the realm of transmigration. In this detachment, the trans-saṃsāric realm is opened up, and ultimate truth is fully realized. However, this does not entail the denial of dependent co-origination; rather, the notion of dependent co-origination is restored in a higher dimension. If ultimate truth is simply distinguished from conventional truth, and the goal of Buddhist life is taken to be beyond mundane life, then it is not the *true* realization of ultimate truth. For this kind of ultimate truth still stands in a relative relationship to conventional truth and is nothing but an extension from conventional truth. Ultimate truth is not merely transcendent, apart from mundane life. Without attaching to the distinction between ultimate and conventional truth, ultimate truth encompasses mundane life and validates its conventional meaning. The two truths theory is not intended merely to be a refutation of worldly, or conventional, truth in favor of ultimate truth, but rather, it indicates the dynamic structure and interrelationship of the two truths.[13]

IDENTITY OF *SAṂSĀRA* AND *NIRVĀṆA*

The identity of emptiness and dependent co-origination and the dynamic interrelation between the two truths in Mādhyamika philosophy are realized fully and religiously in the Mahāyāna teaching of '*Saṃsāra*-as-it-is is *Nirvāṇa*.'[14]

The goal of Buddhist life is *Nirvāṇa*, which is to be attained by overcoming *saṃsāra*. To be emancipated from suffering, one should not be attached to *saṃsāra*. 'Throughout its long history, however, Mahāyāna Buddhism has always emphasized "Do not abide in *Nirvāṇa*" as much as "Do not abide in *saṃsāra*." If one abides in so-called *Nirvāṇa* by transcending *saṃsāra*, it must be said that one is not yet free from attachment, an attachment to *Nirvāṇa*, and is confined by the discrimination between *Nirvāṇa* and *saṃsāra*.'[15] One is still 'selfish because that person loftily abides in his or her own "enlightenment" apart from the sufferings of other *saṃsāra* bound sentient beings. True selflessness and compassion can be realized only by transcending *Nirvāṇa* to return to and work in the midst of sufferings of the ever-changing world.'[16] 'Therefore, *Nirvāṇa* in the Mahāyāna sense, while transcending *saṃsāra*, is nothing but the realization of *saṃsāra* as *saṃsāra*, no more no less, through the complete returning to *saṃsāra* itself. This is why, in Mahāyāna Buddhism, it is often said of true *Nirvāṇa* that, "*saṃsāra* as-it-is is *Nirvāṇa*." ' *Nirvāṇa* is the real 'source of *prajñā* (wisdom) because it is entirely free from the discriminating mind and thus is able to see everything in its uniqueness and distinctiveness without any sense of attachment. It is also the source of *karuṇā* (compassion) because it is unselfishly concerned with the salvation of all others in *saṃsāra* through one's own returning to *saṃsāra*.'[17] Thus, Mahāyāna Buddhism emphasizes 'not abiding in *saṃsāra* for the sake of wisdom; not abiding in *Nirvāṇa* to fulfil compassion.' This completes no-abiding and free moving from *saṃsāra* to *Nirvāṇa*, from *Nirvāṇa* to *saṃsāra* is the true *Nirvāṇa* in the Mahāyāna sense. And this is the soteriological meaning of 'Emptiness.'

5

God, Emptiness, and the True Self

A Zen master said, 'Wash out your mouth after you utter the word *Buddha.*' Another master said, 'There is one word I do not like to hear, and that is *Buddha.*' Wu-tsu Fa-yen (Jap.: Hōen, d. 1104), a Chinese Zen master of the Sung dynasty, said, 'Buddhas and Patriarchs are your deadly enemies; *satori* is nothing but dust on the mind. Rather be a man who does nothing, just leisurely passing the time. Be like a deaf-mute in the world of sounds and colors.' At the close of his life, Daitō (1282–1338) of the Kamakura era of Japan left the following death verse:

> I have cut off Buddhas and Patriarchs;
> The Blown Hair (Sword) is always burnished;
> When the wheel turns,
> The empty void gnashes its teeth.

Or in Kobori Nanrei's translation:

> Kill Buddhas and Patriarchs;
> I have been sharpening the sword Suimo;
> When the wheel turns [the moment of death],
> Sūnyatā gnashes its teeth.

Chao-Chou (Jap.: Jōshū, 778–897), a distinguished Zen master of T'ang China, while passing through the main hall of his temple, saw a monk who was bowing reverently before Buddha. Chao-Chou immediately slapped the monk. The latter said, 'Is it not a laudable thing to pay respect to Buddha?'

'Yes,' answered the master, 'but it is better to go without even a laudable thing.'

What is the reason for this antagonistic attitude toward Buddhas and Patriarchs among the followers of Zen? Are not Buddhas enlightened ones? Is not Śākyamuni Buddha their Lord? Are not the patriarchs great masters who awakened to Buddhist truth? What do Zen followers mean by 'doing nothing' and 'empty void'?

There is even the following severe statement in the *Lin-chi lu* (Jap.: *Rinzairoku*), one of the most famous Zen records of China.

Encountering a Buddha, killing the Buddha;
Encountering a Patriarch, killing the Patriarch;
Encountering an Arhat, killing the Arhat;
Encountering mother or father, killing mother or father;
Encountering a relative, killing the relative,
Only thus does one attain liberation and disentanglement from all things, thereby becoming completely unfettered and free.

These words may remind some readers of the madman described in Nietzsche's *Die Fröhliche Wissenschaft* who shouts, 'God is dead! God stays dead! And we have killed Him.' Are Zen followers who kill Buddhas to attain liberation madmen such as Nietzsche described? Are they radical nihilists in Nietzsche's sense? Are they atheists who not only reject Scriptures but also deny the existence of God? What do they mean by the 'liberation' that is attained only by killing Buddhas and Patriarchs?

To answer these questions properly and to understand Zen's position precisely, let me call your attention to some more Zen sayings.

A Zen master once said: 'Let a man's ideal rise as high as the crown of Vairocana Buddha (highest divinity), but let his life be so full of humility as to be prostrate even at the feet of a baby.'

In the 'Verses of the Ten Ox-Herding Pictures,' Kuo-an Chi-yüan (Jap.: Kakuan), a Zen master of the Sung dynasty, said:

Worldly passions fallen away,
Empty of all holy intent
I linger not where Buddha is, and
Hasten by where there is no Buddha.

What do all these examples mean? When a Zen master said, 'Cleanse the mouth thoroughly after you utter the *word* "Buddha,"' or 'There is one *word* I do not like to hear, and that is "Buddha,"' he sounds like a recent Christian theologian who, by means of linguistic analysis, insists that the *word* 'God' is theologically meaningless. The ancient Chinese Zen master, though unfamiliar with the discipline of linguistic analysis, must have found something odious about the *word* 'Buddha.' The Christian theologian who emphasizes the inadequacy of the *word* 'God' still points to the ultimate meaning realized in the Gospel. In other words, he seems to conclude that not God but the *word* 'God' is dead. Zen's position, however, is more radical. Statements such as 'Buddhas and Patriarchs are your deadly enemies' and 'I have cut off Buddhas and Patriarchs,' and emphasis on 'doing nothing' and the 'empty void' take us beyond the Death-of-God theologians. This seems especially to be true of Lin-chi's above-mentioned saying: 'Encountering a Buddha, killing the Buddha.'

What is the real meaning of these frightful words? The fourth and fifth lines of Lin-chi's saying, about encountering mother or father or a relative and killing them, remind me of Jesus' words:

> If any one comes to me and does not hate his own father and mother and wife and children and brothers and sisters, yes, and even his own life, he cannot be my disciple (Luke 14:26).

With these words Jesus asked his followers to follow him even if this meant opposing earthly obligations.

Lin-chi's words ('Encountering mother or father or relative, kill them') mean much the same as Jesus' words – though Lin-chi's expression is more extreme. The renunciation of the worldly life and the hatred for even one's own life are necessary conditions among all the higher religions for entering into the religious life. Thus Jesus said:

> Truly, I say to you, there is no man who has left house or wife or brothers or parents or children, for the sake of the kingdom of God, who will not receive manifold more in this time, and in the age to come eternal life (Luke 18:29, 30).

In contrast to Jesus' emphasis on doing things 'for the sake of the kingdom of God,' Lin-chi says that by 'encountering a Buddha, killing the Buddha,' and so on, 'only thus does one attain liberation.' This is simply because for Lin-chi to attain real liberation it is necessary not only to transcend worldly morality but also to rid oneself of religious pietism. Zen does not teach that we come to the Ultimate Reality through encountering and believing in Buddha. For even then we are altogether liberated from a dichotomy between the object and the subject of faith. In other words, if we believed in Buddha, Buddha would become more or less objectified. And an objectified Buddha cannot be the Ultimate Reality. To attain Ultimate Reality and liberation, Zen insists, one must transcend even religious transcendent realities such as Buddhas, Patriarchs, and so forth. Only when both worldly morality and religious pietism, both the secular and the holy, both immanence and transcendence, are completely left behind, does one come to Ultimate Reality and attain real liberation.

The fundamental aim of Buddhism is to attain emancipation from all bondage arising from the duality of birth and death. Another word for this is *samsara*, which is also linked with the dualities of right and wrong, good and evil, etc. Emancipation from *samsara* by transcending the duality of birth and death is called *nirvāna*, the goal of the Buddhist life.

Throughout its long history, Mahāyāna Buddhism has emphasized: 'Do not abide in *samsara*, nor abide in *nirvāna*.' If one abides in so-called *nirvāna* by transcending *samsara*, one is not yet free from attachment, namely, attachment to *nirvāna* itself. Being confined by the discrimination between *nirvāna* and *samsara*, one is still selfishly concerned with his own salvation, forgetting the suffering of others in *samsara*. In *nirvāna* one may be liberated from the dualities of birth and death, right and wrong, good and evil, etc. But even then one is not liberated from a higher-level duality, i.e., the duality of *samsara* and *nirvāna*, or the duality of the secular and the sacred. To attain thorough emancipation one must also be liberated from this higher-level duality. The Bodhisattva idea is essential to Mahāyāna Buddhism. Not clinging to his own salvation, the Bodhisattva is one who devotes himself to saving others who suffer from various attachments – attachments to *nirvāna* as well as to *samsara* – by negating or transcending the so-called *nirvāna* which is attained simply by transcending *samsara*.

Therefore, *nirvāna* in the Mahāyāna sense, while transcending *samsara*, is simply the realization of *samsara* as really *samsara*, no more, no less, by a thoroughgoing return to *samsara* itself. This is why, in Mahāyāna Buddhism, it is often said of true *nirvāna* that '*samsara*-as-it-is is *nirvāna*.' This paradoxical statement is based on the dialectical character of the true *nirvāna*, which is, logically speaking, the negation of negation; that is, absolute immanence. This negation of negation is no less than the affirmation of affirmation. The transcendence of transcendence is nothing other than the immanence of immanence. These are verbal expressions of Ultimate Reality, because Ultimate Reality is neither negative nor affirmative, neither immanent nor transcendent in the relative sense of those terms. It is beyond these dualities. *Nirvāna* in Mahāyāna Buddhism is expressed as '*samsara*-as-it-is is *nirvāna*,' and *nirvāna*-as-it-is is *samsara*.' This is simply the Buddhist way of expressing Ultimate Reality. Since *nirvāṇa* is nothing but Ultimate Reality, to attain *nirvāṇa* in the above sense means to attain liberation from every sort of duality.

Zen takes this Mahāyāna position in its characteristically radical way. 'Killing a Buddha' and 'killing a Patriarch' are Zen expressing for 'not abiding in *nirvāṇa*.'

Now we can see what Lin-chi meant when he said, 'Encountering a Buddha, killing the Buddha; encountering a Patriarch, killing the Patriarch.... *Only thus* does one attain liberation and disentanglement from all things.' In this way, Zen radically tries to transcend religious transcendence itself to attain thoroughgoing freedom. Therefore the words and acts of the Zen masters mentioned earlier, though they seem to be extremely antireligious and blasphemous, are rather to be regarded as paradoxical expressions of the ultimate truth of religion.

Since the ultimate truth of religion for Zen is entirely beyond duality, Zen prefers to express it in a negative way. When Emperor Wu of the Liang dynasty asked Bodhidharma, 'What is the ultimate principle of the holy truth?' the First Patriarch replied: 'Emptiness, no holiness.'

In his 'Song of Enlightenment' Yung-chia (Jap.: Yōka, 665–713) said:

> In clear seeing, there is not one single thing:
> There is neither man nor Buddha.

On the other hand, in Christianity, when Jesus emphasized action for the sake of the kingdom of God, the kingdom of God is not simply transcendent. Being asked by the Pharisees when the kingdom of God was coming, Jesus answered them, 'Behold, the kingdom of God is within you.' With this answer Jesus declared that God's rule is a new spiritual principle already operative in the lives of men, and perhaps referred to his own presence in the midst of his followers. We might say, therefore, that the kingdom of God is both immanent and transcendent.

This may be especially true when we remind ourselves of the Christian belief that the kingdom is within only because it has first entered this world in Jesus, who was the incarnation of God. Jesus Christ as the incarnation of God may be said to be a symbol of 'transcending even the religious transcendence.' In the well-known passage of the Letter to the Philippians, Saint Paul said:

> Have this mind among yourselves, which was in Christ Jesus, who, though he was in the form of God, did not count equality

with God a thing to be grasped, but *emptied* himself, taking the form of a servant, being born in the likeness of men. And being found in human form he humbled himself and became obedient unto death, even death on a cross (2:5–8).

As clearly shown in this passage, Jesus Christ is God who became flesh by emptying or abnegating himself, even unto death. It is really through this kenotic negation that flesh and spirit, the secular and the sacred, the immanent and the transcendent became identical in Jesus Christ. Indeed, Jesus Christ may be said to be the Christian symbol of Ultimate Reality. So far, this Christian idea of the kenotic Christ is close to Zen's idea of 'neither man nor Buddha.' At least it may be said that Christianity and Zen equally represent Ultimate Reality, where the immanent and the transcendent, the secular and the sacred, are paradoxically one.

In Christianity, however, Ultimate Reality as paradoxical oneness was realized in history only in Jesus Christ as the incarnation of God. Indeed, Jesus Christ is the Mediator between God and man, the Redeemer of man's sin against God, and the only historical event through which man encounters God. Accordingly, it is through faith in Jesus as the Christ that one can participate in Ultimate Reality.

In this sense, being the Ultimate Reality, Jesus Christ is somewhat transcendent to man. He is the object, not the subject, of faith. Therefore, the relation between Christ and his believer is dualistic. A kind of objectification still remains. In this respect Zen parts company with Christianity.

Of course, as Paul admirably stated: 'I have been crucified with Christ; it is no longer I who live, but Christ who lives in me; and the life I now live in the flesh I live by faith in the Son of God, who loved me and gave himself for me' (Gal. 2:20). Christian faith has a mystical aspect which emphasizes the identification of the faithful with Christ.

Further, as Paul said, 'we are ... always carrying in the body the death of Jesus, so that the life of Jesus may also be manifested in our bodies' (2 Cor. 4:10). Paul died Jesus' death and lived Jesus' life. And this, for Paul, meant being 'baptized into Christ,' 'putting on Christ' (Gal. 3:27), and 'being changed into his likeness' through the Spirit (2 Cor. 3:18).

Being 'in Christ' in this way, i.e., identifying with Christ as Ultimate Reality, is, if I am not wrong, the quintessence of Christian faith. The essence of Zen, however, is not identification with Christ or with Buddha, but identification with emptiness. For Zen, identification – to use this term – with an Ultimate Reality that is substantial is not the true realization of Ultimate Reality. Hence Zen's emphasis on 'emptiness, no holiness,' and 'neither man nor Buddha.'

So far Zen is much closer to the *via negativa* or negative theology of medieval Christianity than to the more orthodox form of the Christian faith. For instance, in his *Mystical Theology*, Pseudo-Dionysius the Areopagite wrote about God as follows:

> Ascending higher, we say ...
> not definable,
> not nameable,
> not knowable,
> not dark, not light,
> not untrue, not true,
> not affirmable, not deniable,
>   for
> while we affirm or deny of those orders of beings
>   that are akin to Him
> we neither affirm nor deny Him
>   that is beyond
> all affirmation as unique universal Cause and
> all negation as simple preeminent Cause,
> free of all and
> to all transcendent.[1]

This is strikingly similar to Zen's expressions of the Buddha-nature or mind.

In Pseudo-Dionysius, identification or *union* with God means that man enters the godhead by getting rid of what is man – a process called *theosis*, i.e., deification. This position of Pseudo-Dionysius became the basis of subsequent Christian mysticism. It may not be wrong to say that for him the Godhead in which one is united is the 'emptiness' of the indefinable One. The words 'nothing, nothing, nothing' fill the pages of *The Dark Night of the Soul*, written by Saint John of the Cross. For him nothingness meant 'sweeping away of images and thoughts of God to meet Him in the darkness and obscurity of pure faith which is above all concepts.'[2]

Despite the great similarity between Zen and Christian mysticism we should not overlook an essential difference between them. In the above-quoted passage, Pseudo-Dionysius calls that which is beyond all affirmation and all negation by the term *him*. Many Christian mystics call God 'Thou.' In Zen, however, what is beyond all affirmation and all negation – that is, Ultimate Reality – should not be 'him' or 'thou' but 'self' or one's 'true self.'

I am not concerned here with verbal expressions but with the reality behind the words. If Ultimate Reality, while being taken as nothingness or emptiness, should be called 'him' or 'thou,' it is, from the Zen point of view, no longer ultimate.

For in this case 'nothingness' or 'emptiness' is still taken as something *outside of* oneself; in other words, it is still more or less objectified. 'Nothingness' or 'emptiness' therefore becomes *something* merely named 'nothingness' or 'emptiness.' It is not true nothingness or true emptiness. True emptiness is never an object found outside of oneself. It is what is really *non-objectifiable*. Precisely for this reason, it is the ground of true subjectivity. In Christian mysticism, it is true that God is often called nothingness or the unknowable. However, if this is taken as the ultimate, or the object of the soul's longing, it is not the same as true nothingness in Zen. In Zen, this is found only by negating 'nothingness' as the end, and 'emptiness' as the object of one's spiritual quest.

To reach the Zen position, one must be reconverted or turned back from 'nothingness' as the end to 'nothingness' as the ground, from 'emptiness' as the object to 'emptiness' as the true subject. Ultimate Reality is not something far away, over there. It is right here, right now. *Everything starts from the here and now.* Otherwise everything loses its reality.

Consequently, while Zen emphasizes emptiness, it rejects mere attachment to emptiness. While Zen insists on killing the Buddha, it does not cling to what is non-Buddha. As quoted earlier, Kuo-an said in his 'Verses of the Ten Ox-Herding Pictures':

> Worldly passions fallen away,
> Empty of all holy intent.

Here both worldly passions and holy intent are left behind. Then he said,

> I linger not where Buddha is, and
> Hasten by where there is no Buddha.

With these words Kuo-an tried to show that if one takes what is non-Buddha as the ultimate, what is non-Buddha turns into a

Buddha. Real emptiness, which is called in Buddhism *śūnyatā*, is not a nihilistic position that simply negates religious values. Overcoming nihilism within itself, it is the existential ground of liberation or freedom in which one finds for himself liberation even from what is non-Buddha, liberation even from a rigid view of emptiness.

Zen's strong criticism of attachment to emptiness or non-Buddha-ness is seen in the following stories:

A monk asked Chao-chou, 'When I bring nothing at all with me, what do you say?'

Chao-Chou said, 'Throw it away!'

'But,' protested the monk, 'I said I bring nothing at all; what do you say I should throw away?'

'Then carry it off,' was the retort of Chao-chou.

In commenting on this D. T. Suzuki says: 'Jōshū (Chao-chou) has thus plainly exposed the fruitlessness of a nihilistic philosophy. To reach the goal of Zen, even the idea of "having nothing" ought to be done away with. Buddha reveals himself when he is no more asserted; that is, for Buddha's sake, Buddha is to be given up. This is the only way to come to the realization of the truth of Zen.'[3]

Huang-Po (Jap.: Ōbaku, d. 850) was bowing low before a figure of Buddha in the sanctuary, when a fellow disciple saw him and asked: 'It is said in Zen "Seek nothing from the Buddha, nor from the *Dharma*, nor from the *saṃgha*." What do you seek by bowing?'

'Seeking nothing from the Buddha, the *Dharma*, or the *saṃgha* is the way in which I always bow,' replied Huang-Po.

But his fellow disciple persisted: 'For what purpose do you bow?' Huang-Po slapped his face. 'Rude fellow!' exclaimed the other.

To this Huang-Po said, 'Where do you think you are, talking of rudeness and politeness!' and slapped him again.

In this way, Huang-Po tried to make his companion get rid of his negative view of non-Buddha-ness. He was anxious to communicate the truth of Zen in spite of his apparent brusqueness. While behaving and speaking in a rude and negative way, the spirit of what he says is affirmative.[4]

As these stories clearly show, the standpoint of emptiness or *śūnyatā* in Zen is not a negative but an affirmative one. Zen affirms the ground of complete liberation – liberation from both the secular and the holy, from both morality and religion, from both theistic religion and atheistic nihilism.

Since the Zen position regarding true emptiness (*śūnyatā*) transcends both the secular and the sacred (through a negation of negation), it is itself neither secular nor sacred. And yet, *at the same time*, it is both secular and sacred. The secular and the sacred are paradoxically identical, coming together as a dynamic whole outside of which there is nothing.

I, myself, who am now writing about the dynamic whole as the true emptiness, do not stand outside of, but within this dynamic whole. Of course, the same is true of those who read what I am writing.

When you see a Zen master, he may ask you, 'Where are you from?'

'I am from Chicago,' you may reply.

'From where did you come to Chicago?' the master may ask.

'I was born in Chicago. Chicago is my hometown,' may be your answer.

'Where did you come from, to your birth in Chicago?' the master may still ask. Then what will you answer?

Some of you may reply, 'I was born of my parents. And their background is Scotland,' and so forth.

Others, falling back upon the theory of evolution, may answer, 'My origin may be traced back to the anthropoid apes and from them back to the amoeba, or a single cell of some sort.'

At this point, I do hope the master is not so unkind as *not* to slap your face. Anyhow, he will not be satisfied with your answers.

Science can answer the question, 'How did I get here?' but it cannot answer the question 'Why am I here?' It can explain the cause of a fact but not the meaning, or ground of a fact.

Socrates' philosophy started from the oracle's admonition: 'Know thyself!' and King David once asked, 'But who am I, and what is my people?' (1 Chron. 29:14)

Zen is also deeply concerned with the question, 'What am I?' asking it in a way peculiar to Zen, that is: 'What is your original face before you were born?' Science seeks for the origins of our existence in a temporal and horizontal sense – a dimension which can be pushed back endlessly. To find a definite answer to the question of our origin we must go beyond the *horizontal* dimension and turn to the *vertical* dimension, i.e., the eternal and religious dimension.

Saint Paul once said, 'For in him [the Son of God] all things were created ... and in him all things hold together' (Col. 1:16–17). In Christianity it is through creation, as the eternal work of the only God, that all things hold together. Zen, however, raises a further question. It asks, 'After all things are reduced to oneness, to what must the One be reduced?' *Śūnyatā* or nothingness in Zen is not a 'nothing' out of which all things were created by God, but a 'nothing' from which God himself emerged. According to Zen, we are not creatures of God, but manifestations of emptiness. The ground of my existence can and should not be found in the temporal dimension, nor even in God. Although this groundlessness is deep enough to include even God, it is by no means something objectively observable. On the contrary, groundlessness, realized subjectively, is the only real ground of our existence. It is the ground to which we are 'reconverted' or turned back by a negation of negation.

In the *Lin-chi lu*, the story is told of Yajnadatta, a very handsome young man who used to look in a mirror every morning and smile at his image. One morning, for some reason, his face was not reflected in the mirror. In his surprise, he thought his head was lost. Thrown into consternation, he searched about everywhere for it, but with no success. Finally, he came to realize that the head for which he was searching was the very thing that was doing the searching. The fact was that being a careless fellow, he had looked at the back of the mirror. Since his head had never been lost, the more he searched for it outside of himself, the more frustrated he became. The point of this story is that that which is sought is simply that which is seeking. Yajnadatta had searched for his head with his head. Our real head, however, is by no means something to be sought for in front of us, but is something that always exists for each of us here and now. Being at the center of one's searching, it can never be objectified.

You can see my head. When you see my head from where you are, it has a particular form and color; it is indeed *something*. But can you see your own head? Unless you objectify your head in a mirror you cannot see it by yourself. So, to you, your head has no particular form and color. It is not *something* which can be seen objectively by you. It is in this sense formless and colorless to yourselves. We call such a thing *mu* or 'nothing' because it is not something objective. It is called 'nothing' not because, in the present case, our heads are missing, but because our heads are now functioning as the *living* heads. As such they are *non-objectifiable*.

The same is true of our 'self.' We often ask ourselves, 'What am I?' and get used to searching for an answer somewhere outside of ourselves. Yet the answer to the question, 'What am I?' lies in the question itself. The answer to the question can only be found in this *here and now* where I am – and which I am fundamentally.

The ground of our existence is nothingness, *śūnyatā*, because it can never be objectified. This *śūnyatā* is deep enough to encompass even

God, the 'object' of mystical union as well as the object of faith. For
śūnyatā is the nothingness from which God himself emerged. Śūnyatā
is the very ground of the self and thereby the ground of everything to
which we are related. The realization of śūnyatā-as-such is precisely
what is meant by the self-awakening of Dharma. Śūnyatā as the non-
objectifiable ground of our existence expands endlessly into all
directions. The same is true of 'awakening in the Dharma.' Can we
talk about the relationship between ourselves and the world without
being, ourselves, in the expanding awakening of the self which
embraces the relationship itself? Can we even talk about the divine–
human relationship without a still deeper ground which makes this
relationship possible? And is not the still deeper ground for the
divine–human relationship the endlessly expanding śūnyatā or self-
awakening?

All I–Thou relationships among men and between man and God are
possible only within an endlessly expanding self-awakening. Zen calls
this our 'Original Face,' the face we have before we are born. 'Before we
are born' does not refer to 'before' in its temporal sense, but in its
ontological sense. The discovery of one's prenatal face – in its ontological
sense – places us within an endlessly expanding self-awakening.

To the extent that we are people, whether from the East or from the
West, this is equally true of all of us. We should not think that we will
come to our awakening at some future time and place and will then
be awakened. On the contrary, we are originally – right here and now
– in the expanding of self-awakening that spreads endlessly into all
directions. This is why we can talk about relationships with the world
and about an I–Thou relationship with God. Nevertheless, just as
Yajnadatta looked for his head outside of himself, we are used to
looking for our true self outside of ourselves. This is our basic illusion,
which Buddhism calls māyā or avidyā, i.e., ignorance. When we realize
this basic illusion for what it is, we immediately find that, in our
depths, we are grounded in endlessly expanding self-awakening.

The 'Song of Zazen' by Hakuin, an outstanding Zen Master of the
middle Tokugawa era of Japan, expresses the point well:

> Sentient beings are really Buddha.
> Like water and ice –
> Apart from water, no ice;
> Outside of sentient beings, no Buddha.
> Not knowing it is near
> They seek for it afar!

Just like being in water –
But crying for thirst!

Taking as form the formless form
Going or coming you are always there
Taking as thought the thoughtless thought
Singing and dancing are *Dharma*'s voice.
How vast the boundless sky of *samādhi*,
How bright the moon of Fourfold Wisdom.
What now is there to seek?
With *nirvāṇa* revealed before you,
This very place is the Lotus Land,
This very body is Buddha.

6

The Concept of Self as Reflected in Zen Buddhist Literature

I

In Christianity, 'Who is God?' is the most important question. In contrast to this, in Buddhism, 'What is the Self?' is the crucial question. A well known anecdote concerning the teaching of the Buddha which appears in the Nikāyas runs as follows: One day sons and daughters of rich families went to picnic in a forest and took a nap after lunch. When they woke up they found that their clothes and jewels were stolen. Being upset they looked around in the forest and happened to meet Gautama Buddha who was meditating under a big tree. They told the Buddha that they were searching for their stolen clothes and jewels and asked if he saw a thief. The Buddha responded by saying that what they should search for is not such objects but the self. This anecdote impressively shows that what is essential in the Buddha's teaching is to seek for and awaken to the true Self.

Christians emphasize faith in God who is the creator, judge and redeemer. To believe in Jesus Christ means to believe in God's redemptive work which forgives even the sinful man through the self-sacrifical love. In Christianity the human self is always understood in relation to God and whether the self is obedient or disobedient to the will of God is crucial. On the other hand, Buddhists talk about self-awakening, i.e., the self's awakening to itself. Buddha is not an object of faith but one who awakened to his own true self. However, what is the true Self in the Buddhist sense?

In ancient India, the Brahmanical tradition propounds *Ātman* which is the eternal, unchanging self and which is fundamentally identical with Brahman, the ultimate Reality of the universe. The Buddha did not explicitly accept or reject the notion of *Ātman* and kept silence. His understanding of the self implied in his silence was later formulated in the doctrine of *anātman*, that is, 'no-self.' Buddhism is quite unique in the history of human thought in denying the existence of an enduring and unchanging soul or self. 'According to the teaching of the Buddha, the idea of self (in the ordinary sense) is an imaginary, false belief which has no corresponding reality, and it produces harmful thoughts of "me" and "mine," selfish desire, craving, attachment, hatred, ill-will, conceit, pride, egoism, and other defilements, impurities and problems. It is the source of all the troubles in the world from personal conflicts to wars between nations. In short, to this false view can be traced all the evil in the world.' However, the notion of no-self, that is, the notion of no substantial, fixed selfhood, does not indicate the mere lack or absence of self, as an annihilationist may suggest, but rather constitutes a standpoint which is beyond both the eternalist view of self and the nihilistic view of no-self. This is significantly illustrated by the Buddha himself when he answered with silence to both the questions 'Is there a self?' and 'Is there no-self?' Keeping silence to both the affirmative and negative forms of the question concerning the 'self', the Buddha profoundly expresses the ultimate Reality of humanity. His silence itself is a great manifestation of the true Self of a person which cannot be conceptualized either in an affirmative or a negative manner.

In the Buddhist tradition, Zen most clearly and vividly demonstrates that the Buddhist notion of no-self is nothing but true Self. Lin-chi I-hsüan's (d. 866) 'true person of no rank' is an example. 'No rank' implies freedom from any conceptualized definition of person. Thus the 'true person of no rank' signifies the 'true person' who cannot be defined either by 'self' or 'no-self.' It is identical with the true Self of the human manifested in the silence of the Buddha. However, unlike the Buddha who is primarily meditative, Lin-chi is active and dynamic, directly showing his own true Self while demanding that his disciple demonstrate this true self. The following event illustrates this active character:

One day Lin-chi gave this sermon: 'There is the true person of no rank in the mass of naked flesh, who goes in and out from your facial gates (i.e., sense organs). Those who have not yet testified (to the fact), look! look!'

A monk came forward and asked, 'Who is this true person of no rank?'

Lin-chi came down from his chair and, taking hold of the monk by the throat, said 'Speak! Speak!'

The monk hesitated.

Lin-chi let go his hold and said, 'What a worthless dirt-stick this is!'

The 'true person of no rank' is Lin-chi's term for the true self. In this event the 'true person of no rank' is taken as a living reality functioning through our physical body. Further, Lin chi is asking his audience to notice that living reality functioning in himself by saying 'look! look!' and demanding the monk who asked 'Who is this true person of no rank?' to demonstrate his own true nature, taking hold of the monk by the throat and saying 'Speak! Speak!' Zen does not intend an explanation or interpretation of the notion of true Self, but rather elicits a direct and immediate testimony or demonstration of it by grappling or negotiating between master and disciple.

II

Zen clearly realizes that the human self cannot be grasped objectively: It is unattainable, and that the 'unattainable' is precisely the true Self. In the Song of Enlightenment, Yung-chia Ta-shin describes the inner light that is the self as follows: 'You cannot take hold of it, nor can you get rid of it; while you can do neither, it goes on its own way.' Lin-chi says of the 'true person,' 'You may try to catch him, but he refuses to be gathered up; you may try to brush him away, but he will not be dispersed. The harder you strive after him the further away he is from you. When you no longer strive after him, lo, he is right in front of you. His supersensous voice fills your ear.'

Unlike animals and plants human existence has self-consciousness. Through self-consciousness human self thinks of itself, reflects upon itself, and even analyzes itself. In this way the self objectifies itself. As soon as the self objectifies itself it is divided into two: Self as an object and self as a subject. And the objectified self is no longer true Self. Nor is the merely subjective self the true one. The true Self is beyond the subject–object dichotomy.

As the ever subjective, the true self is unobjectifiable and yet is the root-source of all objectification, positive and negative. This is the reason, Yung-chia says: 'You cannot take hold of it, nor can you get rid of it: While you can do neither, it goes on its own way.'

Although the true Self is always present it is elusive to our self-consciousness. In order to grasp or awaken the true Self the conscious-self or the ego-self must be broken through. In other words it must be clearly realized that the ego-self is not an unchangeable and enduring entity and is without substance. This is the realization of no-self. Only through the realization of no-self is the true Self awakened.

Unlike other forms of Buddhism in which doctrinal teaching is important, Zen straightforwardly goes to the core of living reality. Nan-ch'üan Pu-yüan (748–835) said 'ordinary mind is Tao' and emphasized 'If you try to direct yourself toward it, you go away from it.' His disciple Chao-chou (778–897) used to point out the true Self in daily activities.

> Chao-chou was once asked by a monk, 'What is myself?'
> Chao-chou said, 'Have you finished the morning gruel?'
> 'Yes, I have finished,' answered the monk.
> Chao-chou then told him, 'If so, wash your bowl.'

Chao-chou's instruction here is not simply to wash a bowl after a meal, but to awaken to the Self in eating and washing. Commenting on this *mondō* D. T. Suzuki says.

> The eating is an act, the washing is an act, but what is wanted in Zen is the actor himself; the eater and the washer that does the acts of eating and washing; and unless this person is existentially or experientially taken hold of, one cannot speak of the acting. Who is the one who is conscious of acting and who is the one who communicates this fact of consciousness to you and who are you to tell all this not only to yourself but to all others? 'I', 'you', 'she', or 'it' – all this is a pronoun standing for a somewhat behind it. Who is this somewhat (behind it)?

Again, Chao-chou's following *mondō* indicates another example along this line:

> Chao-chou once asked a new monk: 'Have you ever been here before?
> The monk answered, 'Yes, sir. I have!'
> Thereupon the master said, 'Have a cup of tea.'
> Later on another monk came and he asked him the same question, 'Have you ever been here?'

This time the answer was quite opposite. 'I have never been here, sir.'

The old master, however, answered just as before, 'Have a cup of tea.'

Afterwards the Inju (the managing monk of the monastery) asked the master, 'How is it that you make the same offering of a cup of tea no matter what one monk's reply is?'

The old master called out, 'O Inju!' who at once replied, 'Yes, master.'

Whereupon Chao-chou said, 'Have a cup of tea.'

It may not be wrong to say that Chao-chou's 'have a cup of tea' is the same as Lin-chi's 'Look, Look!' or 'Speak, Speak!' in that both are trying to help another to awaken to his true 'Self.'

III

In the beginning of this chapter I said that, while in Christianity the human self is always understood in relation to God, in Buddhism, the self awakening to itself is emphasized. In fact *satori* in Zen is nothing but the self-awakening of true Self. To make Zen's understanding of the Self clearer, however, we must ask ourselves how Buddha is grasped in Zen and what is the relation between Buddha and Self in Zen.

In the early history of Zen the term 'Mind' is used for 'Self' and it is emphasized 'Mind' is used for 'Self' and it is emphasized 'Mind is Buddha.' For instance, Fu-Ta-shih (497–569), an eminent Buddhist layman of those days, says 'If you realize the origin, you will attain mind. If you attain mind, you will see Buddha. Mind is Buddha: Buddha is Mind.' In the *Laṅkāvatāra Sūtra* it is said 'The Buddha mind is the basis, and gateless is the Dharma gate. He who seeks after Dharma will certainly attain nothing. Outside mind there is no Buddha: Outside Buddha there is no mind.' It was, however, Ma-tsu Tao-i (709–788) who especially emphasized 'Mind is Buddha.' In *Wu-men-kuan* the following exchange is taken up as a kōan:

Taibai once asked Baso (Ma-tsu), 'What is Buddha?'
    Baso answered, 'Mind is Buddha.'

Referring to this kōan Daitō, Japanese Zen Master of the Kamakura period, comments as follows:

> To see into one's nature (to attain *satori*) is to be awakened to the Buddha mind. Cast all thoughts and consciousness away and see that 'Mind is Buddha'. The one who realizes that his true mind is Buddha is the man who has attained Buddhahood. He neither practices good nor commits evil: He has no attachment to his mind. His eyes see things but he does not become attached to them. This mind that does not become attached to each and every thing is the Buddha mind. This is why Master Baso said, 'Mind is Buddha.'

At a different time, however, Baso gave the same question 'What is Buddha?' a quite opposite answer, that is 'No mind, no Buddha.' This constitutes another kōan of *Wu-men-kuan*, case 33. In his book *Zen Comments on the Mumonkan* Zenkei Shibayama said, 'Earlier, Taibai had come to Master Baso seeking Buddha outside himself, and in order to break through his illusion Baso told him, "Mind is Buddha." Now that Baso sees that many disciples have become attached to "Mind is Buddha" he says "No mind, no Buddha" in order to smash and wipe away their attachment to "Mind is Buddha."'

In his commentary on the kōan 'Mind is Buddha' Wu-men Hui-k'ai (1183–1260) says 'Don't you know that one has to rinse out his mouth for three days if he has uttered the word "Buddha?" If he is a real Zen man, he will stop his ears and rush away when he hears "Mind is Buddha."' Reading this commentary we come to know how severely Zen rejects the attachment to Buddha and emphasizes the importance of freedom even from the notion of Buddha. Through these two kōans referring to Baso's (Ma-tsu) words 'Mind is Buddha' and 'No mind: No Buddha' we come to know the following points:

1. In Zen, Buddha is not transcendent but immanent: Buddha is not an object of faith and worship, but Mind itself. 'Outside mind there is no Buddha.'

2. Yet, any attachment to Mind must be done away with. Mind which is identical with Buddha is not a psychological mind or a metaphysical mind. It is no mind, because the true mind is no mind. Likewise, true Buddha must be no Buddha. Hence 'No mind: No Buddha.'

As I said a little while ago, in the early history of Zen the term mind is an equivalent to the term Self. In Lin-chi's case, 'true person of no rank' is his term for true self. Although various terms have been used for the 'Self' in the history of Zen the problem of self has been constantly a central problem for Zen. And the same basic ideas concerning the self have appeared repeatedly with slightly different modes throughout Zen literature.

IV

This question of selfhood has been formulated in a way peculiar to Zen. 'What is your original face before your parents were born?' 'Before' in this question does not refer to 'before' in the temporal sense but in the ontological sense. However far we may push back the temporal and horizontal dimension we can never reach our 'original face,' because this approach is nothing but an objectification. To see our 'original face' before our parents were born we must go beyond the *horizontal* dimension and turn to the *vertical* dimension, i.e., the eternal and ontological dimension which is transtemporal and transspacial. In other words, the original face 'before' the parents were born can be properly realized *directly below the here and the now*, i.e., at the bottomless depth of the absolute present.

In this bottomless depth of the absolute present 'one's original face before one's parents were born,' i.e., one's true self, is realized. It is the root-source of one's existence. At the same time it is also the root-source of the Universe which includes other people and other things. For in this vertical bottomless depth of the absolute present, one is freed from all kinds of duality including dualities of self and other, self and the world, one and many, time and space, being and non-being. Accordingly in this bottomless depth of the absolute present realized 'before your parents were born' you not only see your original face and awaken to your true self, but also see the other's original face and awaken to his true self. Here the original face of the Universe is disclosed together with your original face. This is the reason Dōgen (1200–1253), Japanese Zen master of the Kamakura period, talks about *dōjijōdō*, i.e., 'simultaneous attainment' of self and others (and the world). If one says 'I have attained enlightenment, but others have not as yet' his enlightenment may not be authentic. When you are in delusion everything is in delusion. When you are in enlightenment everything is in enlightenment. Mahāyāna sutras say

'Grasses, trees, and land without exception attain Buddhahood: Mountains, rivers and the great earth all disclose the Dharma-body,' If one takes these words merely as objective statements referring to mountains, trees and so forth, objectively, apart from one's own enlightenment, these words may sound quite ridiculous. However, the Mahāyāna Buddhist phrases mentioned above express the Buddhist truth that simultaneous awakening of self and others is essential.

V

To understand 'simultaneous attainment' more precisely, we will now examine Lin-chi's words. 'do not seek for Buddha outwardly.' Upon hearing this admonition one may think that one should seek for Buddha inwardly rather than outwardly. Thus one denies the outward approach and engages with the inward approach. As I said before, in Zen, Buddha is not transcendent but immanent. This thought, however, does not hit the mark as yet. For even if one seeks for a Buddha inwardly, in so far as one *seeks for* a Buddha somewhere, the Buddha is understood to be *outside of* oneself. Accordingly the real meaning of the above admonition 'Do not seek for a Buddha outwardly' lies in 'do not seek for Buddha *at all.*' Not only the outward approach but also the inward approach must be done away with. This is because, prior to the very act of seeking for Buddha, whether outwardly or inwardly, one *is originally* a Buddha: he is *originally awakened.* Since one is originally a Buddha one should not and need not seek for Buddha outwardly.

It is in this 'original awakening' that the 'simultaneous attainment' takes place. The original awakening has a twofold aspect: On the one hand (1) it is entirely individual and personal, and on the other (2) it is thoroughly supra-individual and universal.

1. The original awakening is individual and personal because it is opened up and realized as such only through the awakening of a particular individual person to his original face (true Self). Each and every person may realize the original awakening individually and respectively through the realization of no-self. The original awakening apart from individual realization is an abstraction.

2. The original awakening is supra-individual and universal. Although the original awakening can be realized as such only

through an individual person it itself is beyond the individual. As the *original* awakening it is universal and common to everything and everyone. In the light of this original awakening we can say 'grasses, trees, and land without exception attain Buddhahood' and 'mountains disclose the Buddha body: the valley stream is preaching the Dharma.' However, these statements should not be taken as an expression of animism or nature mysticism. While animism or nature mysticism lack the realization of no-thingness these Zen statements are supported by that realization. The realization of no-thingness and no-self is essential to the realization of the true Self and the true World.

7

Education in Zen

To clarify the Zen idea of education at least two aspects should be discussed: one is the group practice among monks in a Zen monastery which is regulated by strict and time-tested precepts; the other is the one-to-one relationship between master and disciple. In this chapter I would like to take up only the second aspect, partly because of limitation of space, and more importantly, partly because the second aspect is the basis for the first. In discussing the second aspect, the relation between master and disciple, I would like to focus on the role of the master in his relationship with his disciples.

To begin with, the relationship between a Zen master and his disciple is ever different from the ordinary teacher–student relation. What the Zen master tries to lead his disciple to and the disciple wants to attain, is not the intellectual knowledge of the natural world nor the understanding of cultural conditions and values, but the disciple's awakening to his original nature. To cause the awakening of his original nature, a Zen student carefully considers which master is the best qualified and most appropriate for him. Once this is handled he visits the master's monastery and asks permission to join. It is only after passing a strict entrance test, which usually lasts five days, to confirm the novice's seriousness and devotion, that he is accepted into the monastery as a member and is allowed to have an interview with the master. Through the interview he formally becomes a disciple of that master. This means that the novice will thereafter follow the guidance of the master even at the expense of his life, and the master will give whatever form of instruction or direction he feels is appropriate for the novice.

In Zen it is extremely important to practice under the guidance of an authentic master. Dōgen, the founder of the Japanese Sōtō Zen tradition says, 'Whether one's *satori* is true or false depends on whether his master is right or wrong.'[1] He even says, 'If you can not find an authentic master you had better not practice Zen.'[2] He defines an authentic master as follows: 'one who regardless of his age or the length of his religious career has awakened to the right Dharma and has been approved by an authentic master. Without giving priority to Scriptures and intellectual understanding he has both extraordinary ability and aspiration. Without clinging to selfish views and without attaching to emotional perceptions his practice and understanding are in complete accord with one another.'[3]

On the other hand, it is noteworthy that however great that master may be, he can not give *satori* to his disciple. This is simply because *satori* is the self-awakening of one's original nature which takes place spontaneously without any external cause. It is the disciple himself who awakens to his own true self. Then what significance does a master have? His role in relation to his disciple may be compared to the role of a midwife in relation to a pregnant woman. In this connection you may recall the 'midwife's art' of Socrates. It is ridiculous if a midwife gives her own baby to an expectant mother. The role of midwife lies in helping an expectant mother give birth to her own baby. According to Socrates, all that the teacher can do is to persuade his pupil to face himself so that the vision of the truth strikes the 'eye of the soul,' and to exercise his mind so as to draw out of it the truth which is being sought.[4]

In the same sense, while a Zen student must have an authentic master, a master is necessary only as a midwife, i.e., not as a *satori*-giver but as a *satori*-helper.

What kind of midwife may a Zen master be said to be? Here again we see some significant affinity between Socrates and Zen. To make his student face himself Socrates shows him the hopeless perplexity, the 'aporia' or position with no way out, in which his ordinary muddle-headed notion about the truth would land him if its implications were worked out. Then he stimulates him gently to discover the right solution.[5] In a similar way a Zen master tries to make his disciple face himself, to get him to return to the root-source of his being, by showing him a kind of 'aporia' in which his analytic reason and intelligence come to a deadlock that can be overcome only by the awakening of his original nature. A Zen master, however, does so more severely than Socrates did.

Let me mention a few examples. A monk asked his master. 'What is the truth of Zen?' The master answered, 'In Zen there is nothing to explain by means of words. Thirty blows whether you affirm or negate .... Do not remain silent; nor be discursive.'[6] Lin-chi (Jap.: Rinzai) asked Huang-po, 'What is the cardinal principle of the Buddha-dharma?' Before he had finished speaking Huang-po hit him. A little while later he went back and asked him again, and

Huang-po again hit him. In all Lin-chi asked the same question three times and was hit three times.[7] This is a well known story about Lin-chi in his younger days.

In such a way a master often thrusts away his disciple and drives him into a corner. He does not impart anything positively nor stimulate his disciple gently, but rather *deprives* him of everything and pushes him into perplexity or aporia. However this perplexity or aporia is not intellectual as in the case of Socrates, but is entirely existential. The disciple's whole existence including intelligence, emotion and volition becomes an aporia. In the midwife's art of Socrates the focus is put on virtue, which to Socrates is knowledge. Accordingly, although Socrates' approach is somewhat existential, it is largely colored by intellectualism. On the other hand, Zen is concerned with the awakening of one's true self and this can take place only by overcoming intellectualism and by breaking through the framework of ego-self. This is the reason a Zen master often uses even harsh and drastic means like shouting and beating. In this way he will deprive his disciple of any conceptual understanding of Zen in order make him go beyond affirmation and negation, cornering him in existential perplexity, and turning his existence into a great block of doubt.

By such means a Zen master is, in the last analysis, trying to destroy the disciple's attachment to Buddha or clinging to *satori*. Since Buddha or *satori* is the central concern of a Zen student, it is natural and inevitable for him to become attached to it. However, Buddha as an object of attachment is not the true Buddha, and *satori* must be free from any form of clinging; so the student must be completely deprived of an attachment to Buddha or clinging to *satori*. Only then will his original nature awaken to itself. The harsh means of a Zen master is thus often compared with 'driving away an ox from a farmer, or depriving a hungry man of food.'[8]

However, beating and shouting is not the only means employed by a Zen master. A Zen master as midwife uses various skillful means to help his disciple give birth to his own baby. To return to the story of Lin-chi and Huang-po, when Lin-chi, in deep perplexity after being hit three times, came to Huang-po to take his leave, Huang-po said: 'You mustn't go anywhere else but to Ta-yü's place. He's sure to explain things for you.' Lin-chi arrived at Ta-yü's temple. Ta-yü said: 'Where have you come from ?' 'I have come from Huang-po's place,' replied Lin-chi. 'What did Huang-po have to say?' asked Ta-yü. 'Three times I asked him just what the cardinal principle of the

Buddha-dharma was and three times he hit me. I don't know whether I was at fault or not.' 'Huang-po is such a grandmother that he utterly exhausted himself with your troubles!' said Ta-yü. 'And now you come here asking whether you were at fault or not!' At these words Lin-chi attained great enlightenment. 'Ah, there isn't so much to Huang-po's Buddha-dharma!' he cried.[9]

As you see, Huang-po sent Lin-chi to Ta-yü, another outstanding Zen master of those days, because he thought an approach from a different angle was necessary to lead Lin-chi to awakening. Meeting his expectations Ta-yü struck Lin-chi's blind spot by saying, 'Huang-po is such a grandmother that he utterly exhausted himself with your troubles! And now you come here asking whether you were at fault or not!' At these unexpected words Lin-chi's ego-structure, which was at that time in deep perplexity, completely collapsed and his original nature awakened to itself. The words Lin-chi uttered at that moment, that is, 'Ah, there isn't so much to Huang-po's Buddha-dharma!' clearly show his independence of his master. At this moment, through awakening of his true self, Lin-chi became a truly independent person who could properly judge his master's Buddha-dharma.

Here we also see the good timing of a Zen master. When Lin-chi said, 'I don't know whether I was at fault or not,' his existential perplexity was so deep that it was ready to be broken through by a proper blow. Not overlooking this Ta-yü told him how kind Huang-po was in hitting him three times. At these words Lin-chi's perplexity was dissolved and his true self manifested itself. This kind of good timing is often called *sottaku-dōji* (啐啄 同時) the simultaneity of a chick's pecking and a mother hen's pecking. If the mother hen pecks the shell of an egg too early the chick inside may die. If the mother hen pecks the shell of an egg too late the chick also may die. Only when the chick's pecking from inside and the mother hen's pecking from outside take place simultaneously is the chick certain to be born. A good Zen master is one who pecks the shell of his disciple's ego-structure at the right time, penetrating it as the disciple is pecking from within. But we should realize that however necessary the pecking by a mother hen may be, it is nothing more than *a condition* for a chick being born as a new bird. What is being born is not the mother hen but the chick who is pecking from inside.

The idea that a newly born baby – as a metaphor for a newly awakened one – is self-dependent and has dignity is well expressed symbolically in the legend of Gautama Buddha's birth. When he was born the Buddha is said to have walked seven steps without another's support and, raising his right hand, to have said 'In heaven and on earth, I alone am to be revered.' As for his enlightenment, the Buddha is said to have attained it by himself without a teacher. These legends reflect the Buddhist idea that enlightenment is nothing but self-awakening to one's original nature which is beyond any external conditioning.

In fact, awakening in Buddhism only takes place if all given conditions are 'transdescended.'[10] In this sense Buddhism is essentially not a religion of faith, but a religion of self-awakening. Of course this self-awakening takes place on a particular occasion under certain conditions. Gautama Buddha attained enlightenment upon seeing the morning star. Hsiang-yen (Jap.: Kyōgen) awakened to enlightenment upon hearing the sound of a pebble striking a bamboo. Ling-yün (Jap.: Reiun) attained *satori* when he saw the peach flowers in bloom. These natural events could become the occasion or condition for their awakenings precisely because their inner spiritual problems had ripened and were ready to be broken through. These cases are not essentially different from the case of Lin-chi. The light of the morning star, the sound of a pebble, the peach flowers, and the words of a Zen master, though indispensable, all are no more than an occasion or condition for awakening – which in Buddhism is essentially *self-awakening*.

In Zen the transmission of Dharma from master to disciple is of great importance. This is why the Dharma genealogy is held in such high esteem in Zen. However, the transmission of Dharma from master to disciple should not be regarded as a mere continuity, or as a direct continuity without discontinuity, but as a continuity which happens through discontinuity. For the Buddha Dharma cannot be transmitted from one person to another as if it were an object. The Buddha Dharma can be transmitted to a disciple only when he attains *satori*, i.e., self-awakening to his original nature. Since a master cannot be a *satori*-giver but only a *satori*-helper, and since *satori* is self-awakening, there is a discontinuity between a master and the disciple who would be his successor. Only when the disciple goes beyond his dependence on his master and attains independence on the basis of his own self-awakening is he qualified as a Dharma successor. Therefore the continuity in terms of Dharma transmission is made possible through the discontinuity between the disciple's new born independence and the master. Only because of this discontinuity can the Buddha Dharma be passed and continued.

This dynamic character of the master–disciple relationship in Zen is well-expressed in the following story of Ikkyū, a Zen master of fifteenth century Japan.

When Ikkyū was twenty-six he was deeply involved in an inner struggle. Late one summer night he was sitting in Zen meditation in a small boat on Lake Biwa, when, hearing the cawing of a crow, he suddenly cried out in wonder. At that instant he felt all uncertainties melt away and a clear awakening took place. Returning to the temple he asked for an interview with his master Kasō. After listening to him, Kasō said merely, 'You've reached the realm of an *arbat*. You still are not a Buddha.' An *arbat* is someone who has attained enlightenment, but who is regarded in Mahāyāna Buddhism as a little lower than Buddha in the sense that he remains attached to his own enlightenment. To this Ikkyū replied, 'If that's the case, I'm delighted to be an *arbat* and have no desire to be a Buddha.' Then Kasō answered, 'You are truly a Buddha.'[11]

If Ikkyū, when he heard his master's negative words, i.e., 'You still are not a Buddha,' had been disappointed or had felt uncertain of his own enlightenment, his enlightenment would not have been a genuine one. As his awakening was, in fact, to him, clear and decisive, he was not only not disturbed by his master's negative reply, but, beyond that, he affirmed his own realization by saying, 'I am delighted to be an *arbat* and have no desire to be a Buddha.' Seeing his firm conviction Master Kasō said, 'You are truly a Buddha,' and thus fully approved him.

It is not the case in Zen that a disciple can be said to attain enlightenment by receiving his master's approval. Instead, it is when a disciple attains enlightenment clear to himself and can stand independent of his master's approval that the master approves him. This is the reason Pai-chang (Jap.: Hyakujō) says: 'One whose insight is the same as his teacher's lacks half of his teacher's power. Only one whose insight surpasses his teacher's is worthy to be his heir.'

Here, in the dynamics of the master–disciple relationship in Zen, and in the focus in Zen education on man's original nature, I think can be found many suggestions and possibilities for education in our time.

Part Two
Zen, Buddhism, and Western Thought

8

Substance, Process, and Emptiness: Aristotle, Whitehead, and Zen

In this chapter, *first*, the philosophy of Whitehead, especially his notion of 'process,' will be discussed in relation to the age-old notion of 'substance" in Western philosophy, particularly Aristotle. *Second*, I will analyze the notion of 'process' in regard to its affinities and differences from the Buddhist notion of 'emptiness.' *Third*, and finally, the Buddhist notion of 'emptiness' will be elucidated in comparison with the notions of 'substance' and 'process.' Accordingly, this chapter is a comparative study of three important philosophical categories, 'substance,' 'process' and 'emptiness.' It is not, however, intended to be a mere comparison of the philosophical doctrines of Aristotle and Whitehead and the teaching of Mahāyāna Buddhism. It is rather concerned with the question 'What is the ultimate Reality for human beings?" This question underlies the above three systems of thought, and has always been central to humankind.

It is even more important for us, who are now living at a historical moment in which the East and West are encountering each other on a scale and at a depth never before experienced. Today the question about the ultimate Reality must be asked again in a broader and more radical way than ever before.

I

We human beings are living in a world in which everything is changing. Everything including ourselves comes to be, exists, for a time, and finally perishes. We, however, cannot find satisfaction with this changing world because, if everything is changeable and perishable our life is quite unstable, uncertain, and restless, with nothing solid upon which to rely. Accordingly, it is quite natural that from ancient times, both in the East and the West, people have searched for something unchangeable, something which truly *is*, something solid and self-existing. 'Substance' is a notion that was arrived at through this pressing quest. The unchangeable being was grasped as 'substance.'

In his *Metaphysics* Aristotle states: 'Indeed the question which was raised of old and is raised now and always, and is always the subject of doubt, namely, what being is, is just the question: what is substance? For it is this that some assert to be one, others more than one, and that some assert to be limited in number, others unlimited. And so we must consider chiefly and primarily and almost exclusively what that is which *is* in this sense.'[1]

In Aristotle, 'Substance' is interpreted in several different senses, but its most distinctive formulation is: 'While remaining numerically one and the same, it is capable of admitting contrary qualities.'[2] It is also defined by Aristotle as 'that which is neither predicable of a subject, now present in a subject.' This means that substance can exist on its own, whereas qualities and relations exist only as the qualities of, or relations between substances.

The Aristotelian notion of 'substance' was further developed by Thomas Aquinas, Descartes, Spinoza, Locke, and others. In one sense the main stream of the history of Western metaphysics has been a metaphysics of 'substance.'

It is against this notion of 'substance' that Whitehead established the notion of 'process.' In this respect, however, the following two points must be carefully noted: first, Whitehead does not simply reject the notion of 'substance' itself, but rather transforms the conception of the *nature* of substance.

> The simple notion of an enduring substance sustaining persistent qualities, either essentially or accidentally, expresses a useful abstract for many purposes of life. But whenever we try to use it as a fundamental statement of the nature of things, it proves itself mistaken. It arose from a mistake and has never succeeded in any of its applications. But it has had one success: it has entrenched itself in language, in Aristotelian logic, and in metaphysics. For its employment in language and in logic there is . . . a sound pragmatic defense. But in Metaphysics the concept is sheer error. This error does not consist in the employment of the word 'substance,' but in the employment of the notion of an actual entity which is 'characterized

by essential qualities, and remains numerically one amidst the changes of accidental relations and of accidental qualities.[3]

As this quotation clearly shows, Whitehead, on the one hand, recognizes that the notion of substance as something self-identically enduring is a useful abstraction for everyday purposes, and that, when employed in language and logic, it is pragmatically well-defended. On the other hand, however, he attacks the notion of substance as something self-identically enduring by saying that 'in Metaphysics it is sheer error,' because the notion does not indicate an actual entity conceived as an activity. Rather, it indicates a substratum or some stuff to which qualities attach and which remains numerically identical throughout qualitative and spatial changes. Criticizing the notion of substance as a substratum enduring unchangingly amidst the flux of events, Whitehead has developed the notion of substance as a process of activity. This is what he means when he says 'the notion of "substance" is transformed into that of "actual entity".'[4] Thus, in his philosophy of organism the existence of an actual entity is constituted by its activity of becoming, so that when this activity is complete an actual entity perishes and ceases to exist. The Aristotelian notion of substance as substratum is thus replaced by the notion of substance as a process of activity. It is in this sense that Whitehead sets up the notion of 'process' against the Aristotelian notion of 'substance.'

Second, with his rejection of the notion of substance as a self-identically enduring substratum, Whitehead also rejects the categories and modes of thought based on that notion. It is the 'subject–predicate' mode of thinking that Whitehead strongly and emphatically rejects as an abstract and irrelevant way of thinking to understand the actual world.

Many philosophers, who in their explicit statements criticize the Aristotelian notion of 'substance,' yet implicitly throughout their discussions presuppose that the 'subject–predicate' form of proposition embodies the finally adequate mode of statement about the actual world. The evil produced by the Aristotelian 'primary substance' is exactly the habit of metaphysical emphasis upon the 'subject–predicate' form of proposition.[5]

This is an extremely important remark because in this remark it is clearly shown that Whitehead's basic concern lies in overcoming the

Aristotelian 'subject–predicate' mode of thinking, and that his rejection of the notion of 'substance' is only a consequence of the basic rejection of the Aristotelian way of thinking, which has become so habitual in the metaphysical thought of the West.

Why does Whitehead so strongly reject the subject–predicate form of thinking? This is because, against the prevailing presupposition that the subject–predicate form of proposition conveys the ultimate characterization of reality, Whitehead believes that it 'is concerned with high abstractions ... This sort of abstraction ... is rarely relevant to metaphysical description.'[6] But in what sense does a subject–predicate proposition express a high abstraction? For that mode of thinking entails the doctrine of the individual independence of real facts and 'the relations between individual substances constitute metaphysical nuances: there is no place for them.'[7] Thus, the Aristotelian view does violence to 'that immediate experience which we express in our actions, our hopes, our sympathies, our purposes, and which we enjoy in spite of our lack of phrases for its verbal analysis.'[8] The 'high abstraction' that Whitehead criticizes as an expression of the subject–predicate proposition may also indicate 'a factor of extreme objectivism in metaphysics.'[9] In so far as the subject–predicate form of proposition is taken as expressing a fundamental metaphysical truth there can be no room for the subjective enjoyment of experience, because perception, feeling, or experience are all here understood to capture a universal quality only through their reference to particular substances. Again, this does not accord with our immediate experience. Thus, Whitehead develops a doctrine of 'feeling' as a positive prehension, and coins a term 'superject' to indicate 'the atomic creature exercising its (an actual entity's) function of objective immortality.'[10] In Whitehead 'the subject–superject is the purpose of the process originating the feelings.' The subjective enjoyment of experience must not be abstracted from the actual entity. However, 'if the subject–predicate form of statement be taken to be metaphysically ultimate, it is then impossible to express this doctrine of feelings and their superject.'[11]

The above reasons for Whitehead's rejection of the Aristotelian subject–predicate mode of thinking have been gathered from his discussion in *Process and Reality*. I interpret these reasons in the following ways: he rejects the subject–predicate mode of thinking because it entails an *objective conceptualization* of reality, and therefore one can never realize the truly ultimate Reality. When one follows that mode of thinking one just contemplates the actual world as a mere objective entity – as if one stood somewhat outside of the actual world; the result is an exclusion of the subjective side in the picture of the world. It is not the ultimate Reality, but an objective reality of the world which is realized only in so far as the world is objectively conceptualized. He also rejects the subject–predicate mode of thinking because it is based on a *dualistic view* of reality by which one again cannot attain the truly ultimate Reality. That his rejections are directed toward the dualistic view can be seen in his frequent references to the 'substance–quality' concept, the 'universal–particular' doctrine, and so forth, in connection with the 'subject–predicate' notion as something to be overcome. The dualistic view leads us into a subject–object structure in which the ultimate Reality is impossible to realize.

In short, in his philosophy of organism, Whitehead rejects the 'subject–predicate' habit of thought which had been impressed on the European mind by the overemphasis on Aristotle's logic during the long medieval period[12] because 'high abstraction' 'extreme objectivism' are the result of that habit of thought, and because the 'objective conceptualization' and the 'dualistic view' involved in it must be overcome. This overcoming is necessary in order to elucidate immediate experience and to realize the ultimate Reality.

As we have seen, in rejecting the Aristotelian 'subject–predicate' mode of thinking, Whitehead emphasizes 'process' rather than 'substance,' and 'becoming' instead of 'being.' However, Whitehead's thoughts on process are not necessarily new. Besides Heraclitus, the notion of process and becoming has been emphasized by many thinkers in the history of philosophy, notably Leibnitz, Hegel, Bergson, and Nietzsche. The unique and novel features of Whitehead's philosophy, however, may be summarized in the following three concepts: (1) the notion of actual entity and the principle of process; (2) an emphasis on relatedness and 'concrescence'; (3) the separation of God and Creativity. Each of the three points is in sharp contrast to the Aristotelian metaphysics of substance and for each there are considerable affinities with the Buddhist way of thinking.

Let us briefly examine these three points.

1. *The notion of actual entity and the principle of process*. As was mentioned above, Whitehead's notion of actual entity is not an entity which endures self-identically as does substance in the Aristotelian sense, but an entity which is a process involving duration, transition, and perishing. This is why he says 'An actual entity is a process, and

is not describable in terms of the morphology of a "stuff"[13]. For Whitehead endurance is nothing but a succession of instantaneous facts. Accordingly, the temporal process is a transition from one actual entity to another. These entities are momentary events which perish immediately upon coming into being. And personal human existence is a serially ordered society of occasions of experience. This view is remarkably similar to Buddhism. In Whitehead, the *being* of an actual entity is constituted by its *becoming*. It follows, as Whitehead says, that '*how* an actual entity *becomes* constitutes *what* that actual entity *is*; so that the two descriptions of an actual entity are not independent. Its "being" is constituted by its "becoming." This is the "principle of process".[14] From the becoming process one can by abstraction derive various static forms of being. But from the notion of being one cannot derive the notion of becoming. Becoming can embrace being, but not vice versa: process can embrace substance, but not vice versa, because the former is more dynamic and more concrete than the latter.

2. *An emphasis on relatedness and 'concrescence.'* Against the doctrine of the individual independence of real facts as derived from the subject–predicate mode of thinking, Whitehead emphasizes the relatedness of actualities. In his philosophy, "Relatedness" is dominant over "quality".[15] Each actual entity is not isolated from another, through its individual substance, but is internally related. For Whitehead, the notion that actual entities are processes not only entails process as 'transition' but also process as what he calls 'concrescence.' Concrescence is 'the real internal constitution of a particular existent,'[16] and the growing together of many into the unity of one. This emphasis on the relatedness between actual entities and the notion of 'concrescence' has parallels in Buddhist teaching. It is not without reason that the Whiteheadian notions of relatedness, especially that of concrescence, are often compared with the Buddhist notion of 'dependent co-origination.'

3. *The separation of God and Creativity.* The most remarkable feature of the Whiteheadian doctrine of process may be said to lie in his separation of God and Creativity. To him the ultimate is not God but Creativity. (Besides 'Creativity,' 'many' and 'one' are two other notions involved in what Whitehead calls the category of the Ultimate). 'Creativity' is the universal of universals characterizing ultimate matter of fact and is the principle of novelty. On the other hand, God is understood as an actual entity and is not an exception to all metaphysical principles, invoked to save their collapse. Thus,

'every actual entity, including God, is a creature transcended by the creativity which it qualifies,'[17] because God is nothing but the outcome of Creativity. This denial of the traditional Christian notion of the one God as the creator, ruler and judge of the universe indicates a great affinity with Buddhism, which is fundamentally non-theistic.

Among the statements made by Whitehead, those that would be most appreciated by Buddhists are the following:

1. It is as true to say that God is permanent and the world is fluent, as that the world is permanent and God is fluent.
2. It is as true to say that the world is immanent in God, as that God is immanent in the World.
3. It is as true to say that God creates the world, as that the world creates God.[18]

As this summary of Whiteheadian philosophy shows, there are considerable affinities between Whitehead and Buddhism. For all these similarities, however, it is also undeniable, in my view, that there are great differences between them. These differences are not just of degree, but essential and fundamental. For instance, Whitehead's notion of 'concrescence,' which is often compared with the Buddhist notion of dependent co-origination, is formulized by him in such statements as 'the many became one, and are increased by one.' On the other hand, in the Buddhist teaching of dependent co-origination it must be said that 'the many *are* one: one *is* the many.' For in dependent co-origination, it is not only that one and the many are dependent on each other in their arising and ceasing, but also that both one and the many are completely without substance and *empty*. Thus it must be realized that although one is one as distinguishable from the many, one *is not* one: although the many is the many as distinguishable from the one, many *are not* the many. This is a realization that there is neither one nor the many. Through this realization of non-substantial emptiness common to one and the many, one as it is is realized as the many: the many are realized as one. This is the dependent co-origination between one and the many. Therefore, although the Buddhist teaching of dependent co-origination has an aspect of becoming, in its essence it does not, as is often misunderstood, indicate 'becoming' but 'being' – 'being' which is realized through the realization of emptiness. Hence, 'one *is* the many' precisely because one *is not* one: the many *are* one precisely because the many *are not* the many. Accordingly, the Buddhist view of dependent co-origination is categorically different from the Whiteheadian notion of becoming or process. 'Isness' or 'being' realized in the Buddhist view of dependent co-origination, however, is different from the Aristotelian notion of 'being' because it is realized through overcoming the notion of becoming. The categorical difference between Whitehead and Buddhism may become clearer when the following point is taken into account, that is, the *character* or *nature* of the 'relatedness' realized in Whitehead and Buddhism. Both in Whitehead and Buddhism the relatedness or relationship, such as between one and the many, is clearly realized. As for the one and the many, Whitehead says 'The term "many" presupposes the term "one," and the term "one" presupposes the term "many"'.[19] There is no 'one' without the 'many' and vice versa. One and the many are interrelated. However, Whitehead's formulation of concrescence ('the many become one, and are increased by one') clearly shows that the relatedness between one and the many is not reciprocal but rather lineal and one-directional. Of course, in concrescence it can be equally said that 'one becomes the many, and is increased by the many.' But this takes place as the next step after the first step in which 'the many become one, and are increased by one.' The many in the second step is different from the many in the first step. Although one and the many are interrelated that interrelationship is taking place step by step in a lineal manner. This is exactly the meaning of 'becoming' in 'process' which essentially implies temporality. Even 'creativity' as the principle of novelty which is non-temporal is understood as unidirectional. Contrary to this non-reciprocal and unidirectional nature of relatedness in Whitehead, the Buddhist notion of relatedness is completely reciprocal by nature. If we must use the term 'become' we can say, 'one becomes the many' and 'the many become one' *at one and the same step*, without temporal succession. But the preferable rendering would be 'one *in* the many; the many *in* one.' Then, interrelatedness between one and the many is grasped as reciprocal and is realized in this non-temporal and ontological dimension. Therefore the terms such as 'becoming' and 'process' are not applicable to indicate the *basic* nature of the relatedness in the Buddhist sense. To indicate the Buddhist notion of relatedness, that is, dependent co-origination, we must say, 'one *is* the many' precisely because one *is not* one; 'the many are one' precisely because the many *are not* the many. Such a statement may be unintelligible to some. This may be the case unless the subject–predicate mode of thinking is completely overcome.

In this brief explanation, we have examined the categorical difference between Whiteheadian philosophy and Buddhist thought. In order to elucidate the difference more clearly, a more systematic explanation of the Buddhist teaching of 'dependent co-origination' and 'emptiness' may be in order.

II

Pratītya-samutpāda ('dependent origination,' or better, 'co-dependent origination')[20] is the most basic perception of Buddhist teaching. It is said that by meditating upon this view of 'co-dependent origination' the Buddha attained Awakening under the Bodhi Tree. In his teaching he said, 'Those who see co-dependent origination see the Dharma, see the Buddha.' It is clear how essential the view of co-dependent origination is to Buddhism. It is identical with the Dharma (truth) and the Buddha (the Awakened One).

To elucidate the meaning of 'co-dependent origination' it may be helpful to compare it briefly with the ancient Greek notion of 'formation' and the Judeo-Christian notion of 'creation.' In Greek philosophy, notably in Plato and Aristotle, a real existence is a thing with a particular form; sheer matter or material without form is something non-existent; only when matter is given a particular form is it understood to come to exist positively. Formation is a key concept of Greek philosophy. Form and matter presuppose each other. And in Aristotle their relationship is grasped dynamically in terms of *dynamis* and *energeia*. Yet, the notion of formation is based on the duality between form and matter. Or at least it may be said that matter depends on form to truly exist, whereas form does not depend on matter; it is self-existing.[21] Contrary to this, Judaism and Christianity emphasize creation rather than formation. The characteristic of the Christian notion of creation is most explicitly defined in terms of '*creatio ex nihilo;*' that is 'creation out of nothing.' It is not that God created the universe out of some given materials, but that he created the universe out of nothing. This indicates the unparalleled, absolute and transcendent nature of the Christian notion of God in which the duality between form and matter as seen in Greek philosophy is completely overcome. In the Christian notion of creation, however, there is another form of duality, that is a duality between the creator and the created. Although the creator and the created presuppose each other and thereby are interrelated with each other there is the essential primacy of God the creator over the created. The created depends on God, the creator, for its existence, whereas God, the creator, does not depend on the created. He is independent. (It is precisely this traditional Christian notion of God, the creator, that process theology is trying to overcome!)

On the other hand, in the Buddhist teaching of co-dependent origination there is nothing independent or self-existing whatsoever apart from other things. Everything is mutually dependent and co-arising and co-ceasing. There can be no exceptions, such as a God standing outside of co-dependent origination. This is the reason Buddhism does not accept the ideas of a God or a Brahman who is self-existing or self-sufficient. In fact, against the Upanishadic notion of Brahman as a substantive, eternal entity underlying the changing, phenomenal world, the Buddha expounded the notion of co-dependent origination to account for the origination and cessation of phenomena. This complete interdependency of everything throughout and even beyond the universe is one of the essential elements of the Buddhist teaching of co-dependent origination.

In his enlightenment the Buddha awakened to this perception of co-dependent origination. Since his primary concern was not with the metaphysical structure of the universe but with human suffering and the release from suffering, he applied this realization to that existential issue. The result was his formulation of the twelvefold co-dependent origination. According to the Pali Vinaya, in his meditation after enlightenment at the foot of the Bodhi Tree the Buddha contemplated the twelve preconditions, running through the chain forward and backward. However, the formulation of the twelvefold co-dependent origination may be the most developed form of the doctrine, probably established after conceiving and preaching the doctrines of the sixfold, the eightfold, and the tenfold co-dependent origination. In the formulation of the twelvefold co-dependent origination, (1) ignorance, (2) dispositions, (3) consciousness, (4) name-and-form, (5) the six sense fields, (6) contact, (7) feeling, (8) craving, (9) appropriation, (10) becoming, (11) birth, and (12) aging and dying are grasped in term of co-arising and co-ceasing. Suffering arises depending first on (12) aging and dying and, running backward in sequence, depending finally on (1) ignorance. Accordingly, when (1) ignorance ceases, then running forward in succession, finally, (12) aging and dying cease. Even this formulation of co-dependent origination does not simply indicate a 'becoming' or 'process.' Twelve items are grasped interdependently in their arising and ceasing *running forward and backward*. Their interdependency does not imply a one-directional but rather a reciprocal movement. Accordingly, is is a mistake to understand the teaching of twelvefold co-dependent origination simply as an analysis of the human, phenomenal world, that is, the realm of *saṃsāra*. The teaching clearly indicates how to overcome *saṃsāra* and attain *nirvāṇa*. The formulation of twelvefold co-dependent origination is a bridge from the realm of *saṃsāra* to the realm of *nirvāṇa*. In reality, it is something more than a bridge between the two realms, it includes both the realm of *saṃsāra* and the realm of *nirvāṇa*, with 'the cessation of ignorance (*avidyā*) *namely* the realization of enlightenment (*vidyā*)' as a hinge. The reason that the teaching of twelvefold co-dependent origination is often misinterpreted as a theory for explaining the realm of *saṃsāra* may lie in an interpretation of it merely as a causal series of twelve chains or links (*nidanas*). When the formulation of co-dependent origination – whether it consists of twelve, ten, eight, or six chains – is interpreted as a causal series of these chains, their interdependency is understood merely as unidirectional, and the formulation appears as a law of causation and a theory for explaining the realm of *saṃsāra*. This misinterpretation is based on a neglect of the reciprocal nature of the relatedness between the chains.

The teaching of co-dependent origination – regardless of the number of chains involved – is more than a law of causation. In this respect the following two points are worthy of note.

(1) *Two kinds of causality.* The term *pratītya-samutpāda*, co-dependent origination, is also translated as causality. In Buddhism, there are two kinds of causality: sequential causality and simultaneous causality. In sequential causality the cause always comes first and the effect later. The movement from the cause to the effect is always unidirectional and non-reciprocal. This notion of causality is connected with temporal sequence and applied to the phenomenal realm, as in biological and historical development. However, in Buddhism, particularly in the formulation of co-dependent origination, things or events are not necessarily grasped in terms of cause and effect, but in terms of cause, condition, and effect. When things or events are grasped in terms of the relationship between these three items, cause, condition and effect, a cause is understood to become an effect only through a condition. What is

called cause and what is called effect can take place only with condition (*pratyaya*) as their mediator:

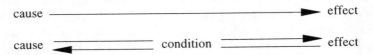

Thus things or events are understood to originate and cease conditionally. And cause and effect take place at the same time through the mediation of condition. This is not a sequential causality but a simultaneous causality in which the relation between what is called cause and what is called effect is not unidirectional but reciprocal. And simultaneous causality can be realized in the non-temporal realm as well as in the temporal realm. It indicates a non-temporal and logical dependency between different things. Although the formulation of twelvefold co-dependent origination includes sequential causality, it also implies simultaneous causality. This is because the very view of co-dependent origination originally implies non-temporal, logical, and ontological structure. Although it has an aspect of 'becoming' and 'process' it indicates something more than them.

(2) *Not the formula of co-dependent origination but the logical ground of co-dependent origination.* The foregoing discussion suggests the need to distinguish between concrete formulas of co-dependent origination such as the twelvefold co-dependent origination and the 'logical ground of dependent origination' implied in them. This difference, though in a loose sense, is somewhat parallel to Heidegger's so-called *Ontologische Differenz*. In Heidegger, *Ontologische Differenz* signifies a difference between *Sein* (Being) and *das Seiendes* (things-that-are or beings). *Das Seiendes* are things given as objects which we can encounter or at least exemplify within our world. On the other hand, *Sein* or being cannot be encountered as an object, because it is that which makes *Seiendes* possible as *Seiendes*, i.e., 'that through which things are.' Making a clear distinction between *Seiendes* and *Sein*, Heidegger calls the way of being of *Seiendes ontisch* or ontic. The way of enquiry into the meaning of *Sein* thematically is called *ontologisch* or ontological because ontology is a discipline which is thematically concerned with the problem of *Sein*, not the problem of *Seiendes*.

Now, in Heidegger, each of the *Seiendes* exist ontically, whereas in Buddhism all *Seiendes* exist in terms of co-dependent origination. And, in Heidegger, it is an ontological, not ontic, standpoint to enquire thematically into *Sein als solches* as the ground of *Seiendes*. Likewise, in Buddhism, it is a task of 'co-dependent originatology' – if such a term can be coined – and not a task of the formula of co-dependent origination, to enquire thematically into the logical ground which makes the existence of *Seiendes* possible in terms of co-dependent origination. To ask for the logical ground or structure of co-dependent origination is possible not in terms of co-dependent origination, but only in terms of 'co-dependent originatology.' Thus, in the mode of Heidegger, I would like to establish a kind of *co-dependent-originatological difference*, so to speak. In Heidegger, *Ontologische Differenz* was necessary to open up the horizon for the true metaphysics to inquire into the meaning of *Sein* as apart from *Seiendes*. In our case the 'co-dependent originatological' difference is necessary to elucidate the logical ground for the notion of co-dependent origination thematically in clear distinction from something which happens in terms of co-dependent origination. Accordingly, 'co-dependent originatology' should no be confused with the formula or formulation of co-dependent origination. For the various concrete formulas of co-dependent origination, such as the twelvefold formula or the tenfold formulas, are concerned with how and what happens in terms of co-dependent origination. On the other hand, 'co-dependent originatology' is concerned with the fundamental structure of the notion of co-dependent origination through which the various formulas of co-dependent origination can be established.

As a clue to the fundamental, logical structure which constitutes the view of co-dependent origination I should like to quote the following four-line statement which appears in *Majjhima Nikāya*, *Samyutta Nikāya* and so forth:

1. When this is present, that comes to be;
2.   from the arising of this, that arises.
3. When this is absent, that does not come to be;
4.   on the cessation of this, that ceases.

This statement indicates the interdependence – often *idampratyayatā* – between 'this' and 'that' in the sense that, on account of the presence or absence of 'this', 'this' comes to be or not to be; on account of the arising or cessation of 'this,' 'this' arises or ceases. In this statement 'this' always precedes 'that' and therefore apparently their relationship seems to be one-sided and not reciprocal. This is, however, not the case. Because both 'this' and 'that' are demonstrative pronouns, particular content is lacking. Accordingly, if we give content to them, the two items demonstrated by 'this' and 'that' become completely reciprocal or reversible. For example, let us consider the content to be 'bigness' and 'smallness.' Then, we may say, 'When "bigness" is present, "smallness" comes to be: from the arising of "bigness," "smallness" arises,' and yet with entirely the same justification we may also say, 'When "smallness" is present, "bigness" comes to be; from the arising of "smallness" "bigness" arises.'

When we examine this statement of co-dependent origination in terms of 'the logical structure of co-dependent origination' we may indicate at least the following three points:

1. Everything in and out of the universe without exception is interdependently related to every other thing; nothing whatsoever is independently self-existing without relying upon something else. And any relationship is reciprocal and reversible; there can be no unreciprocal and irreversible relationship whatsoever.

2. Each items which is mutually related with all other items must have a uniqueness or particularity. This is because, among entities which have no uniqueness or peculiarity, there can be no *mutual dependence*.

3. How is it possible that these two apparently contradictory aspects, i.e., first the complete interdependence, and second the uniqueness of each item, are both implied in the structure of co-dependent origination? This is possible precisely because there is no particular principle, no special reality, such as God, Brahman, Being, which, being beyond, behind, or beneath the co-dependent originational relationship among all things, gives a foundation to it. In other words the above-mentioned two apparently contradictory aspects are working together without contradiction because the relationship of the co-dependent origination takes place in the locus of 'emptiness.'

First, let us consider the third point, that is, emptiness. In the doctrine of co-dependent origination in early Buddhism, the notion of emptiness was not often explicitly discussed, but we may nevertheless say that it was implicit. It is Nāgārjuna who explicitly elucidated the notion of emptiness. Nāgārjuna, who clarified that co-dependent origination and emptiness are synonymous, was the first one to throw light on the 'co-dependent originational' structure of the thought of *pratitya-samutpāda*.

Second, what does it mean to say 'each item which is mutually related with all other items must have a uniqueness or particularity?'

When Buddhism argues 'everything is empty' someone may construe this as attesting that this desk which we can now recognize by our sense organs is in fact non-existent or something like an illusion. This is, however, not the case. When a Buddhist says this desk is empty he does not mean that this desk is like a phantom or apparition or ghost which is unreal and dreamy. He is not denying the sensory and phenomenal self-identity of this desk. Instead he is denying the supersensory and substantial self-identity of the desk that is beyond the sensory and phenomenal dimension. Accordingly, no matter how definitely the sensory and phenomenal self-identity of the desk may be confirmed, the desk must be said to be empty in so far as it is lacking substantial self-identity. This is called 'no-own-being – emptiness.' Now let us call the sensory and phenomenal self-identity 'the self-identity in terms of mark or form' (*lakṣaṇa*) and the supersensory and substantial self-identity 'the self-identity in terms of nature' (*dhātu*).[22] Then, we may say that this desk undoubtedly has a self-identity in terms of 'form' called a desk, but that it does not have a self-identity in terms of 'nature' named a desk. This is what we mean when we say that this desk is empty. Nevertheless we often think of the desk as if it had a self-identity in terms of 'nature,' whereas it has in reality only a self-identity in terms of the 'form' called a desk. Hence, there is an attachment to the desk, a clinging to the desk. Illusion and attachment arise when, being captured by a form, whatever it may be, we misconceive a form for a substantial nature. Everything has its own form, but has no nature to be called 'nature.' This is precisely what 'no-own-being – empty' means. Accordingly it is to indicate this 'selfhood in terms of form' and not the 'selfhood in terms of nature' that I have stated above that each item which is mutually dependent on all other items in the structure of co-dependent origination must have a uniqueness or particularity in some sense or other. If each individual thing has its selfhood in terms of nature it comes to possess a self-sufficient independence by its own nature. As a result its mutual dependence with other individual things becomes impossible. However, since every individual thing has its own 'selfhood in terms of form' respectively, so far as the form is concerned, the interdependence between individual things is quite possible – because a form can be one form only in distinction from or in correlation with other forms. At the same time, every individual thing has a uniqueness in so far as it has selfhood in terms of form. It is precisely because 'selfhood in terms of nature' is denied that a dynamic structure of co-dependent origination is possible in which, due to the selfhood in terms of form, each thing has its uniqueness respectively and yet is mutually dependent. That is to say, it is precisely because the existence of a substantial principle which exists separately beyond 'the selfhood in terms of form' is denied, that, in so far as nature is concerned, everything has no selfhood and therefore is empty.

Now, returning to the first point, let us consider that everything is interdependent: nothing whatsoever is self-existing: there can be no irreversible relationship whatsoever. What must be here especially emphasized is that the principle that everything is interdependent and reversible must be strictly applied to all relationships without even a single exception. Accordingly, not only the relation between husband and wife is interdependent and reversible, but also the relation between father and son, and the relation between God and man as well must be interdependent and reversible. Again, not only are the relations between good and evil, life and death, being and non-being interdependent and reversible, but also the relations between the sacred and the secular, transcendence and immanence, the absolute and the relative must be completely interdependent and reversible.

In the Judeo-Christian tradition the relationship between God and man has not been regarded as a direct and continuous relationship of generation such as begetting and the begotten, but has been grasped as a transcendental relationship in term of *creatio ex nihilo*. It is only in terms of *creatio ex nihilo* that the relationship between man and God as the transcendent one who is beyond all possible immanent relationship becomes clear. Although the notion of creation is based on the interrelationship between creator and the created their relationship is not completely reciprocal. There is a primacy of God, the creator over man as the created. The divine–human relationship is not co-dependent originational. This is more conspicuous when Christianity emphasizes that creation is not 'creation out of something' but creation out of nothing.' This is precisely why Buddhism, which teaches the law of co-dependent origination and regards the interdependence among all entities as the truth, does not accept the doctrine of creation. Speaking from the Buddhist point of view, creatorship is not God's essence or 'nature', but rather a 'form' of him. Likewise creaturehood is a 'form' of man, not his 'nature.' Setting aside Judaism, Christianity must be said to have been aware of this. Accordingly, the core of the Christian faith does not lie in the faith in God the creator but in God the redeemer, that is, faith in salvation through Jesus Christ as the son of God. (God the creator is an occasion of God who himself is free from creation.) This redeemer, Jesus Christ, is none other than the son who was begotten by God the Father within Himself prior to the creation of the universe. This eternal birth of the son within God which is understood as a matter prior to creation represents a much deeper standpoint which takes creatorship not as the 'nature' of God but as merely a 'form' of Him. This overcoming of the concept of God as the creator is clearly realized in process theology, particularly in Professor Cobb's and his colleagues' theological works which, based on Whitehead's metaphysics, take the idea of 'creativity' as the basic category.

III

Nāgārjuna appeared around the second century AD, grounded in the *Prajñāpāramitā Sūtras* of the Mahāyāna Buddhist tradition. It is well-known that during the second century after the death of Gautama Buddha the Buddhist Order split into two sects, the Elders and the Great Assembly. The Elders claimed conservative orthodoxy and emphasized the monastic life isolated from ordinary society. They observed strict asceticism and developed the scholastic doctrine called Abhidharma.

This tradition is called Theravāda or Hīnayāna Buddhism. On the other hand, those of the so-called Great Assembly were more progressive and more sensitive to popular religious values and aspirations. Criticizing the self-righteousness or self-complacency of the Elders, they were much concerned with the salvation of laymen. From this sect developed a new form of the Buddhist movement, beginning about the first century BC. It is not a religion of the monastery but rather a religion of social life, not a religion of the saint, but rather a religion of laymen. This tradition is called Mahāyāna Buddhism. The *Prajñāpāramitā Sūtra* is the first and most basic scripture produced by Mahāyāna Buddhists. Nāgārjuna was historically pivotal for criticizing the Abhidharma Buddhism of Theravāda and elucidating the inner meaning of the Buddha's teaching on the basis of the *Prajñāpāramitā Sūtra*.

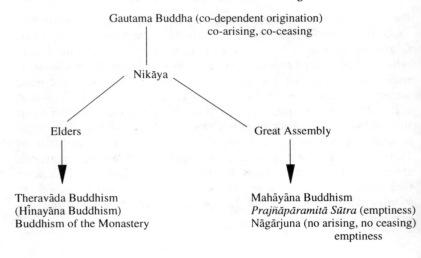

Gautama Buddha (co-dependent origination)
co-arising, co-ceasing

Nikāya

Elders

Great Assembly

Theravāda Buddhism
(Hīnayāna Buddhism)
Buddhism of the Monastery

Mahāyāna Buddhism
Prajñāpāramitā Sūtra (emptiness)
Nāgārjuna (no arising, no ceasing)
emptiness

The *Prajñāpāramitā Sūtra* emphasizes the six paramitas, that is the six virtues of perfection, especially the perfection of *prajñā*, that which is the perfection of wisdom. *Pāramitā* means 'arriving at the other shore' and thus 'perfection.' It also emphasizes the importance of detachment or non-attachment in order to awaken to wisdom. Attachment is objectifying through the will or volition, a process inseparably connected with conceptualization. Love is a positive attachment, hate a negative attachment. We objectify and attach to ourselves, other persons, and other things as if they were something substantial and eternal. This process gives rise to suffering. In Buddhism, as well as in other religions, to be liberated from suffering in this world we must overcome attachment to this secular world and attain the sacred realm. A unique characteristic of the *Prajñāpāramitā Sūtra* is its emphasis on detachment from the sacred realm. In a sense, the sutra places greater emphasis on the harmfulness of the attachment to the sacred realm than that of the attachment to the secular realm. It stresses the necessity of detachment from the 'religious' life. For the realization of wisdom it is necessary to overcome the attachment to this secular world and to attain the sacred realm. However, if one remains in the sacred realm aloof from the secular world, this is not a true wisdom. To realize the perfection of wisdom, i.e. *prajñāpāramitā*, one cannot remain in the sacred world. Rather, by overcoming attachment to the 'sacred,' one must return to the secular world. Only by returning to the mundane world through detachment from the religious life can the perfection of wisdom be truly realized. This is why the sutra emphasizes detachment from the sacred realm. This emphasis is, needless to say, based on the Mahāyānist's criticism of Theravada Buddhists who, renouncing the mundane world, are concerned with their own enlightenment, aloof from ordinary people who are suffering.

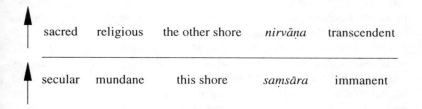

| sacred | religious | the other shore | *nirvāṇa* | transcendent |
| secular | mundane | this shore | *saṃsāra* | immanent |

What, then does detachment from the sacred, transcendent realm indicate? Since everything can be divided into two realms, secular and sacred, immanent and transcendent, detachment from the sacred and transcendent world, which is attained through detachment from the secular and immanent world, indicates nothing whatsoever – nothing-ness, i.e. emptiness. Complete detachment from both the secular and the sacred realms signifies the realization of emptiness, which is neither secular nor sacred. However, the realization of emptiness is not nihilistic. For to realize emptiness by going beyond the sacred realm is none other than returning amidst the secular realm. In the realization of emptiness through complete detachment from both the secular and the sacred worlds one can freely move back and forth between the two worlds without hindrance.

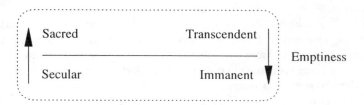

This means that the realization of emptiness is 'both secular and sacred' as well as 'neither secular nor sacred.' The perfection of Wisdom is awakening to this realization of emptiness.

In the *Prajñāpāramitā Sūtras* are found paradoxical statements such as: '*Prajñāpāramitā* is not *prajñāpāramitā*; precisely because this is so, it is called *prajñāpāramitā*.' This means that to arrive at the other shore (in terms of Wisdom) by renouncing this shore is *not* to arrive at the other shore (in terms of Wisdom). Only through this negative realization of 'arriving at the other shore' can one truly arrive at the 'other shore' which is dynamically identical to this shore. In short, 'arriving at the other shore' is not 'arriving at the other shore'; precisely because this is so it is called 'arriving at the other shore' – this is exactly the realization of emptiness.

This is also the reason Mahāyāna Buddhism characteristically emphasizes that '*saṃsāra is nirvāṇa*.' To attain *nirvāṇa* by abandoning *saṃsāra* is not truly attaining *nirvāṇa*; rather by abandoning *nirvāṇa* to return to *saṃsāra* is truly attaining *nirvāṇa*. Hence, *saṃsāra is nirvāṇa* and at the same time *nirvāṇa is saṃsāra*. It is *not* that *saṃsāra becomes nirvāṇa*, nor that *nirvāṇa becomes saṃsāra*. There is no 'process' in this 'isness.' But this 'isness' does not indicate Being or substance in the Aristotelian sense, because this 'isness' is understood trough the realization of emptiness. Specifically, the realization of this 'isness' is nothing but the realization of 'emptiness.'

To be attached to *saṃsāra* means to be attached to *saṃsāra* as something substantial. To be detached from *saṃsāra* means to realize *saṃsāra* as something non-substantial. When we realize the non-substantial nature of *saṃsāra* one can go beyond *saṃsāra* and attain *nirvāṇa*. However, to be attached to *nirvāṇa* indicates being attached to *nirvāṇa* as something substantial. To be detached from *nirvāṇa* means to realize *nirvāṇa* as something non-substantial. When one realizes the non-substantial nature of *nirvāṇa* one can go beyond *nirvāṇa* and return to *saṃsāra*. Hence, the realization that *saṃsāra is nirvāṇa: nirvāṇa is saṃsāra*. In this sense this 'isness' does not indicate 'substance' or 'process,' but 'emptiness.'

For the sake of Wisdom, one must abandon *saṃsāra* to attain *nirvāṇa*. However, if one remains in and attached to *nirvāṇa* one cannot be said to have awakened to the true wisdom. Accordingly, for the sake of compassion one should abandon *nirvāṇa* together with wisdom to return to *saṃsāra*. Then one can be said to have awakened to the true wisdom. Therefore, true wisdom is at once true compassion. (Compassion in *saṃsāra* before attaining *nirvāṇa* is not true compassion. True compassion is realized only through abandoning wisdom together with *nirvāṇa*). This realization that 'true wisdom is at once true compassion' is nothing but the realization of 'emptiness' because in this realization both wisdom and compassion are realized as non-substantial. This signifies the realization that 'wisdom is not wisdom; precisely because this is so it is called wisdom' and the realization that 'compassion is not compassion; precisely because this is so it is called compassion.'

This is the import of the *Prajñāpāramitā Sūtras*. In this way it emphasizes the perfection of wisdom, which is nothing other than the wisdom of *śūnyatā* (emptiness). In the *Prajñāpāramitā Sūtra*, however, the wisdom of *śūnyatā* was intuitively realized. A paradoxical statement such as *'prajñāpāramitā* is not *prajñāpāramitā;* precisely because this is so it is called *prajñāpāramitā'* comes directly from intuitive wisdom and heartfelt compassion. It was Nāgārjuna who gave this intuitive wisdom of emptiness a logico-philosophical foundation. And, in Nāgārjuna, this logico-philosophical foundation of the wisdom of emptiness was inseparably connected with the reinterpretation of the Buddha's view of co-dependent origination.

In the first stanza of *Madhyamikārikā* (Middle Stanza) Nāgārjuna says: 'I offer salutation to the best of preachers, the Buddha, who has taught that co-dependent origination has no ceasing, no arising, no nullification, no eternity, no unity, no plurality, no coming, no going, that is quiescent of all verbal fabrication, that is blissful.' This is well known as Nāgārjuna's 'Eightfold Negation.' Here, four pairs (1) ceasing and arising, (2) nullification and eternity (3) unity and plurality, (4) coming and going, which may be taken as the basic categories representing our daily thinking, are mentioned.

In this respect, the following points may be worthy of note:

1. All of the four pairs indicate an interdependency between two items which are *mutually opposing* and *negating,* such as ceasing and arising, nullification and eternity, and so forth. And both sides of these mutually opposing items are *equally negated* in such a manner as *no* ceasing, *no* arising, *no* nullification, *no* eternity, and so forth. This is significantly different from an interdependency between 'this' and 'that' as seen in the four line statement of co-dependent origination cited above. In the latter case, the interdependency between 'this' and 'that' indicates that between A and B, the negation of both still implies the possible existence of C, D, E, and so forth. Thus, the double negation does not necessarily indicate 'emptiness.' On the other hand, in the latter case the interdependency signifies that between A and *non-A,* and thereby the negation of both (the double

negation of A and non-A) clearly indicates 'emptiness.' There can be
no possibility of the existence of C, D, E, and so forth.

2. The teaching of 'co-dependent origination' is here understood to
have the double negation of these mutually negating pairs, such as
'no ceasing, no arising' and so forth – that is 'emptiness.' This is the
reason Nāgārjuna takes 'co-dependent origination' and 'emptiness'
synonymously as we see in the 18th and 19th stanzas of Nāgārjuna's
The Middle Stanza as follows:

18. The 'co-dependent origination' we call 'emptiness.' This
apprehension, i.e. taking into account [all other things],
is the understanding of the middle way.
19. Since there is no *dharma* ('factor' or 'element' of existence)
whatever originating independently, no *dharma* whatever
exists which is not empty.

In his book *Emptiness*, Professor Frederick J. Streng comments on
these stanzas by saying:

Considered in the context of emptiness (*śūnyatā*), co-originating
dependently loses its meaning as the link between two 'things';
rather it becomes the form for expressing the phenomenal
'becoming' as the lack of any self-sufficient, independent
reality.[23]

In Nāgārjuna co-dependent origination does not indicate 'co-arising, co-
ceasing,' but rather, 'no arising, no ceasing.' Thus we may say 'co-
dependent origination is not co-origination; just because this is so it is
called co-dependent origination.' This is the realization of true co-
dependent origination which is nothing but the realization of emptiness.

Now, let us summarize the remaining discussion as follows:

1. Nāgārjuna also emphasizes Fourfold Negation, for example, the
negation of the following phrases:

Being,
Non-being,
Both being and non-being,
Neither being nor non-being.

This is a complete negation of all possible propositions which is
essential for the realization of emptiness.

2. The pivotal point of the realization of 'emptiness' is the double negation implied, for instance, in 'neither arising nor ceasing' or 'neither being nor non-being.' This double negation, that is, the negation of the negation, is affirmation at the same time. This is because, as the negation of negation in this case is the double negation of two mutually negating items, that is A and non-A – this is absolute negation – there can be no possibility of third or fourth negation and thus for an endless repetition of negations. The double negation must thus turn into an affirmation. This is, however, not an affirmation in the relative sense, but rather an affirmation in the absolute sense, because this is an affirmation realized through the double negation. Thus it can be said:

> Negation of negation is affirmation of affirmation;
> double negation is double affirmation;
> absolute negation is absolute affirmation.

This is a logical formulation of the realization of emptiness.

3. The absolute affirmation implied in the realization of emptiness is essentially different from the affirmation implied in *via eminentiae*. *Via eminentiae* indicates the highest rank which can be reached or in which one can participate through *via negativa*. It is realized over there, not down here, and thus is somewhat teleological. On the other hand, the absolute affirmation implied in the realization of emptiness does not indicate the highest rank but rather 'no rank' which is realized down here, right now – as seen in Lin-chi's words, 'There is a true Man of no rank who is coming in and out through your sense organs. Those who have not witnessed the Man, Look! Look!' To awaken to this true Man without rank is the realization of emptiness which is not teleological.

4. This difference of 'affirmation' in between the realization of emptiness and *via eminentia* depends on whether or not the affirmation is realized through the absolute negation, that is, the double negation of the two mutually negative items.

5. 'Emptiness' is also termed 'formlessness' because it completely overcomes 'form.'

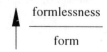

However, if formlessness is simply distinguished from form by negating the latter, and remains with itself, it is not true formlessness, because, being distinguished from form, formlessness turns into a 'form' merely named 'formlessness.' To be truly formless, formlessness must negate itself and must return to form, taking forms freely. Being formless, to take various forms freely; taking various forms freely to always keep formlessness – this is the realization of true formlessness.

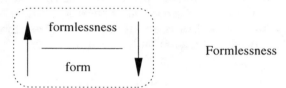

Formlessness

6. The same is true with emptiness. Emptiness is realized by the double negation of being and non-being. Emptiness is neither being nor non-being.

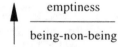

If emptiness, however, is simply distinguished from 'being-non-being' it is not true emptiness because it stands against being-non-being and thus turns into something merely called 'emptiness.' To be true emptiness, emptiness should not attach to itself and must empty itself. Only when emptiness empties itself and takes forms of being and non-being freely can it be called true emptiness.

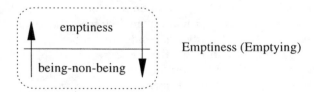

Emptiness (Emptying)

Accordingly 'emptiness' (*śūnyatā*), although expressed in terms of a noun, should be understood in terms of a verb. In other words, true emptiness is *pure activity of emptying* which empties everything including itself.

7. This means that, emptying itself, emptiness can take 'this' form or 'that' form or every form freely in their distinctive manner and yet every form is emptied and thereby interpenetrates others without hindrance.

Since emptiness as the pure activity of emptying incessantly empties everything including itself, there is nothing outside of this pure activity of emptying. Everything is included in this activity of emptiness and each, at each place and at each time, is absolutely negated as well as absolutely affirmed.

8. This pure activity of emptying is the True Self. That is to say, the realization of this activity of emptying is the realization of one's True Self. If the activity of emptying is realized somewhat outside of the Self, it will again turn into something, because it is then looked at from outside and is objectified by the self. It becomes something dead. In so far as it is the pure *activity* of emptying, it must be said that true emptying is the Self and the True Self is the subject of emptying. This is what Lin-chi describes as the 'True Man of no rank who is coming in and out through your sense organs.'

9. When emptiness as True Self empties itself it becomes 'Vow.' Emptiness which does not become vow is not true emptiness. At the same time, if vow remains with itself and does not empty itself, it is not true vow. True vow must empty itself and always become 'practice.' Thus in the pure activity of emptying, emptiness becomes vow, and vow becomes practice. However, this does not mean that emptiness becomes something else or that emptiness goes out of itself. The whole process of emptiness → vow → practice is nothing but the pure activity of emptying itself and is included by that activity. There is no outside for the activity of emptying. In the realization of the activity of emptying, 'become' is not 'become.' Precisely because this is so it is 'become.' 'To go out of itself' is not 'to go out of itself' (but rather 'to return to itself'). Precisely because this is so it 'goes out of itself.'

10. Just as 'becoming' can embargo 'being,' but not vice versa 'emptiness' can embrace 'becoming' but not vice versa. Since 'becoming' can embrace 'being,' 'emptiness' as the pure activity of emptying can embrace both 'being' and 'becoming.' 'Emptiness' is at once 'being' and 'becoming.' This is realized only when the Aristotelian form of the 'subject–predicate' mode of thinking is completely overcome. Ultimate Reality is realized in the dynamic realization of emptying. However, as soon as the pure activity of emptying loses its function of self-negation, that is, negation of

negation, it turns into 'emptiness' in noun form and the Ultimate Reality will be lost. Incessant self-emptying is essential to the realization of true emptiness.

9

The Problem of Death in East and West: Immortality, Eternal Life, Unbornness

The highest death is to die without having thought about it in advance,' writes Montaigne (*Essais*). It might be possible for some to ignore death by *not* thinking of it and *not* questioning its meaning. Again, even if one knows that death is inescapable, one might not dwell on it, but rather think primarily of life and seek after life. A death met precisely in the midst of the earnest pursuit of life and unconcern for death may be called the highest death. The present age is one of fulfillment and enjoyment of life. Nevertheless, due to the appearance of absolute weapons, the present age has at the same time become an age of anxiety over death and of nihilism. Indeed, does not anxiety and nihilism characterize humankind's present existential situation? People grieve over the fact that they must die, rather than over death itself. This brings to mind Pascal's profound words: 'Death is easier to endure for the man who does not think of it than for the person who, though he is not directly in danger of dying, still thinks about it' (*Pensées*). For animals, even if there is 'the fact of death,' there is no 'problem of death.' Only for humans, who consciously face 'the fact of death,' does it become an intense 'problem.'

Consequently, wherever man has existed, in the East and the West, there have appeared various self-conscious attitudes toward death, and different ways of solving the problem of death have been proposed. Just as only humans question death, it appears that only humans can truly experience death. Only those who truly die can truly live. Self-consciousness of dying is then ultimately bound up with self-consciousness of living. Among the various forms of the self-awareness of death in human history, I would like to take up the notions of the immortality of the soul, eternal life, and unbornness as the most fundamental understandings of the problem of death realized by human beings.

I

The idea that the soul does not die even though the body perishes has arisen in people's minds since ancient times. This widely shared idea is perhaps crystallized in its purest form and attains an extremely profound 'self-awareness of death' in Plato's doctrine of the immortality of the soul.

To Plato, death is nothing other than the release of the imperishable soul from the perishable body. Death is the separation of soul from the body: the body separates from the soul and becomes body only. The soul separates from the body and becomes the pure soul itself (*Phaedo* 64c). The body (*sōma*) is frequently likened to the tomb (*sēma*) of the soul (*Gorgias* 493a). From such a point of view it can be said that for Plato, death is not the body entering the tomb; on the contrary, it is the release of the soul from the tomb of the body. Through death, the soul rids itself of the bonds of the flesh and becomes pure; it returns to itself, eternal and imperishable. Consequently, the true *philosophos* longs for death, and believing in happiness after death (*Phaedo* 64a), faces death calmly. The philosopher believes that apart from the realm of the dead, he cannot encounter that which is his own *raison d'être*, the attainment of pure wisdom.

The death of Plato's teacher, Socrates, seems to have functioned as a very powerful force behind this kind of self-consciousness of death in Plato. His self-awareness of death was in fact conjoined with a clear concept of the immortality of the soul.

Yet the concept of the immortality of the soul is not peculiar to Plato. It is found in the Orphic religion of his day, and also in the Pythagorean school. The Pythagoreans, however, understood the soul as not being itself eternal and imperishable, but as eternal because it transmigrates from one body to another. Within that limitation, the soul could live forever by depending on the body, without being eternal in itself. In Plato, on the other hand, the soul is understood as eternal in itself, preceding the body and independent of the body. It is seen as having the character of 'something divine, immortal, that which becomes the object of intellect, has a simple form, indivisible, a permanent existence that never changes the way of being of itself' (ibid., 80b). Plato believes that the soul is apart from the body, eternal and immortal in itself. But Plato can also be said to recognize the fact of transmigration of the soul when he says that the soul changes many bodies like a tailor who replaces his old worn-out coats (ibid., 87d). Plato's concept of the immortality of the soul, however, still differs from that of the Pythagorean school. In Plato's case, it is not that the soul is immortal and eternal because it changes bodies, but that it is able to transmigrate precisely because it is immortal and eternal in essence.

At this point, we can see that the Platonic soul possesses the character of Platonic Ideas. The soul partakes of eternal existence. It exists not through the body but through itself. Transcending all change and birth and death, it partakes of the transcendent nature of the Ideas which always exist in themselves. It differs in essence from the body, which is subject to change, birth and death, and which does not possess a permanent nature in itself. At the root of Plato's theory of immortality of the soul in the *Phaedo*, his theory of Ideas is clearly evident; without a grasp of his theory of Ideas it would be impossible to understand his concept of the immortality of the soul. He sought that which is invisible beyond the visible and phenomenal, the permanent and unchanging above and beyond whatever changes, the pure and simple behind the many, and the eternal and imperishable beyond the perishable. This is the reason he distinguished the Ideas from the phenomenal. In Plato's case, discussion of the soul, which is imperishable by transcending the death of the body, at the same time entails the imperishability of the Ideas. To clarify the immortality of the soul is to prove the existence of the Ideas, and conversely the immortality of the soul is demonstrated from the existence of the Ideas. This point, Plato's clear grasp of the Idea-like character of the soul, may be considered the reason why Plato differs from the Pythagoreans and goes a step beyond them, even though they both teach the same immortality of the soul.

This point can be clearly read within Plato's argument developed through the mouth of Socrates, in his response to the doubt raised by Cebes, himself a student of the Pythagorean school. The argument can be called the climax of *Phaedo*. Cebes' doubt is as follows. He recognizes that the soul is stronger and longer lasting than the body and transmigrates through many lives, but this does not necessarily prove *the immortality of the soul itself*. For the possibility remains that the soul gradually deteriorates as it passes through many transmigrations and, finally, in a 'death' somewhere along the line, it completely perishes. If no one can know of the 'death' which brings final extinction to the soul, and unless the soul can be proven to be immortal and imperishable in the perfect sense, who could prove that a belief which precludes the fear of death is not the result of foolishness? (ibid., 88a, b). Against this keen doubt, which perhaps is grounded in the thought of the Pythagorean school, Plato has Socrates make the following rebuttal.

Just as everything beautiful is beautiful by means of 'Beauty in itself,' so too a Form exists for everything and is called the same name as the Form by virtue of participating in this Form. Thus, while the number three does not oppose 'even numbers,' it does not partake of 'even numbers.' For three has as its form 'oddness' which is opposed to 'even numbers.' Again, fire is not directly opposed to 'cold' but does not partake of 'coldness,' for fire has the form of 'hotness' which is the opposite of 'coldness.' Similarly, the soul itself which brings life to the body by occupying it is not directly opposed to 'death' but, as the principle of life, it does not partake of death. According to this logic, the soul must possess a character opposite to 'death,' namely, 'death-less-ness.' Consequently when death invades a man, his mortal part dies, but his immortal part, ceding the place to 'death,' goes away while it itself is not affected nor does it perish (ibid., 100b–106e).

As is plainly evident in this rebuttal to Cebes' argument, immortality for Plato is essential to the soul and is grounded in his theory of Ideas. Accordingly, in Plato's case, his self-consciousness of death must also be said to be based on his theory of Ideas. Death is neither something like a dream wherein every kind of sensation has merely disappeared, nor is it the extinction of existence. It is precisely death which brings about distinction between Ideas and phenomena by the separating of soul and body. Conversely, in death, the immortal soul and the realm of Ideas become manifest.

Yet as long as we are living, the soul exists together with the body; and as long as it exists together with the body, the soul cannot purely know the realm of Ideas. Rather, when housed in the body, the soul often goes astray, becomes confused, and is deceived. In order to realize the truth of things and attain to their reality, the soul must strive to become pure soul itself, without being agitated by anything physical – neither hearing, nor sight, nor sufferings and pleasures (ibid., 65c). Only when the soul get rids of bodily contamination and becomes pure, and simply contemplates things by itself, does it have a relation with the permanent and immutable Ideas, and preserves a permanent and immutable way of being itself. This condition of the soul is called wisdom (phrónēsis) (ibid., 79d). Clear knowledge or pure thinking can only be attained by the pure soul uninfected by the corruption of the body. But it is precisely death that releases the soul from the bonds of the body and makes it free and pure. Consequently, the philosopher, the lover of wisdom, must of course be one who does not fear death. If a man grieves and becomes afraid when facing death, he is not a philosopher who loves and pursues wisdom; he would be someone attached to the body, perhaps one who loves money and fame as well (ibid., 98b, c). The task towards which the philosopher in the true sense strives is nothing other than to go to death and complete it. He is one who 'practices dying' (ibid., 64a, 67c). This is, for Plato, the understanding of wisdom and the soul, and also the way of the philosopher.

II

In Plato's case, however, immortality of the soul does not merely pertain to life after death. It is at the same time related to a person's life prior to birth. Plato firmly believes that as long as it is immortal, the soul exists apart from the body even before it dwells among us. Plato's fundamental standpoint is that the soul has an existent nature akin to the transcendent nature of the Ideas, and a permanent nature apart from the body. The soul's pre-existence is proven by the theory of recollection (*anámnēsis*), but here too we see that the immortality of the soul is grounded in the theory of Ideas.

Plato already in the *Meno* (81d) held the position that learning is actually nothing but recollecting. In the *Phaedo*, he grasps recollection as the function that recognizes the Ideas to be essentially different from individual things which come into being and pass away, and attempts thereby to prove the pre-existence of the soul. In other terms, the Idea of 'Equality in itself' is completely different in essence from any 'equal thing.' Indeed, when we have known that two stones are equal through sensation, we have known 'Equality in itself' by taking the sensation of 'equal things' as occasion. In such a way, is not embracing B in the mind on the occasion of perceiving A an act of recollection? Such Ideas as 'Equality in itself,' 'The Good in itself,' and 'The Beautiful in itself' are recollected in this way by taking sensation of individual things as *occasions*: but still the sensation of individual things does not *ground* the reality of the Ideas. Those which we grasp through sensation are merely imperfect things, from which 'Equality in itself' and 'the Good in itself' cannot be extracted. Sensation of individual things is only an occasion that causes that which cannot be grasped immediately in itself to be only indirectly recollected; but the

Ideas, on the contrary, precede things and constitute their ground. In other words, the Ideas are certainly recognized by taking the sensation of individual things as occasion, but things sensed can rather be called 'equal things' or 'good things' in reference to those Ideas. If we consider that what is known by recollection in this way – for example, 'Equality in itself' – becomes the standard in terms of which a judgment is made that things sensed are truly equal to one another, it should be clear that the Ideas precede individuals.

The soul must, therefore, have knowledge of what 'Equality in itself' and 'Good in itself' is before we begin to use the senses, that is, prior to birth; and consequently it must be said that the soul necessarily has existed even prior to our being born, and has pre-existed with such knowledge of the Ideas. This is the reason Plato has Socrates say that 'The soul has existed separate from the body even before dwelling in the form of man, and had power of knowledge' (*Phaedo* 76c). Recollection is nothing other than the fact that the soul, while possessing such knowledge prior to birth, has lost it when it comes to be born, and later on regains that former knowledge through the clues of sensation. Recollection is neither a mere association of ideas nor a calling up of the remembrances of the past. It is the soul's returning to itself, and the intuition of the Ideas thereby. Recollection always takes sensation of individual things as occasion, but therein the realm of Ideas comes to be called up within the soul.

In this way Plato asserted not only the immortality of the soul after death but its pre-existence before birth as well. This assertion was based on his belief in the eternal and immutable nature of the soul which transcends the birth, death, and changes of the body. I have already mentioned that Plato's theory of the immortality of the soul is based on this Idea-like nature of the existence of the soul. But Plato did not merely seek the eternal and the immutable in the past or future. Rather, he sought it within the present. He neither wished for the immortality of the world after death by fleeing the present reality, nor yearned for the purity of the world prior to birth through recollection. He attempted to live in purity of soul while possessing a body within present reality. This is why Plato says that the true philosopher 'practices dying.' For Plato, to philosophize meant to purify (*kathársis*) the soul bound by the body within the present reality of this world from bodily corruption, to make the soul pure while it exists with the body, and thus to think the world of Ideas. For Plato, who holds that death brings about release of the soul from the prison of the body, to philosophize is nothing other than precisely to 'practice dying' while living. It is to live through dying, to practice dying while living. Herein is the way of the philosopher for Plato – the way in which death is overcome.

In Plato, the question of death is certainly grasped subjectively and practically, but it is clear that at its root there is a kind of dualism of body and soul, and a two-world theory which separates the world of phenomena and the world of Ideas. Immortality of the soul is also grasped through pure thinking and *anámnēsis* while the soul has a body in this world, but it ultimately is based on the world of Ideas in the background of present reality. Even if it is said that the Ideas appear within present reality, it is still held that they transcend present reality. In that respect his standpoint is one of an a-temporal, a-historical eternity, of eternity in the sense of endlessness (*Unendlichkeit*). Accordingly, his self-consciousness of death, no matter how subjectively it is grasped, still retains that which is seen objectively.

III

In contrast to this view, there is a standpoint which does not view the relation between body and soul dualistically, as in Plato, or teach immortality on the basis of considering death as the separation of soul from body. Instead it grasps the body and soul as a unity and believes in the death of man – who is this unity of body and soul – and his *eternal life*. Let us now turn our attention to the self-consciousness of death in Christianity as the teaching which, while assuming this standpoint, has developed a very profound religious nature.

Even among the Hebrews there were words such as *rûaḥ* and *nephesh* to express the spirit distinguished from the flesh (*bāsār*), and to express the spirit after death. Spirit and body are not, however, understood as entities dualistically opposed, as in the case of Plato. They are considered an organic unity. Man is simultaneously soul and body. Therefore there is no concept corresponding to the Greek idea that the body is the prison of the soul and death the separation of the soul from the body. In his book, *What is Man?* Wolfhart Pannenberg states: 'In the sense of the concept that a part of man continues beyond death in an unbroken way, the idea of immortality cannot be held ... The inner life of our consciousness is so tied to our corporeal functions that it is impossible for it to be able to continue by itself alone' (pp. 49–50). For the Hebrews, people descended after death to the netherworld as both body and soul. The one sleeping in the grave is not the soul of the dead person, but the deceased himself. Thus it would seem natural that body and soul are considered as a unity both in life and death in the Judaic-Christian standpoint which understands a person as a creature of God. For the Christians, since both soul and body originate in the creation of God, the body is not the prison of the soul but rather a 'temple of the Holy Spirit' (1 Cor. 6:19). What must be essentially distinguished in Christianity is not soul and body, but God and man.[1]

For Christianity, the life of a person is grasped not as a substantial entity that exists in itself, but as something in vital connection with God the creator. For the prophets of the Old Testament, when the God Jehovah turns away his face, it signifies his wrath and judgment (Jer. 44:11; Ezek. 15:7). In contrast to this, when God and man meet face to face, God and man are related not only vitally but personally. The God who speaks therein is like a person, and man who answers is also a person. This relation between God and man is linked by the *word*. Indeed, death for man is nothing other than a severance of this vital and personal link with God. For the people of the Old Testament, death in fact cut off the bond between God and person rather than between person and person, and one fears death not because of returning to nothingness but because the relation with God is sundered.

In Christianity, indeed, the origin of sin lies in human disobedience to God, and rebellion against the *word* of God constitutes the essence of sin. Accordingly, it is natural that, due to committing the sin of rebelling against God's word, it is ordained that man must die by the severance of his vital bond with God based on the word. Loss of the relation with God is nothing other than the result of sin. 'The wages of sin is death' (Rom. 6:23) may be thought truly to have had this meaning. Original life is uncorrupt as something given from God; consequently, death menaces people not as something natural but only as the result of sin. Herein lies the distinct characteristic of the self-consciousness of death in Christianity.

For the Christian, then, 'death' has at least two meanings. First, death severs the vital and personal bond with God the creator. Second, death is repayment for the sin of rebelling against God and is the judgment given by God for sin.

First, a fear of death is expressed throughout the Old and New Testaments. The reverse side of the fear of death would seem to be attachment to life. However, the attachment to life which appears in the Bible is essentially different from the attachment to life which many modern men exhibit. It is not attachment to life itself, but rather an attachment in the sense of a person not wanting to lose the fundamental bond with God, the creator of his or her own life. To fall into the hands of death is to be abandoned by God. Even Jesus, faced with death in the garden of Gethsemane, was 'greatly distressed and troubled' and complained to his disciples that 'my soul is very sorrowful, even to death' (Mark 14:33–34). On the cross he emitted the sorrowful cry, 'My God, my God, why hast thou forsaken me?' (Mark 15:34). At that point, Jesus' death is the diametrical opposite of Socrates who, conceiving of death as the soul entering the world of Ideas by being released from the body, calmly accepted the hemlock and personally practised the philosophy of the immortality of the soul. Even Jesus' prayer in Gethsemane, 'Yet not what I wilt, but what thou wilt' (Mark 14:36), did not mean that his fear of death had gone, but seems to mean that if this most horrendous death derives from God's will, he would dare to obey it too.[2] Since Jesus as the son of God is more profoundly linked to God than anyone else, he feels the fear of death which would cut him off from God more deeply than any other man. Precisely because he obeys the will of God to the very end, he accepts his death. Even for Christ who put all his enemies under his feet, death is truly 'the last enemy' to be feared (1 Cor. 15:26).

Second, however, death is not merely the last enemy for man, but at the same time is 'the wages of sin.' The body, too, which is the subject of desires and evanescently perishes, is not something evil in itself, but has only come to have the fate of such destruction as the result of sin. The sin of Adam who disobeyed the word of God extends to the whole of the existence of man who is a unity of soul and body, and death also extends to all creatures as the result of that sin. 'Therefore as sin came into the world through one man and death through sin, so death spread to all men because all men sinned' (Rom. 5:12). In Christianity, death is essentially linked to sin. Death does not become problematic merely in itself. What becomes problematic is not death as death, but death as sin.

This is a theme which is completely absent in the Greek Platonic philosophy. It can be said that in Plato, too, death is not treated as a problem merely in itself. What becomes problematic for Plato is not death as death – even less is it death as sin – but death as release of the soul to the world of Ideas. Death is not repayment for sin enjoined by God, but the release of the soul from the body in order for it to return to the realm of the pure Ideas. Therein death does not pertain to the soul but only to the body; similarly, evil does not pertain to the soul but only to the body. Evil exists in the sensory, and not within the Idea-like soul. Though evil is due to an absence of the soul and insufficiency of education, it is not personal sin – even less is it personal sin as rebellion against the will of the creator. In Plato, death, as that which causes release of the immortal soul to the realm of the ideas, has a positive meaning – this is precisely the reason why Socrates met death calmly – but the problem of human evil is only negatively understood. Consequently, even if there is pure yearning for the realm of Ideas by transcending even death, there is no consciousness of personal sin by subjective individuals. Therefore, although death becomes the moment which causes the world of Ideas to become manifest, it is not linked to sin.

In Christianity, on the contrary, death is in all respects the result of sin as rebellion against the word of God. The fact that man, the creature of God, instead of believing and obeying the word of God, becomes an autonomous existence independent of God and freely willing – that is, that man becomes man himself – is the insolence (*hybris*) of man. Death, the severance of the vital bond with God, is enjoined by God as repayment for this sin. Without sin there would be no death in which the vital bond with God is severed. Thus in Christianity, death is not something which pertains only to the body and not the soul, as in the case of Platonic philosophy. It pertains to the whole being of man. The consciousness of 'sin' which causes man to die is linked to the very self-consciousness of human autonomous existence. Therein differing from Plato's philosophy, death in Christianity is grasped as a problem truly pertaining to a person's entire being – moreover, within the personal dialogue with God the absolute, as a problem pertaining to the deepest source of human nature.

IV

How is death conquered in Christianity? It cannot be separated from the faith which believes in the fact of Jesus' death and resurrection. The belief that Jesus is the incarnation of the *Word* of God, that human sins are redeemed through his death on the cross, and that the severed relationship between God and man is also restored through his death and resurrection may be called the kernel of Christian faith. That Jesus Christ conquers sin and death in this world through his crucifixion and resurrection, becoming the complete victor, and that thus a new age is begun, is the belief which runs throughout the New Testament. According to Karl Barth, the significance of Christ's death is that on the one hand it is the curse, judgment, and protest of God, but at the same time the sanction, sacrifice, and victory of God.[3]

1. Christ's crucifixion, death, and burial (*sepultus*) signify that as a man, Jesus took upon himself and personally experienced the suffering of death as repayment for sin. There may be nothing which more vividly makes us ponder the severity of the suffering of death than Christ's agonized cry, 'My God, my God, why hast thou forsaken me?' However, according to Barth, Jesus' death is 'the self-sacrifice of God for the existence and destiny of man.'[4] Christ's crucifixion is nothing other than the deepest form of the hidden God. The Son of God 'emptied himself, taking the form of a servant,' and again 'humbling himself and became obedient unto death, even death on a cross' (Phil. 2:6–8). Christ's crucifixion is indeed God's own judgment upon himself, and at the same time the judgment given for the sin of people *in Christ*. Only as something crushed by the anger of God in Jesus Christ does man himself become self-conscious of his sin. The hidden God is for man the face of death.

2. However, at the same time, in the crucifixion of Christ, God empties himself and embraces within himself even human unpardonable original sin, and by causing his only son to die accomplishes redemption of sin in man's place. This is nothing other than reconciliation with God. The painful concealment of the cross where he himself agonized is the revelation of the absolute mercy of God who is hidden in Christ. The absolute death in which God himself takes on the sin and blame of man is absolute life. Jesus' death, indeed, signifies the revelation of true life as eternal life which is now immortal. This is the resurrection of Christ.

Belief in Jesus is nothing other than belief in the fact of his death and resurrection. In Jesus Christ, death is for the first time converted into life. Faith entails the fact of continuous dying together with the crucifixion. 'Let him deny himself and take up his cross and follow me. For whosoever would save his life will lose it, and whosoever loses his life for my sake and the Gospel's will save it' (Mark 8:34–35). By taking up one's own cross and 'being buried with Christ' – that is the meaning of baptism – the Christian also participates in Jesus' death and resurrection.

Barth writes: 'God became mortal man in Jesus Christ, restored the destruction of the relation with man in his obedience, and in his death carried man's sin and eternal death which is its results ... Precisely this God is the immortal God with whom man can be united in death, ... is the hope of all men.' Again: 'God assumed the death of man through Jesus Christ, caused him to have immortality, and gave eternal life.'[5]

Karl Rahner, although with somewhat different connotations, also states, 'The mystery of the Incarnation must be in God himself, and precisely in the fact that, although he is immutable in and of himself, he *himself* can become something in another.'[6] 'The *Logos became* man – the history of the becoming of his human reality became *his own* history – our time became the time of the eternal One – our death became the death of the immortal God himself.'[7]

In Christianity both life and death, and eternal life as their conquest, is grasped in all aspects in relation with God. Death is not the release of the soul from the prison of the body, as in Plato. It is a severance of the vital and personal bond with God the creator, a severance as the result of sin which is rebellion against the word of God. Moreover, in Plato's case, the conquering of death appears within the way of the philosopher who, while firmly believing in the immortality of soul that has an Idea-like transcendent nature, purifies the soul while in the bonds of the body, and practices dying while living. In the case of Christianity, through faith in the death and resurrection of Jesus as the redemption of sin, the severed relation with God is restored and a new life is received that is established by transcending even death. It is not a philosophical self-consciousness of the immortality of the Idea-like soul, but faith in the resurrection of the dead as the righteousness of God – faith in eternal life based on the restoration of one's relation with God.

For the Christian who is self-conscious of the fact that he is determined to die because of sin, the possibility of *anámnēsis* which is a return to the eternal essence, to pure soul, would seem to be ultimately inconceivable. The Christian is profoundly self-conscious that an eternal essence which conquers evil and death cannot be discovered within himself. The Christian participates in the eternal not by recollection (*anámnēsis*) but by revelation (*Offenbarung*). Only through Jesus Christ as the revelation of the word of God does a person recover the link with eternal life that has been lost as the result of sin. 'The word of God that was in the beginning, the word of God who creates us, comes to us again as Jesus Christ.... However, not as the human possibility of *anámnēsis* but as the divine possibility of *restitutio imaginis*.'[8]

That this *restitutio imaginis* (restoration of the image) is possible, needless to say, has been demonstrated by the fact of the resurrection of Jesus Christ. The Christian 'resurrection' differs in essence from the Platonic 'immortality of soul.' Just as death in Christianity is not merely the perishing of the body but death as unity of soul and body, so too the Christian resurrection is not merely resurrection of the soul, but of the dead person who is a unity of soul and body. As Paul says, 'Christ, who will change our lowly body to be like his glorious body' (Phil. 3:21), it is not a bodiless Idea, but resurrection as a 'spiritual body.' Consequently the resurrection is not merely the overcoming of the bodily nature, but of death itself. It is the receiving of a new life by conquering death. The resurrection is the work of God (for example, 1 Cor. 15:15–16), and is not something demonstrable by pure philosophic thought. It is the fact that the entire existence of a person is rescued from death by the working of a new creation by God. For the Christian, the hope of resurrection is not based on any kind of speculation – philosophical or apocalyptical – but to the very end is based on the fact of Christ's resurrection. Jesus Christ is not merely a man, but 'the man' who represents all people, the second Adam, and in his resurrection all humankind fundamentally conquers death. This is the reason it was written: 'Death has been swallowed up by victory. O death, where is thy victory? Death, where is thy sting?' (1 Cor. 15:55–56). The history of the human fall begins from the first Adam. But the sin of humankind is redeemed, death as the 'wages' of sin is conquered, and a new age is begun by the death and resurrection of Jesus Christ, the second Adam. 'For as in Adam all die, so also in Christ shall all be made alive' (1 Cor. 15:22). This is the definite significance of the historical incidents of Christ's death and resurrection.

V

However, it is not that all of humankind immediately lives again and receives a 'glorious body' together with the resurrection of Christ. In Christ's resurrection, it has been demonstrated *in principle* that death can be conquered. Christ truly is its 'first fruits' (1 Cor. 15:23), and a new age *has begun* in Christ. Neither does the Christian, who believes that death has been fundamentally conquered in Christ's resurrection, by his faith change immediately from corruptible body into an incorruptible one, or from perishable body to the 'glorious body.' The resurrection does not occur immediately after the death of each person. It must be awaited until the end of time when Christ will come again. In his second coming, Christ 'will judge the living and the dead' (1 Pet. 4:5). At this end of time, the hidden Christ will reveal his complete power and glory, and before his judgment all the deeds done within history will be openly judged and will be realistically repayed according to the reality of faith or non-faith. The believers will arise from the dead, and attaining 'glorious bodies' will rise again and receive eternal life; the unbelievers will be handed over to eternal punishment. Therefore, the last judgment for the Christian is a hope rather than fear. The Christian is presently living in the 'middle-time' (*Zwischenzeit*) between this resurrection of Christ (the beginning of the new age) and the second coming (its end).

For the Christian who is living in this middle-time, however, the hope in the resurrection in the end of time is hardly a contentless, empty hope. For those who believe in the resurrection of Jesus Christ 'are buried together with Christ through baptism into death,' and this is entirely 'so that as Christ was raised from the dead ... we too might walk in newness of life' (Rom. 6:4). In other words, in baptism the Christian does not believe in the fact of Christ's death and resurrection as a mere object, but he dies together with Christ, and lives together with Christ. The following famous words of Paul would seem to express this fact most powerfully: 'I have been crucified with Christ, it is no longer I who live, but Christ who lives in me, and the life I now live in the flesh, I have to live by faith in the Son of God, who loved me and gave himself for me' (Gal. 2:20). For Paul, baptism was not merely being baptized in the name of Jesus Christ, but being baptized *into Christ* (Gal. 3:27). This is the reason that one dies together with Christ and participates in his resurrection. Here we realize the existence of a *mystical experience* which is not restricted to what is called faith. The 'old man' has been crucified together with Christ (Rom. 6:6) and is revived as the 'new man' created in the image of God (Eph. 4:13–14; Col. 3:10).

For the Christian, therefore, it is precisely dying together with Christ that is the beginning of resurrection into eternal life. While for the Christian, the resurrection is a hope to be realized at the end of history, the resurrection is experienced in advance in the present. As it is written, 'our inward man is renewed day by day' (2 Cor. 4:16) by the working of the Holy Spirit through faith. The new life has already begun. But just as Paul says, 'I die every day' (1 Cor. 15:31), this new life takes the form of constant dying. The living behavior wherein one perfectly lives the new life is always at the same time the experience of dying (*mortificatio*).[9] In the practice of the Christian, so-called life appears as death, and new life is perfected within constant dying. Here we may call to mind Plato's teaching that 'philosophy is a practicing of dying.' For Plato, too, the practicing of dying while living is the highest way for a person. But in Plato's concept of practicing dying, there is no encounter with history. It is not obstructed by the corruption of the body while living; it takes place a-temporally, unrelated to history and transcending birth, death, and change, in seeing the eternal Ideas.

For the Christian, on the contrary, the progress of his new life that is dying and resurrecting day by day is deeply bound up with history. It also possesses an eschatological seal. The Christian participates in the new life of the resurrection by being baptized into Christ and dying together with Christ; but his complete resurrection and new life that is 'to be like his glorious body' must wait for the end of history. Through Christ's death and resurrection, sin and evil have been conquered and the decisive battle is now over, but the day of final victory when all of humankind is reborn has not yet come. The Christian is always within the tension of the middle-time. Accordingly, the progress of new life that is a daily dying and resurrecting is the practice of *love* in the present of this middle-time which is supported by *faith* and *hope*.

Faith believes in the resurrection of Jesus Christ, the second Adam, who has redeemed, by his death on the cross, the history of the human fall beginning with the first Adam and begun a new era by conquering even that death. The hope is to be resurrected in complete glory by the second coming of Christ at the end of history. The practice of love is bound up with the task of history in the rebirth of all humankind and, ultimately, is based on God who is hidden in Christ. The self-consciousness of death and the conquering of it in Christianity must be understood within this kind of practice of love. Therein we find a standpoint of faith deeply related to history, and immanently linked with ethical practice. This differs greatly from the a-historical intellectual, contemplative standpoint of Plato to whom philosophizing is a practicing of dying.

VI

It can be said that humankind has crystallized within Buddhism a self-consciousness of death which differs from the self-consciousness of death in Platonic philosophy and in Christianity which we have reviewed to this point.

It is a well known story that the Buddha, when asked about the existence of the soul after death, answered with silence. Buddhism teaches neither the imperishability of the soul nor the extinction of the soul. Buddhism originally did not recognize the existence of the soul distinguished from the body, and the problem of death was not understood to be solved merely in terms of immortality or non-extinction, and of eternal life. In Buddhism, resolution of the problem of death is sought in terms of no-birth and no-extinction, or unbornness and undying, that is, in terms of transcending 'birth and extinction' or 'birth and death' itself.

The 'Verse on the Impermanence of All Things' (*Shogyō mujō ge* 諸行無常偈) in the *Nirvāṇa Sūtra* directly articulates the essence of Buddhism; it consists of the four lines:

諸行無常	All things are impermanent:
是生滅法	They appear and disappear;
生滅滅己	When an end is put
	to this appearance and disappearance,
寂滅為楽	The bliss of *nirvāṇa* is realized.

The first two lines – 'All things are impermanent: They appear and disappear' – express the Buddhist's cognition of actuality (the realities of the world). The third line – 'When an end is put to this appearance and disappearance' – does not merely teach that there is non-extinction or immortality when *extinction* is overcome, but emphasizes the need to overcome *both* birth (appearance) and extinction (disappearance) as a duality. The last line – 'The bliss of *nirvāṇa* is realized' when this very fact of appearance and disappearance is transcended – teaches the attainment of *nirvāṇa* which is the ultimate goal of Buddhism. Therefore the third line, 'When an end is put to this appearance and disappearance,' must be said to be the pivot causing present reality to be converted into *nirvāṇa*.

'Appearance and disappearance' (*shōmetsu* 生滅) would seem to be an expression referring broadly to organic and inorganic things, but in reference to beings that have life, it is of course 'birth-and-death' (shōji 生死). Consequently, the standpoint of Buddhism can be understood not from the perspective of attaining immortality by extinguishing death relative to life, but as the attainment of no-birth and no-death by extinguishing *birth and death* themselves – of that which has transcended birth and death (saṃsāra) itself. The standpoint of Buddhism vividly comes out in the term '*no birth*' or 'unborn' (fushō 不生) which means neither immortal, nor non-extinction, nor eternal life, but a freedom from the duality of birth and death.

When human existence is said to be impermanent, it does not merely mean that it is impermanent because death exists over against life; it must mean that the very fact that there is birth-and-death is the true reality of impermanence. We are impermanent not merely because we are *perishable* existences, but precisely because we are existences that constantly are *born and die*. This constant being born and dying is called saṃsāra. The essential point, then, is not release from death, but *release from birth-and-death*. When Plato speaks of immortality, he takes as his premise the fact that a person is mortal, that is, a perishable existence; and when Christianity speaks of eternal life, it takes life as the foundation. Certainly immortality could be attained if death could be extinguished. Eternal life could be realized if death could be conquered. But must we not say that these views are still one-sided, and that what is sought therein is still the extension of life in some form – that is, in a different transcendent dimension?

In Plato's case, however, immortality of the soul is not merely related to life after death, as we have seen above, but to pre-existence before birth as well. The soul is thought to transcend birth, death, and the changes of the body, and to be immortal and eternal through its existence before birth and after death. The soul, being permanent and unchanging, has an Idea-like character. Indeed, when Plato says that the true philosopher practices dying while living, we find a common aspect between Plato's standpoint and Buddhism. But in Plato's case, to the extent the meaning of death is questioned, the meaning of birth and the meaning of coming to be born as a person is not deeply questioned. The dualistic theory which conceives of the realm of the Ideas behind phenomena and the infinite behind the finite does not avoid causing Plato's grasp of the problem of death to be objective and contemplative. Therefore, is not non-being ultimately a kind of being, and the immortal nothing other than a transformed form of life?

On that point Christianity, which does not conceive of body and soul as merely dualistically opposed, but rather attempts to grasp human existence as a unity and understand it as a creature created from nothing, must be said to have been more thoroughgoing in its understanding of death. In Plato, who taught that when death presses upon a person, that which perishes is the body, while the soul concedes the place to that which must die and goes away and preserves its own Idea-like permanent nature, the human finitude and temporality cannot be said to have been fully realized. Christianity, on the contrary, holds that human beings and history begin together with the original sin as rebellion against the word of God, the absolute. The Christian is self-conscious, in an extremely acute way, of the finitude and temporality of man who is destined to die. All the more, the faith that one's sin and death are vanquished by the death of Jesus on the cross and his resurrection, and the hope in eternal life based thereon, must be said to be extremely profound.

Nevertheless, in that Christianity sets up God as creator, it has no place for 'no-birth,' or the 'unborn.' Fundamentally the creator expresses absolute life. God, the creator, is eternal life itself. It may be thought that for the Christian, while there is death and the hope of eternal life as victory over it, there is no self-consciousness of unbornness. But in the case of Christianity, can it not be understood that the character of being unborn applies to God, though not to man who is a creature? For God, the creator, creates all things while himself being uncreated. In other words, if we follow the phraseology of John Scotus Erigena, there is God who creates and is not created: *natura creans et non creata.* (In orthodox Christianity, however, God is not 'neither creating nor created' – *natura nec creata nec creans.*) But this uncreatedness is said only of God and not of man, the creature. Concerning us human beings, even though the phrases life and death, eternal life and new life, are used, in the case of Christianity they take the absolute life of God the creator as foundation, and possess the character of realization of divine life within history. The axis of realization of the will of this living God within history is precisely the cross of Jesus Christ. God who is the lord of life and death (2 Cor. 1:9) has had his only son Jesus Christ die on the cross and rise again from the dead. It can even be understood that in this death and resurrection of Christ, God himself experiences the test of death and thus crushes death.[10] Therein death is truly vanquished and the new age (*aiōn*) of the resurrection begins. This is, however, realized in Jesus Christ, the son of God, and does not apply directly to all people.

Although it does not take a dualistic relation of body and soul, Christianity nevertheless grasps God and man in a special kind of dualistic relation, that is, as creator and creature or as redeemer and the redeemed. In other words, the horizontal dualism between body and soul is overcome, but the vertical dualism between God and man is retained. In the cross of Jesus Christ, the transcendence of God and the immanence of man interpenetrates in perfect concreteness. In his death and resurrection, a subjective standpoint of transcendence-qua-immanence is revealed, and taking this point as pivot, history is transformed into eternal life by overcoming sin and death. These things themselves, however, are all possible within the transcendent nature of God. This transcendent nature of God, in the present case, is the eternal life of God. Herein would seem to lie the reason why 'no-birth' or 'unborn' never becomes seriously problematic in Christianity.

VII

In Buddhism, on the contrary, both 'undying' and 'unborn' have become important issues. The Buddhist seeks not merely no-death (the immortal), but 'no-birth-and-no-death.' As I have stated above, this is precisely because the Buddhist does not understand human existence merely as subject to death, but grasps it as *that which is birth-and-death* or *living-dying*. Throughout the Buddhist scriptures we meet with expressions which regard the reality of human being as that which is born and dies. In early Buddhism, it is well known that included in the 'noble truth of suffering' there is the teaching of the four sufferings of birth, old age, sickness, and death; and in the 'twelve causes,' there is the teaching of old age, dying, and birth as the point of departure for investigating human illusions. In the *Śūraṇgama sūtra*, it is written: 'After birth there is death, after death there is birth, birth and birth, death and death, like a wheel of fire, it never stops' (vol. III). In the *Vijñaptimātratasiddhi-śāstra* it is written: 'While one has not yet attained true enlightenment, he is always in a dream; therefore the Buddha teaches the long night of birth and death' (vol. VII). Again in the *Sukhāvatī-vyūha*: 'Birth and death turn in endless cycles' (vol. I). Other such expressions which grasp the form of human beings who are birth-and-death are too numerous to cite: 'The realm of birth and death,' 'The cloud of birth and death,' 'The shore of birth and death,' 'The ocean of birth and death,' 'The sorrowful ocean of birth and death,' 'The prison of birth and death,' 'The mud of birth and death,' 'The bonds of birth and death,' 'The stream of birth and death,' 'The wheel of birth and death,' etc. It seems to go without saying that the aim of Buddhism lies in 'plucking out the root of all the hardship and suffering of birth-and-death' (*Sukhāvatī-vyūha sūtra*).

How, then, can one pluck out 'the root of the hardship and suffering of birth-and-death'? Birth-and-death as suffering signifies attachment to the existence of the self that is ceaseless birth-and-death, and thereby signifies a bondage by birth-and-death. That all things are impermanent is one of the fundamental teachings of the Buddha. There is nothing permanent and unchanging, nothing that endures as it is. Within such impermanence, however, we ceaselessly seek what is permanent and infinite. This fundamental desire is called 'longing' (*taṇhā*). All sufferings arise as a result of this longing, for the dissatisfaction of longing is suffering. What, then, is this longing based on? It is based precisely on ignorance (*avidyā*) of the true nature of human life that is impermanent. It is precisely this fundamental ignorance that lies at the root of human existence; it is the ultimate condition that is not grounded on anything more ultimate. Accordingly, when this fundamental ignorance is extinguished, longing is extinguished as well, and all suffering in turn disappears.

In reference to the question of birth-and-death, if one is not attached to the existence of the self which is birth-and-death, and if one clearly awakens to the fact of birth-and-death and impermanence, one should be able to transcend the sufferings of birth-and-death. It is written in the earliest Buddhist scriptures:

> Seeing the terrible results of attachment produced and caused by birth and death, they achieve unattachment to the causations of birth and death, and experience release.
>
> Achieving peace and composure they rejoice and experience *nirvāṇa* in this life; they transcend all anger and fear, and transcend all sufferings. (*Majjhima Nikāya*, III, p. 187-g)

In Buddhism, there is no thought of struggling with death, overcoming it, and thereby becoming victorious over it. For the Buddhist, death is, of course, painful and sorrowful, but as long as he or she is a person, who is birth-and-death, death is totally unavoidable. Neither disgracefully attached to life nor audaciously attempting to conquer death, the Buddhist attempts quietly to thoroughly realize the stark 'principle of birth-and-death.' The Buddhist is fully aware of the fact of birth-and-death and impermanence. Therein lies the way along which one transcends birth-and-death while living in birth-and-death. The Buddhist does not conquer death; he frees himself from – is emancipated from – birth-and-death. In that sense, the death of the Buddha under the twin *śāla* trees is diametrically opposed to the death of Jesus on the cross. In the death of the expiring Jesus who, while nailed to the cross, emitted the endless agonizing cry, 'My God, my God, why hast thou forsaken me?', people cannot fail to be deeply moved by personally feeling the severity of the suffering of death symbolized by the man Jesus. I have already elaborated the point above that the Christian faith consists in believing that in this death and resurrection of Christ, 'Jesus our Lord ... was put to death for our trespasses, and raised for our justification' (Rom. 4:24–25). But in the case of the Buddha, there is no such anguish of death and no victory over death by resurrection.[11]

In his entering into *nirvāṇa*, his death seems to have been far closer to the death of Socrates who calmly took the hemlock and quietly met death. Socrates willingly died believing that by death the soul is released from the body, returns to the world of the pure Ideas, and participates in eternal wisdom. But from the original standpoint of Buddhism I have cited above, Socrates' death is still not a true awareness or right seeing of the principle of birth-and-death and impermanence; even if it is Idea-like, the desire for the immortal soul in the next life cannot avoid being a 'longing.' This seems to be unavoidable as long as Plato sees the Ideas as existing behind present reality, while taking the perspective of a contemplative dualism.

VIII

It seems entirely natural for Buddhism, which seeks not mere overcoming of death but release from birth-and-death, to thematize not the immortal, but the unborn and undying, that is, *nirvāṇa* which is beyond birth and death. Although the Buddhist clearly perceives birth-and-death, he or she does not understand the unavoidability of birth-and-death contemplatively or follow the determination of birth-and-death negatively. Rather the Buddhist is taught to awaken to the original nature that is free from birth and death. Dōgen's statement 'To clarify birth and to clarify death is for the Buddhist the single most important issue,' also exhibits this kind of positive sense. Consequently, the Buddhist notion of 'no-birth' or 'unborn' does not indicate the notion of *not being born*. It means to transcend and be released from birth-and-death. Not merely no-birth relative to no-death, but no-birth-and-no-death (*fushō fushi* 不生不死) constitutes the true meaning of 'no-birth' or 'unborn' (*fushō* 不生). Only when precisely this kind of 'unborn' becomes the existential subject does there arise the experience of true release which is emancipated from birth-and-death while being birth-and-death. The resolution of the problem of death which Buddhism seeks lies herein.

In Buddhism, the expression 'unborn' is widely employed. For example, at the outset of the Mādhyamika philosophy, which is considered to have clarified the fundamental standpoint of Mahāyāna Buddhism, Nāgārjuna expounded the Middle Way of the eightfold negation and clarified the reason why all dharmas 'have no self nature and are empty' thereby.[12] The Middle Way of the eightfold negation can be condensed into one phrase: 'unbornness' (*fushō*). In the Hua-yen (Kegon) school it is said: 'No-birth of a single thought (*ichinen fushō* 一念不生), precisely this is the Buddha' (*Kegon gokyōsho*, I). Again, in the Shingon school, it is said: '*A-kāra* (ultimate Reality) is originally unborn' (*a-ji honfushō* 阿字本不生). In the Shingon teaching of the Ten Stages of Mind, the seventh stage, 'The awakened mind is unborn mind' (*kakushin fushōshin* 覺心不生心), teaches that 'one who awakens to the fact that this mind is essentially unborn gradually enters into the gate of *a-kāra* (*a-ji mon* 阿字門)' (Kūkai, *Jūjū shinron*). In the Pure Land teaching, T'an-luan writes that 'being born in the Pure Land' (*ōjō* 往往) has the meaning of the birth of 'no-birth' (*Ching-t'u lun chu*). In Shinran's *Kōsō wasan* there are the words: 'Since depending on the Tathāgata's pure original vow, there is the birth of no-birth' (*Nyorai shōjō hongan no mushō no shō narikereba* 如来清浄本願 の無生の生なりければ).

Indeed in Ch'an, or Zen, 'unborn' is strongly emphasized in an extremely subjective and realistic form. Bankei expounds *Fushōzen* (the unborn Zen) in the words: 'In everyone there is the clear and unborn Buddha mind. Do not darken it; be unborn.'[13] Passing over this quote for the moment, even the words used as a *kōan* since ancient times, 'See your Original Face before the birth of your father and mother,' do not merely mean to awaken to the self of no-birth relative to no-death, but to awaken to the self of no-birth-and-no-death, the original Self which transcends birth-and death. Huang-po said that 'if there is no seeking, that is the unborn mind; if there is no attachment that is the undying; unborn and undying are precisely the Buddha.' He then warned a monk: 'If you desire to attain the becoming of Buddhahood ... only study non-seeking and non-attachment' (in *Ch'uan-hsin fa-yao* 伝心法要). Indeed, 'when emotion and cognition are extinguished, birth-and-death are empty, when birth-and-death are empty, the way of Buddha is attained' (in *T'ien-mu Chung-feng ho-shang kuang-lu* 天目中峯和尚広録). The words of Kanzan Egen, 'Within myself there is no birth-and-death' would also be an expression of the self-awakening to unbornness in the true sense. This kind of realization of no-birth-and-no-death is *nirvāna* in the Buddhist sense.

However, if one empties this birth-and-death and goes no further than a *nirvāna* which has escaped from birth-and-death, one is descending to a realization of no-birth-and-no-death *relative* to birth-and-death. In that case, no-birth-and-death, unbornness itself, would be grasped objectively and would be attached as 'unbornness.' In this limitation, that would precisely be to go no further than a negative kind of quietism. However, Buddhism does not teach one to escape from birth-and-death and to enter into *nirvāna* by not dwelling in birth-and-death, but to return to the world of birth-and-death by *not dwelling even in nirvāna*. To enter into *nirvāna* and yet not remain there, but to sojourn in the garden of birth-and-death, is *true nirvāna*. Consequently, even though we speak of transcending birth-and-death, or emptying birth-and-death, this hardly means to get out or flee from birth-and-death. It means to penetrate birth-and-death itself through and through. By doing so, one transcends birth-and-death from within. Accordingly, *nirvāna* cannot be something apart from birth-and-death. Instead *birth-and-death as it is, is nirvāna*. Therein lies the self-awakening to unbornness. Dōgen writes:

> This present birth and death itself is the Life of Buddha. If you attempt to reject it with distaste, you are losing thereby the Life of Buddha. If you abide in it, attaching to birth and death, you also lose the Life of Buddha, and leave yourself with [only] the appearance of Buddha. You only attain the mind of Buddha when there is no hating [of birth and death] and no desiring [for *nirvāna*].[14]

Consequently in true *nirvāna*, the subject of unbornness is birth-and-death precisely as no-birth-and-no-death, and functions in the realm of *samsāra*. A poem of Shidō Bunan, Zen master of seventeenth-century Japan, says,

> While living, become a dead man
> Thoroughly dead
> Then do as you will;
> All will be all right.

This is a direct expression of the point I am trying to make. It differs both from Plato's 'practicing of dying' and from the death and resurrection of Jesus Christ. Do we not find therein the most thoroughgoing self-consciousness of death and a way of resolution which transcends every kind of dualism and which is directly verified in the immediacy of the present?

IX

Nevertheless, is not this kind of Buddhist standpoint reducible, like the standpoint of Plato, to an a-temporal, a-historical world? And in that case, is not the meaning of history ultimately robbed, and ethics also excluded? The reservations have often been brought against Buddhism in comparison with Christianity; they are problems to which Buddhists must earnestly address themselves.

Christianity is a religion based upon the revelation of God; it rests upon faith that the word of God has been revealed *within history*. On that faith is grounded a view of history and an eschatological view of ethics in which the meaning, direction, and purpose of history is given by revelation. It is only natural that Buddhism, which stands not on the revelation of God but on human self-awakening, does not have a view of history and a view of ethics in the same sense as Christianity. Is there, then, a historical view and an ethical view special to Buddhism? It may be thought that, at least up to the present time, Buddhism has lacked a theologically systematized view of history. Profound philosophies of time have existed in Buddhism for a long time, but it would seem that human existence has not been understood as essentially historical existence, and the truth of Buddhism has not been accepted as linked to historical self-consciousness – with a notable exception of the doctrine of the three stages of the Dharma.[15] This would certainly seem to indicate a lack of historical consciousness. But it may be thought that a very thoroughgoing self-consciousness of primal-history (*Urgeschichte*) is implicit within Buddhism. I should like to touch upon this point very briefly in relation to the problem of birth-and-death.

I stated above that, in Buddhism, man is grasped not merely as a perishable being, but as an existence which is birth-and-death. *To be birth-and-death* fundamentally is understood as the 'birth-and-death of the moment' (*setsuna-shōji* 刹那生死). The 'birth-and death of one life time' (*ichigo no shōji* 一期の生死) can be understood only on the basis of this 'birth-and-death of the moment.' Accordingly, that we human beings are existences that are birth-and-death, means that we are existences which *are born and die at every moment*. This is the 'principle of birth-and-death.' Being attached to life and loathing death, to be deluded in birth-and-death, arises from a lack of self-awakening to this principle of birth-and-death. On the other hand, to enter into *nirvāṇa* by transcending birth-and-death is nothing other than self-awakening to this principle of momentary life-and-death. Therein the Buddhist is born and dies moment after moment and enters into *nirvāṇa* moment after moment. Accordingly, the Mahāyāna emphasis that birth-and-death *saṃsāra* is *nirvāṇa* does not mean that *saṃsāra* is simply identical with *nirvāṇa*. Rather birth-and-death is thoroughly birth-and-death; *nirvāṇa* is thoroughly *nirvāṇa*. When it is, however, truly subjectively or existentially realized that *saṃsāra* is the birth-and-death at each and every moment that cannot be objectified and substantialized, *saṃsāra* is transcended from within and turns into *nirvāṇa* at each and every moment. *Nirvāṇa* is fundamentally *nirvāṇa of the moment* (*setsuna-nehan* 刹那涅槃). If that were not the case, then *nirvāṇa* itself would thereby be substantialized. True *nirvāṇa* is '*nirvāṇa* of the moment,' which is realized moment after moment. *Saṃsāra* ceaselessly turns into *nirvāṇa* because it is *saṃsāra* of the moment. *Nirvāṇa* ceaselessly returns to *saṃsāra* precisely because it is *nirvāṇa* of the moment. *Saṃsāra* and *nirvāṇa* are united through mutual negation at each moment. The unextended, subjective point where *saṃsāra* and *nirvāṇa* are mutually united through negation is nothing other than the *moment* (*kṣaṇa*). This moment is the place where we are born and die in actual reality, and is the openness in which *nirvāṇa* subjectively takes place.

Indeed, moment in this sense is not an extremely small amount of time. It is the moment of the 'now' wherein the infinite past and infinite future are self-consciously included and self-consciously transcended. All time of past, present, and future are transcended precisely in the moment of the 'now.' The eternal is realized at present, and the wheel of birth-and-death which has no beginning or end is broken and converted into the silence and purity of *nirvāṇa* which is boundless and inexhaustible. Moreover, as long as the moment is the moment, there is transition from moment to moment while each moment is thoroughly independent in itself. There is endless passage. That, however, is not a simple immediate *continuity* (*renzoku* 連続) but discontinuous *succession* (*sōzoku* 相続).

Precisely because moments are essentially discontinuously successive, the birth-and-death of the moment incessantly turns into *nirvāṇa*, and nirvana incessantly returns to birth-and-death. Birth-and-death is emptied moment after moment; *nirvāṇa* is realized moment after moment. The expression, 'Only after experiencing the Great Death is one reborn' also indicates the decisive moment in which birth-and-death is transcended and the dialectical identity of *saṃsāra-is-nirvāṇa* is subjectively realized. The moments before the Great Death are the moments of flux; the moments after the Great Death are the moments of release. The former are moments grasped by substantializing them such that they are immediately continuous. Consequently, the momentariness of birth-and-death cannot be realized therein; birth-and-death becomes an object of attachment. The principle of momentary birth-and-death is realized in the moment of release. The mutual conversion of *saṃsāra-is-nirvāṇa* is subjectively and existentially realized to be successive, moment after moment, in spite of the discontinuity of each moment.

X

This kind of Buddhist standpoint, even if it thematizes the relation of time and eternity, may perhaps be still unable to grasp the problem of history, the essence and meaning of history. Time is not directly history. The nature of time and the nature of history must be distinguished. Time only becomes 'history' when the factor of spatiality (concretely, 'worldhood,' *Weltlichkeit*) is added to it, and is permeated by the self-consciousness of the uniqueness (*Einmalichkeit*) of time.

Since ancient times, Buddhism has used the terms *loka* and *lokadhātu*, which mean 'society' (*seken* 世間) or 'world' (*sekai* 世界). The word *seken* simultaneously connotes spatiality as a *place* and temporality as *flux*, and is, needless to say, the world in which sentient beings dwell. 'The impermanence of the world' is a fundamental thesis of Buddhism, and it cannot be separated from the birth-and-death and impermanence of sentient beings. That all sentient beings undergo the flux of birth-and-death means that they exist in society (*seken*) or the world (*sekai*) as sunk down into the flux. Thus, the expression, 'to leave or transcend the world' (*shusseken* 出世間) truly means to transcend this kind of flux, to be released from the flux of birth-and-death.

For Buddhism, history is 'the history of "*lokadhātu*" (the world),' 'the history of being sunk down in the flux.' It is the 'history of the impermanence of the world,' the 'history of the flux of birth-and-death of sentient beings.' This flux is beginningless and endless. Because there is neither creation nor an end of time, history for Buddhism does not have a particular direction. It has no direction, yet history is not directionless. Therein lies the profundity of the impermanence of history. However, when we once truly penetrate the birth-and-death of the moment and transcend it, the history of the flux of birth-and-death is also transcended. What is revealed therein is no longer 'the history of the world' but the 'history of transcending the world' (*shusseken no rekishi* 出世間の歴史), no longer 'the history of *saṃsāra*' but 'the history of '*nirvāṇa*' which is emancipation.

As stated above, however, just as *saṃsāra* and *nirvāṇa* are mutually united through negation and succeed each other moment by moment in the self-consciousness of the Buddhist, so too the history of birth-and-death and the history of emancipation are mutually united through negation in the moment and are subjectively (discontinuously) successive. Accordingly, 'the history of transcending the world' does not take place on the other-shore at the end of the 'history of the world.' We self-awaken to the impermanence of the world and the flux of birth-and-death of all sentient beings by penetrating the *birth-and-death of the present moment of the self*. In *that present moment*, although the history of the world is thoroughly the history of the world, its impermanence is transcended from within and it turns into the history of transcending the world. Moreover, at the same time, the history of transcending the world, while completely being the history of transcending the world, turns into the history of the world in which one experiences the process of birth-and-death. It is precisely the subject of this dialectical interchange of the history of the world and the history of transcending the world who experiences the momentary *nirvāṇa* while experiencing the momentary birth-and-death. It is this subject who acts while bound by neither *saṃsāra* nor *nirvāṇa*, yet freely goes out and enters into both *saṃsāra* and *nirvāṇa*. Therein lies the foundation that grounds creative activity which creates history by transcending history; therein lies the basis of the Buddhist ethic: 'However innumerable sentient beings are, I vow to save them.'

Indeed, there is neither a beginning nor an end to history in Buddhism, which takes the impermanence of the world and self-awakening to the momentary birth-and-death as its foundation. The moment and history dialectically co-arise and co-perish. In *any moment* of the endless development of history there is the endless return of history. In every moment, development toward the historical future is at the same time a return to the origin of history. History in Buddhism is 'the history of the moment.' It is also 'the history of discontinuous succession,' which is a succession being neither of the past as in Platonic reminiscence nor of the future as in Christian resurrection. It is of the absolute present as a discontinuous succession of the moment. Thus may we not conclude the following? Greek history is a history of return and reminiscence; Christian history is a history of instants[16] and of repetition. Buddhist history, in contrast, is the history of the moment and discontinuous succession.

We have gradually come this far in our enquiry into the self-consciousness of death in the East and the West. Yet the problem of death, no matter how much words are piled up, cannot in the end be touched in its reality. In reference to the question of birth-and-death, as Tao-wu answered to the question of Chien-yüan, 'I won't tell! I won't tell!' must be the only correct answer.[17]

10

Śūnyatā as Formless Form: Plato and Mahāyāna Buddhism

I

According to Plato, beyond the realm of phenomena perceptible by our senses and subject to time and to change, there exists a realm of 'Forms' which are immutable, timeless, and knowable only by the pure intellect. This realm exists independently and transcends the phenomena that participate in the Forms. Forms are realities and prototypes which make individual things what they are – as the copies of the former.

Like Plato, Mahāyāna Buddhism insists that everything in this world is mutable, transient, and subject to time and to change. Unlike Plato, however, Mahāyāna Buddhism does not expound the existence of an immutable, eternal, and transcendent realm beyond this world. There is *nothing* eternal, transcendent, and real behind or beyond this transitory world. In spite of the fact that the human intellect desires and expects to find the existence of an immutable, eternal, and transcendent world beyond this mutable, temporary, and immanent world, if we are to awaken to the Ultimate Reality we must overcome such a dualistic way of thinking. What is real in Mahāyāna Buddhism is not eternal, self-existing 'Forms' but *Śūnyatā*, which literally means emptiness, and which is without any form whatsoever.

Let us discuss in greater detail the affinities and differences between Plato and Mahāyāna Buddhism on this point.

II

For Plato this actual world perceived by our senses is a perpetual flow of ever-changing appearances of which no real knowledge is possible.[1] It is the world of earthly phenomena, a mutable and unreal shadow-show. Plato arrived at the theory of Forms in an attempt to determine the real nature of moral goodness which, according to Socrates, is the *same for all*. Since only by really knowing goodness can one become truly a good man, it became a serious problem to know the true and unchangeable reality of things. In this connection, Plato employed the Pythagorean doctrine that the soul can realize its divinity and contemplate eternal numerical truth which transcends our sense perception.[2] Thus Plato's theory of Forms might be said to be motivated by the problem of moral goodness and the problem of knowing reality. He insisted that 'there certainly are self-existent forms unperceived by sense, and apprehended only by the mind.'[3]

And thus he clearly and definitively presumed the existence of a realm of Forms which, existing of themselves, are eternal, unchangeable, and real, and which is to be distinguished from that of sensual phenomena. It is his idea of *methexis* (participation) that bridges the gulf between the supra-sensual realm of Forms and the realm of sense. Plato's doctrine of the soul, which is inseparably connected with the doctrine of Forms, and particularly with the famous doctrine of *anamnesis* (recollection) also shows a kind of relation between the two realms. Being immortal in its own right, the soul has known the Forms before incarnation in a body, and is 'reminded' of them by perceiving through the senses those particular things in this world which 'participate' in them.[4]

For Buddhism as well this actual world is an unceasing flow of ever-changing phenomena which is unreal and illusory – that is, *māyā*. Hence everything's impermanence or transiency is one of the basic doctrines of Buddhism. So far there is a great affinity between Plato and Buddhism. Buddhists, however, do not share the doctrine of Forms, for Buddhists do not accept the existence of supra-sensual and unchanging reality beyond this world. From the earliest times Buddhists emphasized *pratītya-samutpāda*, which means 'dependent origination,' 'relationality,' 'relational origination,' or 'dependent co-arising.' This means that everything is dependent upon something else without exception, nothing whatsoever in the universe being independent and self-existing. Through his long existential struggle the Buddha came to realize this principle by going beyond the traditional Hindu idea of *Brahman* as the sole basis underlying the universe, which is ultimately identifiable with *ātman*, the eternal self at the core of each individual. The conception of *Brahman*, the Hindu expression for the absolute, was replaced by the Buddha with the notion of dependent origination, and its accompanying notions of 'impermanence of everything,' and of *anātman* – that is, no self. The denial of *Brahman* is inseparably accompanied by the denial of *ātman*.

Thus we may say that the interdependence emphasized in the Buddhist notion of dependent origination is realized in the most strict sense by rejecting both transcendence and immanence. Accordingly, there can be nothing whatever, at least in the sense of any substantial thing such as soul, that is more real and eternal, and that lies behind or beyond the interdependence of everything. This is true whether one speaks of the temporal or non-temporal realms, sensual or supra-sensual realms. In Buddhism one cannot emphasize too strongly the interdependence of everything. Therefore when we say that there can be 'nothing' whatever that is real and eternal and beyond this world of complete interdependence we must notice the following two points:

1. This 'nothingness' should not be taken as simply distinguished from 'somethingness.' If so, it is merely 'relative nothingness' in contrast to 'somethingness.' It is still 'something' called 'nothingness' and not 'true and absolute nothingness.' The Buddhist idea of dependent origination therefore implies that there can be *absolutely* nothing whatsoever that is real and eternal – behind this actual world.

2. This 'nothingness' is neither directly graspable by the conceptual intellect nor objectively observable. It is properly understood only through existential and non-objective awakening.

We now see that the Buddha's doctrine of dependent origination was supported by an existential realization of 'absolute nothingness,' and we maintain that it remains today supportable by such direct experience. It was Nāgārjuna, the formative expositor of Mahāyāna Buddhism, who *explicitly* realized and enunciated this *implicit* notion of 'absolute nothingness' in terms of *śūnyatā*.

Thus the realization of *śūnyatā*, or 'emptiness,' may be said to be the fundamental foundation for the doctrine of dependent origination. Complete interdependence of everything throughout the sensual and non-sensual world is possible only in and through the realization of *śūnyatā*, which is boundless, limitless, and without form. This formless *śūnyatā*, in Mahāyāna Buddhism, best describes ultimate Reality.

III

Now we must clarify the likenesses and the differences between Plato's idea of 'Forms,' and the Mahāyāna idea of śūnyatā. A Form is the universal quality common to all things belonging to a 'kind' of being. It is ever immutably the same, simple, and everlasting, and becomes the standard, eternal model or paradigm for the particular group of phenomena over which it presides. Being distinct from phenomena, it is an intellectual and normative idea not only in terms of knowledge but also in terms of moral practice. This is why the Form of the Good is also the highest and most universal Form of all, by which the mind may ascend through the hierarchy of Forms to find 'an abiding city' for its final rest. Accordingly Plato's Forms, particularly the hierarchy of Forms with the form of the Good at its summit, have a teleological or paradigmatic significance. The Form of the Good is the end to be reached by *eros*, the instinctive and unceasing longing of the mind. Here, however, a question arises: Can the mind actually reach the Form of the Good for Being? The answer must be negative. In order to explain why, we must deal with the dualities of body and soul, phenomenon and Form in Plato's philosophy.

First, let us consider the duality of body and soul. For Plato, as already mentioned, the body can perish, but the soul cannot. In so far as the soul is embodied and belongs to this actual world, it cannot reach, although it may approximate, the Form of the Good, because the Form of the Good is essentially transcendent beyond the realm of this actual world. The soul, however, may reach the Form of the Good after its separation from the body after death – hence Plato's idea of the duality of the body and the soul. But is there a justifiable ground for the body–soul duality? Isn't is merely an assumption that Plato posited idealistically? The unreal nature of the body–soul duality conception will become clearer when we ask why the soul has to be embodied, which Plato never explains clearly.

If the idea of the body–soul duality is called into question the idea that the soul can reach the Form of the Good is questioned along with it. The soul must be said to be always 'on the way' to reaching the Good. There is an essential gap between the soul and the Form of the Good. It is a paradox and dilemma for the soul that searches for the abode of the final rest in the Form of the Good to have to be always on the way to it. The final rest can never be found 'on the way' to the abode of the final rest. Once this dilemma implied in the Platonic approach to the Form of the Good is fully realized, the very approach tends to collapse. Here we come to examine a wider and more basic form of duality than that of body and soul – that is, the duality of phenomenon and Form.

For Plato Forms are realities whereas particular things in this world are unreal and only participate in the former. Forms are common qualities, and universal, absolute existence, being paradigms for particular things. Here a series of problems arise which include at least the following three difficulties, all of which disclose the limitation of the duality of phenomenon and Form.

1. When two particular things owe their similarity to an idea, to what must we ascribe the similarity between the idea and the two particulars? This is the difficulty which Aristotle in his criticism of the theory of Forms called the problem of the third man. This leads to a *regressus in infinitum*.[5]

2. Plato's theory of the Forms as the universal idea for things seems logically to compel us to admit even Forms corresponding to negative universal terms, denoting absence of good – sickness, ugliness, evil and so forth. But their existence is very difficult to reconcile with the function of the Forms as universal standards, with his doctrine that all Forms derive their being from the Good, and with his conviction that evil belongs entirely to the lower world and has no place in the realm of real being.[6]

3. The third difficulty derived from the duality of phenomenon and Form is the problem of participation. If the Forms are essentially separate from particular things, how can the latter at the same time participate in them? Participation is only possible when both one can be many, and many one. But how can one Form be in the many things which participate in it?[7]

At least these three difficulties clearly show the limitation of Plato's idea of the duality between phenomenon and Form. They especially undermine his claim that the Form of the Good is real. When we admit the Forms as *the universal idea* for things we are logically required to admit the Form of Evil. Considering the paradigmatic and teleological nature of the Form, the idea of the Form of Evil is self-contradictory, so Plato's theory inevitably falls into a dilemma.

We can of course understand the idealistic motivation of Plato's ideas of the body–soul duality and the Form of the Good. But no matter how much they are idealistically motivated, it remains another question whether they are really based upon the reality of human existence. To reach the ultimate Reality we must go beyond all duality, including dualities between body and soul, good and evil, Form and phenomenon.

Buddhists strongly insist upon the necessity of going beyond dualistic ways of thinking to awaken to the ultimate Reality. For the dualistic way of thinking always conceptualizes reality by analyzing and distinguishing it into two entities. Naturally Buddhists do not accept the duality of body and soul, or Plato's idea of the immortality of the soul. In Buddhism it is not that the soul is immutable and self-existing apart from the mutable body, but that body and soul are equally mutable, perishable. In other words the soul is not excluded from the teaching concerning the impermanence of everything whatever. This will be clear when we recall the rejection by Buddhists of the Hindu idea of *ātman*, which is an eternal and unchangeable self. Emphasizing the non-dualistic oneness of body and soul, Buddhists insist that it is an illusion, or at least an unreal conception to believe in the pre-existence of the soul and thus to posit a duality between body and soul.

Again, Buddhists do not accept the duality between phenomenon and Form, and thereby between phenomena and the Form of the Good as well. There is absolutely nothing that is real and unchangeable apart from this changeable world. and everything in this changeable world is dependently related for its origination and for its ceasing to be. Like Plato, of course, Buddhists speak of the sensual and supra-sensual realms. For Buddhists, however, the supra-sensual realm does not, ultimately speaking, have superiority over against the sensual realm. In Buddhist understanding the sensual and the supra-sensual realms are mutually participating in one another. It is not the supra-sensual realm itself which is real, but rather this dynamic relationality of mutual participation between the sensual and supra-sensual realms. The so-called sensual and supra-sensual realms as rigidly distinguished from one another are merely conceptual productions derived from this primary Reality of mutual participation. This mutual participation or interdependence is also true of the relation between good and evil, life and death, being and non-being, and so forth.

Idealistically speaking we should seek for the good. Realistically, however, the more we seek for the good the more we realize how far we are away from the good. A search for the good inevitably discloses our evil nature. Not only conceptually but also existentially good and evil are inseparably connected with one another. This dynamic conflict between good and evil is realized by Buddhists as an endless *karma*. Once Buddhists fully realize this endless *karma* through the conflict between good and evil within themselves, they are led to go beyond *karma* and to awake to the Reality which is neither good nor evil – that is, to the Reality of *śūnyatā*. For Buddhists the solution does not lie in an approach to the Form of the Good, but in an awakening to *śūnyatā*, which is beyond the duality of good and evil.

IV

We now realize that, although both Plato and Buddhists are aware of the mutability of this world, Buddhists are more deeply aware of it than Plato, as can be noted in the thoroughgoing application by Buddhists of the doctrines of universal transiency, and of dependent origination. With the realization of complete transiency and dependent origination, a teleological approach to the Form of the Good is replaced by a fundamental awakening to *śūnyatā* in which good and evil are mutually participating in one another and which in itself is neither good nor evil. In this respect Plato is strongly oriented by an intellectual morality, whereas Buddhists are faithful to the actuality of man and the world. Therefore the question is not whether Buddhists are pessimistic or optimistic, but whether they are realistic or non-realistic.

For Plato Form has a positive significance. It indicates a universal definition and a clear intellectual limitation of an idea. On the other hand, for Buddhists form is something negative, and the formless *animitta* (freedom from form and color) has a positive significance. This is because for Plato Reality must be knowable and definable by human intellect, but for Buddhists Reality is undefinable and unlimited by human intellect. Buddhism, however, is not a mysticism in the Western sense nor an agnosticism.

Although Buddhists emphasize *śūnyatā* as the ultimate Reality, which is without any form whatever, if it simply remains formless it is involved in a kind of duality – that is, a duality between form and formlessness. In order to attain *śūnyatā* as the ultimate Reality we must go beyond formlessness together with a duality between form and formlessness. Formlessness remaining dualistically distinguished from Form becomes a Form named 'Formlessness.' True *śūnyatā* is formless not only in the sense that it is beyond any form or any definition such as good and evil, but also in the sense that it is free from both form and formlessness. This indicates that, being formless in itself, true *śūnyatā* does not exclude forms, but freely and unrestrictedly takes any form as its own expression. True *śūnyatā* is not statically formless but has a dynamic structure, being freely form and formless at one and the same time.

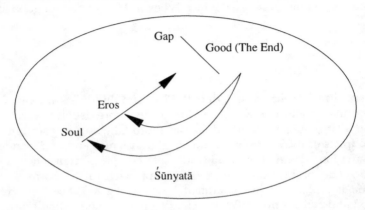

An arrow in the solid line toward Good illustrates Plato's idealistic philosophy of Form whereas the oval line indicates the Buddhist notion of formless śūnyatā. Two curved lines express the idea that the Form of the Good can be realized not over there, but right here, now, at any point of the ascending process, including the starting point, the soul.

This is not a conceptual play, nor a state objectively understandable. Instead it is a most serious religious issue in the Buddhist tradition, which can take place only through the complete negation of one's ego-self and the subjective and existential awakening. Mahāyāna Buddhists often emphasize 'Do not abide in *saṃsāra* nor in *nirvāṇa.*' It is essential for Buddhists to go beyond *saṃsāra* – transmigration of life and death – and to attain *nirvāṇa*. However, if we simply abide in *nirvāṇa*, forgetting fellow beings who are still suffering in *saṃsāra*, it can never be true *nirvāṇa*. Although we should transcend *saṃsāra* we should not abide in and cling to *nirvāṇa*, just as we should go beyond form, but should not be attached to the formless. To attain true *nirvāṇa*, we should go beyond even *nirvāṇa* and return into the midst of *saṃsāra* to save others. In true *nirvāṇa*, in the Māhāyana sense, one freely moves from *saṃsāra* to *nirvāṇa*, from *nirvāṇa* to *saṃsāra*, without abiding in either to save others as well as oneself. *Nirvāṇa* in this dynamic sense is simply another term for *śūnyatā* as the formless form.

As I suggested earlier, the Platonic approach to the Form of the Good, as the goal to be attained, although idealistically necessary, realistically cannot but end short of reaching it. Because of its dualistic assumption of the Forms transcending this actual world, the approach must necessarily fall finally into a dilemma in which, despite the idealistic intention of the approach to the goal, it cannot go beyond being 'on the way.' Thus Plato's ascending approach to the Form of the Good inevitably collapses. With the collapse of Plato's teleological approach which intensively converges to the Form of the Good which is One, the boundless field of *śūnyatā* is opened up, a field of emptiness which is without any form whatever.

Once the teleological structure converging on the Form of the Good disappears, every point of the ascending approach is realized as the end. Goal or end is not over there. It is right here at our feet. This means that ultimate Reality is not to be found far away from here, sometime in the future, but is realized right here and right now. This is true not only with any point of the process, but also with its very beginning and lowest point. It is not that ultimate Reality stands in front of us, but that we are standing *in* the ultimate Reality. The ultimate Reality is not an *object* to be reached, but the *ground* which is unobjectifiable. Hence it is without form.

Śūnyatā precisely indicates this unobjectifiable ultimate Reality. Plato regards the Form of the Good as the ultimate Reality and takes it as the object to be attained. Plato, however, seems to realize that ultimate Reality is unobjectifiable when he thinks that the Good is the Form of Forms, that is, something more than a Form. Here we see a slight implication of formlessness, and thereby the unobjectifiable nature in Plato's idea of the Form of the Good. However, formlessness implied in the Form of the Good is conceived in Plato as somewhat beyond, or at the summit of, the hierarchy of various Forms. Accordingly that formlessness is still to this extent objectified. Since Buddhists insist that ultimate Reality is *completely* unobjectifiable it is not the Form of the Good but the formless *śūnyatā*.

When the Platonic approach to the highest collapses, and the boundless field of the formless *śūnyatā* is opened up we then come to know the following two points. First, each and every point of the process of our movements and activities is an end and a beginning at one and the same time. This is possible because the process is now taking place in the field of boundless emptiness and therefore the process in itself is without end and without beginning. In other words, since the process of our activities is beginningless and endless every and each point of the process is immediately realized as beginning and end at once. Here Aristotle's criticism of Plato's theory of Forms in terms of *regressus in infinitum* is overcome through the realization of emptiness. Second, each and every thing in the universe is completely interdependent. This complete *inter*dependence is possible when each and every thing has its individuality and uniqueness. A combination of these apparently contradictory aspects – the aspect of interdependence and the aspect of universal individuality – is possible not in a teleological and hierarchical structure but in the boundless field of emptiness. A difficulty concerning Plato's theory of Forms – namely, how one can be many and many one, is solved in the field of emptiness. As Buddhists often say: 'flowers are red; willows are green,' or 'mountains are mountains; rivers are rivers,' and as I should like to put it, 'you are you and I am I,' everything and everyone exists together, lives together without losing individuality – that is, with its own particular form, in the field of formless emptiness.

But as soon as we take this formless *śūnyatā* as a *goal* to be attained and thereby objectify it, as has often happened in the history of the Mahāyāna tradition, it will lose its dynamic nature and turn into a superficial affirmation of or an uncritical indifference to this actual world. Formless *śūnyatā* should not be taken merely as a goal but as the fundamental *foundation* on which we base our being, and as the point of departure from which we can properly begin to live freely and to start creative activities. Formless *śūnyatā*, taken as the fundamental basis, is not merely formless. It is full of forms because it is the boundless field or bottomless ground which lets everything exist and work with its particular form within itself.

In this dynamic structure of *śūnyatā* nothing is excluded. You and I and everything else are existing and living together with particular forms, without losing individualities in this *śūnyatā* as formless form.

11

The Self in Jung and Zen

I

The most conspicuous difference between Buddhism and Western psychology is perhaps found in their respective treatments of the concept of 'self.' In Western psychology, the existence of a 'self' is generally affirmed; Buddhism denies the existence of an enduring 'self' and substitutes instead the concept of *anātman*, 'no-self.'

In Western spiritual traditions one of the classical examples of the affirmation of an enduring self is Plato's notion of the immortal soul. The basis of the modern Western conception of the self was established by Descartes' *cogito ergo sum*, which led to a dualistic interpretation of mind as thinking substance and matter as extended substance. Christianity, which is not based on human reason but divine revelation, emphasizes man's self-denial or self-sacrifice in devotion to one's God and fellow human beings. Even so, as a responsible agent in an I–Thou relationship, the human self is affirmed as something essential. Although it is a relatively new scientific discipline, modern Western psychology shares with older Western spiritual traditions the affirmation of the existence of a self.

In ancient India, the Brahmanical tradition propounded the idea of Ātman or the eternal, unchanging self which is fundamentally identical with Brahman, the ultimate Reality of the universe. The Buddha did not accept the notion of *ātman* and discoursed instead about *anātman*, no-self. As Walpola Rahula states:

> Buddhism stands unique in the history of human thought in denying the existence of such a Soul, Self, or Atman. According to the teaching of the Buddha, the idea of self is an imaginary, false belief which has no corresponding reality, and it produces harmful thoughts of 'me' and 'mine', selfish desire, craving, attachment, hatred, ill-will, conceit, pride, egoism, and other defilements, impurities and problems. It is the source of all the troubles in the world from personal conflicts to wars between nations. In short, to this false view can be traced all the evil in the world.[1]

Throughout his life, the Buddha taught the means to remove and destroy such a false view and thereby enlighten human beings.

To those who desire self-preservation after death, the Buddhist notion of no-self may sound not only strange but frightening. This was true even for the ancient Indians who lived in the time of the Buddha. A bhikkhu once asked the Buddha: 'Sir, is there a case where one is tormented when something permanent within oneself is not found?' Not unaware of such fear, the Buddha answered, 'Yes, bhikkhu, there is.' Elsewhere the Buddha says: 'O bhikkhus, this idea that I may not be, I may not have, is frightening to the uninstructed worldling.'[2] Nevertheless, the Buddha preached the notion of no-self tirelessly until his death, simply because the doctrine is so essential to his teaching: to emancipate human beings from suffering and to awaken them to the fundamental reality of human existence.

To properly understand the Buddhist notion of no-self, it would be helpful to consider the following five points:

1. The doctrine of no-self is the natural result of, or the corollary to, the analysis of the five skandhas or five aggregates, that is, matter, sensation, perception, mental formations, and consciousness. According to Buddhism, human beings are composed of these five aggregates and nothing more.[3]

2. The notion of no-self, that is, the notion of no substantial unchanging own-being, is applied not only to human beings, but also to all beings. This is why one of the three essentials peculiar to Buddhism is that 'all dharmas [i.e., all entities] are without self.' Thus, not only conditioned, relative things, but also unconditioned, absolute things are understood to be without self, without their own-being. Accordingly, not only *saṃsāra*, but also *nirvāṇa*, not only delusion, but also enlightenment, are without own-being. Neither relative nor absolute things are self-existing and independent.

3. The notion of no-self entails, therefore, the denial of one absolute God who is self-existing, and instead forwards the doctrine of dependent origination. That is, in Buddhism, nothing whatever is independent or self-existing; everything is dependent on everything else. Thus, all unconditioned, absolute, and eternal entities such as Buddha or the state of *nirvāṇa* co-arise and co-cease with all conditioned, relative, and temporal entities, such as living beings or the state of *saṃsāra*.

4. In accordance with these teachings, the ultimate in Buddhism is neither conditioned nor unconditioned, neither relative nor absolute, neither temporal nor eternal. Therefore, the Buddhist ultimate is called *śūnyatā*, that is, 'Emptiness.' It is also called the 'Middle Way,' because it is neither an eternalist view which insists on the existence of an unchanging eternal entity as the ultimate, nor an annihilationist view which maintains that everything is null and void.

5. If one clearly understands that the Buddhist notion of no-self is essentially connected with its doctrine of dependent origination and *śūnyatā* or Emptiness, one may also naturally understand that the Buddhist notion of no-self does not signify the mere lack or absence of self, as an annihilationist may suggest, but rather constitutes a standpoint which is beyond both the eternalist view of self and the nihilistic view of no-self. This is forcefully illustrated by the Buddha himself when he answered with silence both the questions 'Is there a self?' and 'Is there no-self?' Keeping silence to both the affirmative and negative forms of the question concerning the 'self,' the Buddha profoundly expressed the ultimate Reality of humanity. His silence itself does not indicate an agnostic position, but is a striking presence of the true nature of human being which is beyond affirmation and negation.

In the light of these five points, I hope it is now clear that the Buddhist notion of no-self does not signify a mere negation of the existence of the self, but rather signifies a realization of human existence which is neither self nor no-self. Since the original human nature cannot be characterized as self or no-self, it is called No-self. Therefore, No-self represents nothing but the true nature or true Self of humanity which cannot be conceptualized at all and is beyond self and no-self.

In the Buddhist tradition, Zen most clearly and vividly emphasizes that the Buddhist notion of No-self is nothing but true Self. Lin-chi's phrase, the 'true man of no rank' serves as an example. 'No rank' implies freedom from any conceptualized definition of human being. Thus the 'true man of no rank' signifies the 'true man' who cannot be characterized either by self or no-self. 'True man of no rank' is identical with the true nature of human being presenting itself in the silence of the Buddha. Unlike the Buddha who emphasizes mediation, however, Lin-chi is an active and dynamic Zen master, directly displaying his own 'true Self' while demanding his disciples to actively demonstrate this 'true Self' in themselves. The following exchange vividly illustrates this dynamic character:

> One day Lin-chi gave this sermon: 'There is the true man of no rank in the mass of naked flesh, who goes in and out from your facial gates [i.e., sense organs]. Those who have not testified [to the fact], look! look!'
>
> A monk came forward and asked, 'Who is this true man of no rank?'
>
> Lin-chi came down from his chair and, taking hold of the monk by the throat, said, 'Speak! Speak!'
>
> The monk hesitated.
>
> Lin-chi let go his hold and said, 'What a worthless dirtstick this is!'[4]

In this exchange, 'true man of no rank' represents a living reality functioning through our physical body. Furthermore, Lin-chi is asking his audience to notice the living reality functioning in himself by saying 'Look! Look!' and demanding from the monk a demonstration of his own true nature, taking him by the throat and saying 'Speak! Speak!' Zen does not intend to provide an explanation or interpretation of the nature of true Self, but rather to precipitate a direct and immediate testimony or demonstration of it through a dynamic encounter between master and disciple.

II

In seeking to point out the similarities and dissimilarities between modern Western psychology and Buddhism, especially Zen, with regard to their understanding of the concept of the 'self,' let us examine a dialogue between Hisamatsu Shin'ichi (1889–1980) and Carl Gustav Jung (1875–1961).

Hisamatsu Shin'ichi was a professor of Buddhism at Kyoto University. He is regarded as one of the outstanding Zen thinkers of contemporary Japan. But Hisamatsu was also a Zen layman who had attained a very profound, clear-cut Zen awakening, and his subsequent thinking and way of life were deeply rooted in this awakening. He was an excellent calligrapher, tea master, and poet as well. In all, he was a real embodiment of the Zen spirit, outstanding even among contemporary Zen masters in Japan.[5] This dialogue with

Carl Jung took place at Jung's home at Küsnacht, on the outskirts of
Zurich, on May 16, 1958.[6] While there were many stimulating
exchanges and many interesting points raised in the course of the
dialogue, I would like to focus here on the issue of self as understood
by Jung and Hisamatsu.

After a discussion about the relation between consciousness and
the unconscious, Hisamatsu asked, 'Which is our true Self, the
"unconscious" or "conscious"?' Jung replied,

> The consciousness calls itself 'I', while the 'self' is not 'I' at all. The
> self is the whole, because the personality – you as the whole –
> consists of the 'conscious' and the 'unconscious'. That is the
> whole, or the 'self'. But 'I' know only the consciousness. The
> 'unconscious' remains to me unknown. (p. 27)[7]

This is Jung's well known distinction between I or ego, and self. To
Jung, 'ego' is the center of the field of consciousness and the complex
entity to which all conscious contents are related, whereas 'self' is the
total personality which, though always present, cannot fully be
known.[8]

Later in the dialogue, the following exchange occurs:

> HISAMATSU: 'Is the "I-consciousness" (ego-consciousness)
> different from the "self-consciousness" or not?'
> JUNG: 'In the ordinary usage, people say "self-consciousness",
> but psychologically it is only "I-consciousness". The "self" is
> unknown, for it indicates the whole, that is, the conscious and the
> unconscious ...'
> HISAMATSU: 'What! The "self" is not known?'
> JUNG: 'Perhaps only the half of it is known and it is the "I". It is
> the half of the "self".'

Hisamatsu's surprise is understandable, because in Zen practice
the self is to be clearly known. *Satori* is 'self-awakening,' that is, the
self awakening to itself. The awakened self is characterized as
ryōryōjōchi 了々常知 , that is, 'always clearly aware.'

Here we can see an essential difference between Jung and Zen. In
Jung, self as the total personality consists of the consciousness as 'I' or
'ego,' which is known to itself, and the unconscious, which remains
unknown. Furthermore, the unconscious includes the personal
unconscious which owes its existence to personal experience, and

the collective unconscious, the content of which has never been conscious and which owes its existence exclusively to heredity. Whereas the personal unconscious can sooner or later present itself to consciousness, the collective unconscious, being universal and impersonal, consists of pre-existent forms, or archetypes, which give definite form to certain psychic contents, but which can only become conscious secondarily.[9] It would therefore be appropriate to say that in Jung, the collective unconscious, as the depth of the self, is seen from the side of the conscious ego as something beyond, or as something 'over there,' though not externally but inwardly. It is in this sense that the unconscious is unknown. In contrast to this, according to Zen, the self is not the unknown, but rather the clearly known. More strictly speaking, the knower and the known are one, not two. The knower itself is the known, and vice versa. Self is not regarded as something existing 'over there,' somewhere beyond, but rather is fully realized right here and now.

We must therefore recognize clearly that although both Jung and Zen discuss the concept of the self, the entity of the self is understood by them in fundamentally different ways. According to Zen, in order awaken to the true Self, it is necessary to realize No-self. Only through the clear realization of No-self can one awaken to the true Self. And the realization of No-self in Zen would reflect the realization of the non-substantiality of the unconscious self as well as the conscious ego, to use Jungian terminology. In Jung, self is the total personality which cannot be fully known. It consists of the conscious and the unconscious. But in Zen the true Self is awakened to only through overcoming or breaking through the self in the Jungian sense. I will try to clarify later how this process can occur, but at this point I would merely like to observe that there is no suggestion of the realization of the No-self in Jung. Since the No-self, that is the non-substantiality of self, is not clearly realized in Jung, it therefore remains as something unknown to the ego.

III

The dialogue now turns to the case of a patient's mental suffering and the method of curing the infirmity. Hisamatsu asked, 'How is the therapy connected with the fundamental "unconscious"?' Jung replied, 'When a disease is caused by things which we are not conscious of, there is the possibility that it might be cured by making these causes conscious. While the cause does not always exist in the "unconscious", there are cases where the symptoms show that the psychic causes have existed [in the "unconscious"].' Emphasizing the existence of the worries and difficulties in our daily life, Hisamatsu then raises several other questions. 'If the essence of cure is freedom from worry, what sort of changes in the sphere of the "unconscious" correspond to this freedom?' 'Is it possible or not possible for psychotherapy to shake off the thousand and one worries of human life all at once?'

> JUNG: 'How can such a method be possible? A method which enables us to free ourselves from suffering itself?'
> HISAMATSU: 'Doesn't psychotherapy emancipate us from suffering all at once?'
> JUNG: 'Free man from his suffering itself? What we are trying to do is to reduce the suffering for human beings. Still some suffering remains.'

At this point in the conversation, Jung's reaction to the possibility of sudden emancipation from suffering itself was quite negative. Referring to Jesus Christ and Gautama Buddha, Hisamatsu says, 'The intention of these religious founders was to emancipate us from our fundamental suffering. Is it really possible for such great freedom to be achieved by psychotherapy?' Jung's response to this question is not simply negative.

> JUNG: 'It is not impossible if you treat your suffering not as a personal disease but as an impersonal occurrence, as a disaster or an evil ... Patients are enmeshed by *kleśa* (passion) and they are able to be freed from it by their insight. What [psychotherapy] aims at is all the same with the aim of Buddhism.'

This leads to a crucial point in the dialogue:

> HISAMATSU: 'The essential point of freedom [from suffering] is how we can be awakened to our fundamental Self. That fundamental Self is the one which is no more confined by a myriad of things. To attain this Self is the essential point of freedom. It is necessary, therefore, to free oneself both from the "collective unconscious" and from the bondage caused by the "collective unconscious".'

JUNG: 'If someone is enmeshed by a myriad of things and confined in them, it is because he is caught in the "collective unconscious" at the same time. He can be freed only when he is emancipated from both of them ... After all, man must reach, to the degree that he is able, freedom both from "he must", being obligated to chase after things, and from being obligated inconveniently to be ruled by the "unconscious". Both are radically the same and *nirvāṇa*.'

HISAMATSU: 'In what you have just said before about the "unconscious", Professor Jung, do you mean that the "collective unconscious" is something from which, in its nature, we can free ourselves?'

JUNG: 'Yes, it is.'

HISAMATSU: 'What we generally call self is the same as the "self" characterized by Professor Jung. But it is only after the emancipation of the self that the "Original Self" of Zen emerges. It is the true Self of *dokudatsu mue* 独脱無依 , absolute freedom, independent from everything.'

At this point, Jung answered affirmatively Hisamatsu's question as to whether the collective unconscious is something from which one must be emancipated for real freedom. Earlier in the dialogue, he answered negatively a question concerning the possibility of gaining freedom from suffering all at once. Towards the end of the conversation, however, Jung clearly agreed with Hisamatsu on the need of overcoming even the collective unconscious for a complete cure of the patient. According to Tsujimura Kōichi, who acted as interpreter for the dialogue, Jung's affirmative response surprised people in the room, for if the collective unconscious can be overcome, then Jung's analytical psychology must be fundamentally re-examined.

IV

Looking back over the dialogue, I would like to make three remarks.

First, the psychotherapeutic method of relieving a patient's suffering and the Zen method of dissolving a student's suffering are different. In Jungian psychotherapy, to cure a patient's suffering, the analyst tries to help the patient become aware of the causes of his suffering, which previously had been unconscious, or he tries to help the patient realize the aim or meaning of his life, or he tries to help change the patient's attitude towards psychic worry and make him more accepting and positive. But as Jung says in the conversation, there is no universal rule or method for the cure. There are only individual cases, and in psychotherapy the analyst must cure the patient's worries as fully as possible in each individual case. As Hisamatsu points out in his additional note, however, 'If each disease is cured separately and individually, we shall not be completely cured of disease, for when one disease is gone, another disease comes. This in itself may be said to be a disease in a very profound sense' (p. 31).

Hisamatsu calls this 'the vicious endlessness' of psychoanalytic therapy. Unless the root of all possible diseases is dug out and cut away, the vicious endlessness of psychoanalytic therapy will not be overcome. What, then, is the root of all possible psychic diseases? According to Jung it is the collective unconscious or the unknown self which is responsible for hindering us psychically. Instead of analyzing psychic diseases one by one, Zen tries to dig out and cut away the very root of the human consciousness beyond consciousness, including the Jungian or any other hypothesized realm of an unconscious. Zen insists that only then can complete emancipation from human suffering be achieved and the true Self be awakened. The realization of No-self, which is indispensable for the awakening to true Self, is simply another way of describing 'cutting away' the root of human consciousness.

Second, in Jung, the collective unconscious is something unknown which must be intensively analyzed to discover the cause of a patient's suffering, but it is at the same time a realm that can never be completely known. By definition, the collective unconscious remains an unknown 'x' for both analyst and analysand. In Zen, through zazen and kōan practice with a Zen master, the Zen student not only digs out the root of the unknown 'x' but also becomes one with it. For the Zen student the unknown 'x' is not something 'over there.' It comes to be realized as 'here and now.' In other words, it is totally, completely and experientially realized by the student *as the unknown 'x.*' In this total, experiential realization, it ceases to be an *object* to the student, and instead the two become one with each other. Now, the student *is* the unknown 'x' and the unknown 'x' *is* the student. Only in this way can the student overcome the unknown 'x,' 'cut off' its root, and awaken to his true Self.

This event can be illustrated by a *mondō* (a question and answer exchange) between Bodhidharma, the first patriarch in the Zen tradition, and Hui-ko, who later became the second patriarch. In deep anguish and mental perplexity after many years of inner struggle, Hui-ko approached Bodhidharma and asked him:

'My mind is not yet pacified. Pray, Master, pacify it.'
'Bring your mind here and I will pacify it,' said Bodhidharma.
'I have sought it for many years,' Hui-Ko replied, 'I am still unable to take hold of it. My mind is really unattainable.'
'There! Your mind is pacified once and for all,' Bodhidharma confirmed.[10]

Instead of analyzing the causes of Hui-ko's suffering, Bodhidharma asked Hui-ko to bring forth his mind. Confronted with this straightaway command, Hui-ko, who had sought after his mind for many years, clearly realized that the mind is unattainable. Suddenly, he totally and experientially realized the mind to be the unattainable and the unattainable to be the mind; there was no longer even the slightest gap between himself and the unattainable. His internal perplexity was resolved in this existentially complete realization of the mind as the unattainable. Recognizing this, Bodhidharma immediately said, 'There! Your mind is pacified once and for all.'

In Jung, the depth of mind is *objectively* regarded from the side of the conscious 'I' as the unknown collective unconscious. In contrast, by overcoming such an objective approach, Zen straightforwardly enters into the depth of mind and breaks through it by becoming completely identical with it. In Zen, this breaking through is called the Great Death – Because it signifies the complete denial of human consciousness, including any such Jungian notion of the collective unconscious. And yet the Great Death in Zen is at one and the same time a resurrection in the Great Life – because in this breaking through of mind, not only is the realization that mind is unattainable or unknowable included, but also the realization that the unattainable or the unknowable is precisely the true Mind or true Self. This is why 'No-mind' in Zen is not a negative but a positive entity. That is to say, unlike the Jungian unconscious, No-mind in Zen is not an extra-conscious psyche, but rather is the true Mind or Original Mind which is realized beyond Jung's framework of the mind.

A significant aspect of Zen in this connection is perhaps the emphasis in kōan practice on the Great Doubt. Most kōans, such as

Jōshū's *Mu* and Hakuin's 'Listen to the sound of the single hand,' are designed to drive a Zen student into a mental corner, to break thought the wall of the human psyche, and to open up an entirely new spiritual dimension beyond analytic or dualistic thinking. For example, the kōan, 'Show your Original Face before your parents were born,' does not refer to one's pre-existence in a temporal sense, but rather asks of a student to demonstrate his or her original nature which can be *immediately* realized at the depth of existence. Only when the student demonstrates it can he or she break through the framework of a self-centered psyche. The phrase, 'Original Face *before your parents were born*' can be understood to refer to that which lies beyond even the hypothesized collective unconscious and which is impersonal, universal, and yet is the root-source of your own being and which is unknown to the 'I' which is limited by time and space.

Zen emphasizes the importance for a Zen student to become a 'Great Doubting Mass': 'At the base of Great Doubt lies Great Awakening.' This emphasis on Great Doubt implies that a Zen student must dig up and grapple with the unknown 'x' so thoroughly that he turns into the unknown 'x' itself. To become a Great Doubting Mass is to turn into the unknown 'x.' To turn into the unknown 'x' is to come to know existentially that the unknown 'x' is nothing but the true Self. And that knowing is the Great Awakening to the true Self, characterized as *ryōryōjōchi*, 'always clearly aware.' Kōan practice has proved an effective way to lead a student to the Great Awakening through Great Doubt.

Third, despite the essential differences between Zen and Jungian psychology in their understandings of self and their respective methods of curing human suffering, I believe there are also points at which these two disciplines can profitably learn from each other, although the scope and depth of their mutual learning may perhaps not be equal. Since Zen is so overwhelmingly concerned with cutting off the root of the human consciousness in order to attain No-self as true Self, or to attain No-mind as true Mind, it tends on the whole to neglect psychological problems that occur sometimes in the process of Zen practice, in particular the delusory apparitions known as *makyō*.[11] But if Zen learns from Jungian psychology about the theory of the archetype as an unconscious organizer of human ideas, and the process of individuation, it might help the Zen practicer to better understand such mental fabrication.

Modern Western psychology, and particularly Freudian and Jungian psychology, have claimed to discover the existence of a psyche outside consciousness. With this discovery the position of the ego, until then absolute as the center of human consciousness and the active source of man's spiritual act, was relativized.[12] In Jung, the ego is no longer identical with the whole of the individual but is a limited substance serving as the center of non-unconscious phenomena. If this relativization of the ego is strengthened, that is, the substance of the ego is understood to be even more limited, it could help open the way to the realization of No-self. But in Jung, instead of a relativization of the position of ego, the position of the self as the total personality based on the collective unconscious is strongly maintained. If the collective unconscious is something ultimate in which human suffering is rooted, then, as Hisamatsu suggests in his dialogue with Jung, Jungian psychotherapy may not be free from an inevitable 'vicious endlessness,' because even though it can relieve a particular disease separately and individually, other forms of psychic disease may recur endlessly. Only when the true source is reached beyond such possible psychological realms as the collective unconscious, can human beings go beyond the root of suffering itself and be released from the 'vicious endlessness' of particular manifestations of suffering. Zen offers a way to break through even the collective unconscious and similar theories about the structure of the mind.

In this respect, it is extremely significant that in his dialogue with Hisamatsu, Jung seemed eventually to agree with the possibility and necessity of freedom from the collective unconscious. Ultimately, Jung and Zen seem to agree that there is hope for human beings to be emancipated from suffering itself, rather than their being destined to remain in a samsaric cycle, finding relief from one suffering only to be faced with another.

Part Three
Current Issues in Buddhism

12

Time in Buddhism

It is often said that the Buddhist view of time is cyclical whereas the Christian view of time is linear. In Christianity time began with God's creation and will end at the last judgment with the event of Jesus Christ as the center of history. Time is thus understood to be linear, fundamentally unidirectionally moving from the past to the future.[1] By contrast, according to some scholars, in Buddhism which talks about endless transmigration, time is understood to be repeatable and cyclical.

It is true that in Hinduism time is viewed to be cyclical but unlike Vedantic philosophy, Buddhism which emphasizes *pratītya-samutpāda*, that is 'dependent co-origination', does not view time as cyclical. In my understanding, the Buddhist view of time is neither linear nor cyclical. How then does Buddhism view time? In the following I would like to clarify the basic view of time in Buddhism in comparison with that of Christianity.

I

Buddhism does not regard time as an objective entity or independent reality apart from our consciousness. Nor does it grasp time as an abstract category with which we measure the duration of various objects. In Buddhism time is realized in and through the realization of the impermanency of everything in the universe, especially through the realization of our own living-dying. As a religion, Buddhism is concerned with human salvation, salvation from the problem of life and death. And the human problem of life and death is grasped in Buddhism as a part of the more universal impermanency common to all things in the universe. Unless the impermanency common to all things is overcome the human problem of life and death cannot be properly overcome. This is the reason Buddhism emphasizes *sabbe saṅkhārā aniccā*, that is 'all conditioned things are impermanent,' as one of the three fundamental doctrines of Buddhism.[2]

Time is thus understood in Buddhism always to be inseparable from things as ever-changing. There is no time apart from things in the universe. Time and things are completely non-dual. Objective time or absolute time is an abstraction from this living real time.

Accordingly, it is not that spring comes in the framework of time nor that flowers bloom in a time called spring. Instead, flowers blooming in themselves are spring coming. Flowers blooming, birds singing, and the warm wind blowing in themselves are the time called spring. There is no spring apart from these things, and no time apart from phenomenal things. In our lived reality time is recognized in and through the transition of things. In short, it is not that there is time a priori in which the transition of things take place. Time and things are inseparably connected with one another. This is why Dōgen, a Japanese Zen master of the thirteenth century, states:

Mountains are time and seas are time. If they were not, there would be no mountains and seas. So you must not say there is no time in the immediate now of mountains and seas. If time is destroyed, mountains and seas are destroyed. If time is indestructible, mountains and seas are indestructible. Within this true Dharma, the morning star comes to appear, the Tathāgata comes to appear, eye-pupils come to appear, the holding up of the flower comes to appear. This is time. Were it not time, things would be not-so.[3]

Since time and things are inseparable, time is understood in Buddhism to be non-substantial and empty because things are understood to be non-substantial and empty. The non-substantial nature of time is a characteristic of the Buddhist view of time.[4]

In this regard the Buddhist view of time is essentially different from the Christian view of time. In Christianity time is understood to be real because time is a creation of God. Augustine raises the question of whether God created the world in time or not. His answer is that if God created the world in time God and his creation must be limited by time. But this understanding is contrary to the transtemporal nature of God. Accordingly, Augustine insists, God created time itself in the creation of the world. Time itself is a part of creation and God is the maker of time.

In Christianity this sacred time was spoiled and became sinful time through the rebellion of Adam and Eve against the word of God. However, the death and resurrection of Jesus Christ on the cross redeemed the sinful time and turned it into the time of salvation. The time of salvation will be completely fulfilled in the universal scale of humankind at the end of history and the original sacred time will be reconstructed through the last judgment. As this brief description indicates time in Christianity is a reality created and ruled by God. By contrast time in Buddhism is not a reality but an unreal non-substantiality. This is because in Buddhism God as the creator and ruler of the universe does not exist. Time as well as the universe are not creations of God.

II

Then how does time arise in Buddhism? In Buddhism our ordinary notion of time is regarded as a conceptual attachment. *Aṣṭasāhasrikā Prajñāpāramitā* speaks of it in this way: Ordinary people discriminate everything by alternative judgment and attach to the discrimination as if it is real. Regarding time, people discriminate past, present, and future, and substantiate them in their fixed form through attachment. In attaching name and form discriminated of the phenomenal world they are involved in transmigration without realizing ultimate reality.[5] This process of transmigration is called *saṃsāra* and time realized in the process is samsaric time which is unreal.

Although discrimination offers a sort of clear knowledge of the objective world it hinders the manifestation of reality just as it is. True reality can and must be realized prior to discrimination. Since the discrimination, that is everyday knowledge based on alternative judgments, is understood in Buddhism to be rooted in *avidyā* (fundamental ignorance), the notion of time ultimately arises from *avidyā*.[6] Because of *avidyā*, the twelve links of causation[7] arise. It indicates this actual empirical world which arises from *avidyā* and ends with birth, old age, and death. Time comes into being through this actual experience. In order to awaken to true reality one must break through the ordinary concepts of time by overcoming attachment and realize the non-substantiality of time. To overcome time, the attainment of *prajñā* (wisdom) or *nirvāṇa* is required.

In Christianity as well, sinful time spoiled by Adam and Eve's rebellion against God's word must be overcome. It is redeemed through pure faith in Jesus Christ's redemptive event on the cross. This event of Christ took place in time. It is a *kairos*, the fullness of time of Christ, through which sinful time has been transformed into the salvational time. The reality of time originally created by God has thus been resurrected although its complete fulfillment will be realized only at the end of history.

By contrast in Buddhism samsaric time is overcome not by faith in divine redemption but by emancipation from *avidyā* (fundamental ignorance innate in human nature). Unlike Christianity in which the overcoming of sinful time brings us to the Kingdom of God in which eternal life will be fulfilled, in Buddhism the overcoming of samsaric time entails attainment of *nirvāṇa* which is timeless or transtemporal.

Nirvāṇa, however, is not simply timeless. It is timeless in the sense that it is beyond time and eternity. Being beyond time and eternity, *nirvāṇa* includes time and eternity without being limited by them.

In *nirvāṇa* as the realization of *śūnyatā*, time is realized anew as time on the basis of the realization of its emptiness and non-substantiality. The distinction between past, present, and future is reaffirmed without attachment. In other words, samsaric time is regrasped in the light of *prajñā* and *nirvāṇa*.

III

How can we overcome the attachment to time and the notions of past, present, and future? As I stated above, in Buddhism time is realized in and through the realization of the impermanency of everything in the universe, especially through the realization of our living-dying. Buddhism does not regard life and death as separate, but as one indivisible reality, that is, living-dying. For if we grasp our life not objectively from the outside, but subjectively from within, we are fully living and fully dying at each and every moment. There is no living without dying, and no dying without living. According to Buddhism, we are not moving from life to death, but in the process of living-dying. This must be clearly realized.

We must also realize that the process of our living-dying is without beginning and without end. The process extends itself beyond our present life both into the direction of the remote past and into the direction of the distant future. Due to the absence of God as creator and ruler of the universe, in Buddhism there is no beginning in terms of creation and no end in terms of final judgment. Accordingly, we must realize the beginninglessness and endlessness of *saṃsāra*, that is, the transmigration of living-dying. This realization is essential to overcome time because it implies at least the following two things.

First, each and every moment can be understood to be a beginning and an end. Time begins and ends at each moment. Accordingly time is not understood to be an unidirectional movement but a sheer series of independent moments that can move reciprocally. A sort of reversibility of time is realized here. (Further discussion about reversibility will be given later.)

Second, if we clearly realize the beginningless*ness* and endless*ness* of living-dying *at this moment*, the whole process of living-dying is concentrated into this moment. In other words the moment embraces the whole process of beginningless and endless time within itself. Thus one can transcend time at this very moment.

This implies the following three points:

1. Through the clear realization of the beginninglessness and endlessness of the process of living-dying (*saṃsāra*) at this moment in *saṃsāra*, one transcends *saṃsāra* into *nirvāṇa*: *nirvāṇa* realized in the midst of *saṃsāra*, not beyond *saṃsāra*.

2. Through the realization at this moment in time one transcends time into eternity: eternity is realized in the midst of time, not at the end of time.

3. This transcendence or transdescendence is possible by cutting off the process of living-dying and opening up the bottomless depth of the transtemporal, eternal dimension. This cutting off is possible not by our speculation but by our religious practice, e.g. meditation and the 'death' of the ego-self.

IV

The cutting off of the beginningless and endless process of living-dying in time and the opening up of the bottomless depth of eternity have the following two meanings:

1. Through the cutting off and the opening up one goes down or transdescends into the bottomless depth of the transtemporal dimension and realizes eternity right 'below' the present. This is the aspect of wisdom in which time is overcome. From this depth of eternity one can grasp or embrace the entire process of living-dying without beginning and without end and thus can reverse the process. The unidirectionally of time is thus overcome and the reversibility of time is realized from this bottomless depth of eternity.

2. Through the cutting off of time and the opening up of eternity, one rises up from the bottomless depth to the dimension of temporality and moves forward toward the endless end along the process of living-dying. But now, coming from the bottomless depth of eternity, one is not confined by living-dying while one is working for others in the midst of living-dying. This is the aspect of compassion in which one tries endlessly to save others.

In the cutting off of the process of time and the opening up of the depth of eternity, the going down into and coming up from the depth of eternity work together. This is the structure of this moment, the 'now' – which is dynamically related to the bottomless depth of eternity, that is, *nirvāṇa*. One's movement from this moment to the next moment always involves this dynamic structure.

Accordingly, we must say that time has two aspects: the aspect of continuity or forward movement and the aspect of discontinuity or transdescending movement. And these two aspects are dynamically linked together at each and every moment.

The usual understanding of time as a continuity or a unidirectional forward movement represents only one aspect of time and is thus not sufficiently real. We must ask several questions to those who embrace this understanding. Where does one take one's stand when one understands time as a unidirectional continuity and a forward movement from the past, through the present, and into the future? Does not the person stand somewhat *outside* of time when he or she talks about time in terms of undirectional continuity? Isn't this understanding an objectification and conceptualization of time?

If we grasp time not from outside, but existentially from within, we realize the discontinuity of time at each moment, that is, the depth of time rather than the expanse of time. The continuity of time without the realization of its discontinuity is an abstraction. Real continuity of time is realized only through the realization of discontinuity. discontinuous continuity is real continuity. Passageless passage is real passage. An unrepeatable, undirectional forward movement is not a real forward movement. Real forward movement must include its self-negation, that is the repeatability and reversibility of time.

Time dies and is reborn at each and every moment. Buddhism is not closed to the possibility of a forward moving and irreversible historical time: further, it affirms anew every possible reality of history and time on the basis of the transtemporal depth of eternity.

To a Buddhist, in any moment of the beginningless and endless process of history, to move forward toward the future is nothing but to return to the source of time and history, and to return to the source of time and history is to move forward toward the future.

Accordingly, as I suggested in the beginning, the Buddhist view of time is neither linear nor cyclical and yet – or more precisely speaking, because of this – it is dynamically linear as well as cyclical.

13

On the Occasion of Buddha Day 1990: The Future Task of Buddhism

INTRODUCTION

Northern California is a unique area in the world where almost all living forms of Buddhism are represented. Included are not only Theravāda Buddhism from Sri Lanka, Burma, Thailand, and Cambodia, but also other important schools of Buddhism form China, Tibet (including Kagyu, Nyingma, Sakya, and Gelug orders), Korea, Japan (including Rinzai and Sōtō Zen, Nichiren and Jōdo-Shinshū), and Vietnam. Most of them have their own centers or temples with leading monks or priests and a sizable number of followers. A cooperative organization was formed to represent these groups called the Buddhist Council of Northern California, and every year they have gotten together to celebrate the Vesakha Festival in May. Originating in the Theravāda tradition, the Vesakha Festival commemorates Buddha's birth, enlightenment, and *parinirvāṇa*. Under the name of 'Buddha Day' this Vesakha Festival has been held by the Buddhist Council of Northern California as the most important event common to all member schools.

In 1990, they celebrated the 12th Annual Vesakha Festival on May 6 at Dwinelle Hall, University of California, Berkeley. The following text is the key address which I was asked to deliver on that occasion. My main concern in this address was to clarify the most appropriate way to celebrate Buddha Day for all of us despite the great diversity of various Buddhist traditions, especially in regard to the difference in the view of Gautama Buddha held by Theravāda, Mahāyāna, and Vajrayāna Buddhism, and also to show the future task common to all Buddhists in this turbulent world situation. I was pleased that after my address two Theravāda monks, one from Sri Lanka, the other from Thailand, came up to me and equally expressed their agreement and appreciation.

ADDRESS

Distinguished representatives, priests and laymen from various Buddhist groups all over Northern California! Today, we gather together here to celebrate the Buddha Day, Vesakha ceremony. On this occasion, we celebrate the birth of Śākyamuni Buddha, but also commemorate the Buddha's enlightenment and *parinirvāṇa*. This is an important Buddha Day for all Buddhists and this year we have the 12th Annual Buddha Day festival.

It is important, however, for us to think about what is the most appropriate way to celebrate Buddha's birth, enlightenment and *parinirvāṇa*. Of course, we would like to honor the Buddha as the founder of Buddhism, our Lord and Great Teacher. Is it, however, good enough for us to honor Śākyamuni Buddha as the object of our worship and celebration? I don't think it is good enough. Should we not, in truly honoring him, awaken to the Buddha Dharma by ourselves, and begin to walk on the same Buddha path as Śākyamuni Buddha? We should not take Śākyamuni Buddha merely as an object that we honor, but, rather, we would follow and live Buddha's Way by ourselves, subjectively and existentially. To me, this is the most appropriate way to celebrate Buddha Day.

According to the *Mahaparinibbana Suttanta*, shortly before his death Śākyamuni addressed Ananda, one of his ten great disciples, and others who were anxious at the prospect of losing their master:

> O Ananda be ye lamps unto yourselves. Rely on yourselves and do not rely on external help. Live the Dharma as a lamp. Seek salvation alone in the Dharma. Look not for assistance to anyone besides yourselves.

Obviously, when he said to his disciples, 'Do not rely on external help,' and 'Look not for assistance to anyone besides yourselves,' he included himself in the term 'external help' and he also included himself in 'anyone besides yourselves.' He said this despite the fact that he, Śākyamuni Buddha, had been a teacher of Ananda and others for many years. It may not, however, be clear at first how the following two passages in the set A and the set B in his statement are related to each other:

> Set A: 'Rely on yourselves,' and 'seek salvation alone in the Dharma.'
> Set B: 'Be ye lamps unto yourselves,' and 'Live the Dharma as a lamp.'

In this address, Śākyamuni did not mention his own identity with the Dharma in some exclusive sense. Instead, he explicitly identified the Dharma with the individual disciple. All this implies that the identity with the Dharma is not unique to Śākyamuni Buddha, but is common to all people. Further, he emphasized in the concrete situation of his death everyone's direct identity with the Dharma and this identity is without external help or mediator.

And, yet, in Buddhism, despite the identity of a particular individual with the Dharma and despite the identity of Śākyamuni himself with the Dharma, the Dharma is beyond everyone – beyond even Śākyamuni Buddha, the founder of Buddhism. The Dharma exists by itself universally apart from any human existence. Śākyamuni Buddha is not a creator of the Dharma, but a discoverer of the Dharma. This is the reason the *Samyutta Nikāya* states:

> Regardless of the appearance or non-appearance of the Tathāgata (Śākyamuni Buddha) in this world, the Dharma is always present.

Yet, who is rightly qualified to talk about the Dharma in its absolute universality? Is one who has not realized the Dharma qualified to talk about it? Certainly not! For, if it is the case that one does not realize the Dharma in her- or himself, then one understands the Dharma and its universality merely conceptually, and thereby the total universality of the Dharma becomes an empty or dead universality. Hence, only one who has realized the Dharma with his or her whole existence can properly talk about it in its total universality. Although the Dharma transcends everyone, including Śākyamuni Buddha, and is present universally, there is no Dharma without someone to realize it. Apart from the realizer, there is no Dharma. In other words, the Dharma is realized *as the Dharma* in its universality only through a particular realizer. Śākyamuni Buddha is none other than the *first* realizer of the Dharma of our era. He is not, however, the *only* realizer of the Dharma. But, it is also true that without Śākyamuni no one would have known the existence of the Dharma functioning throughout the world. He is indeed the *first* realizer of the Dharma. This is why he has been regarded as the founder of Buddhism.

In the sense that Śākyamuni is a realizer of Dharma in its total universality, he may be said to be *a* center, not *the* center of the Buddhist religion. The significance of Śākyamuni's historical existence is equal with that of every other realizer of the Dharma, except that Śākyamuni was the first, and supremely realized the Dharma.

How can we hold to those two apparently contradictory aspects of the Dharma: that is its total universality, on one hand, and its dependency upon a particular realizer, on the other? The answer lies in the fact that the realization of the Dharma is nothing but the *self-awakening of Dharma itself*. Your awakening of the Dharma is, of course, your own awakening. It is your awakening to the Dharma in its complete universality. But this awakening is possible only by overcoming our self-centeredness, i.e., only through the total negation of ego-self. Our self-centeredness is the fundamental hindrance for the manifestation of the Dharma. Originally the Dharma is present universally, but due to our self-centeredness, it does not become manifest to us. Therefore, when the self-centeredness is overcome and the selflessness is attained, i.e., *anātman* is realized, the Dharma naturally awakens to itself. Accordingly, the self-awakening of the Dharma has the following double sense. First, it is *your* self-awakening on the Dharma in your egoless true Self. Secondly, it is the self-awakening of *Dharma itself* in and through your whole existence. In other words, a particular individual's self-awakening to the Dharma and the Dharma's self-awakening are not two, but one.

It was on the basis of this self-awakening of the Dharma that Śākyamuni said, without any sense of contradiction, 'Rely on yourselves,' and 'seek salvation alone in the Dharma.' His statements, 'Be ye lamps unto yourselves,' and, 'live the Dharma as a lamp' are complementary and not contradictory. To ultimately rely on one's self is not to rely on the ego-self, but rather on the 'true self' which realizes the Dharma. Just as Śākyamuni's awakening was the self-awakening of the Dharma in the double sense mentioned above, that is, on the one hand, it is *his own* self-awakening of the Dharma, and, on the other, it is *the Dharma's* self-awakening, so anyone's awakening to the Dharma can and should be the self-awakening of the Dharma in the same sense.

This is the basic standpoint of Buddhism, which after his awakening was clarified by Śākyamuni himself throughout his life and particularly, as mentioned before, as he approached death. Some time after the *parinirvāṇa* of the Buddha, Buddhism began to experience various schisms and thus it developed into Theravāda, Mahāyāna, Vajrayāna, and so forth. However, all forms of Buddhism are fundamentally based on the above basic standpoint of Buddhism, that is the self-awakening of the Dharma in the double sense, as discussed above. Considering this basic standpoint of Buddhism clarified by Śākyamuni himself, I think the most appropriate way of celebrating Buddha Day is not to merely honor Śākyamuni Buddha as the object of our worship and celebration, but for each one of us to awaken to the Buddha-Dharma by ourselves and live and practice Buddha-Dharma subjectively and existentially.

Then, what is the Dharma which we should awaken to, live and practice? It is the law of *pratītya-samutpāda*, that is the law of dependent co-origination. This law means that everything in the universe is co-arising and co-ceasing and is interdependent with each other, that nothing exists independently; nothing has its own enduring fixed own-being. I believe this law of dependent co-origination is a very powerful and effective principle for the word, and that this is true not only for the past, but also for the future.

In harmony with the law of *pratītya-samutpāda*, Buddhism is not a monotheistic religion which is based on one absolute God. It does not reject the standpoint of others. Again, Buddhism is not some kind of pluralism, or some kind of polytheistic religion which has many deities without one integral principle. Being based on the law of dependent co-origination, Buddhism is neither monotheistic nor polytheistic, but non-dualistic. It can give life to everything, without reducing everything into one substantive principle. And yet, at the same time, Buddhism can embrace everything in the dynamic oneness of non-duality.

The contemporary world is rapidly shrinking due to the remarkable advancement of technology. Jet airplanes fly everywhere, and electronic communication happens almost instantly. In this shrinking world, however, the difference and opposition among various value systems and ideologies becomes more and more conspicuous. How to integrate this pluralistic world situation without marring the features of the culture and religion of various nations? This is the urgent issue which human kind is facing today. The future task of Buddhism is to apply the law of dependent co-origination to this world situation and to try to establish a dynamic and yet harmonious world. For the Buddhist law of dependent co-origination can serve as a powerful and effective principle to cope with the above urgent issue for the future of humanity.

Let us take on, then, the future task of Buddhism! Let us awaken to the Buddha-Dharma and become fully and compassionately human. Let us join hands in fellowship and live and practice the law of dependent co-origination and in this way let us build a better world where all beings in the ten quarters, including self and others, men and women, nations and faces, humans and nature, all may live harmoniously and peacefully.

Gate, Gate, paragate, parasamgate bodhi, svaha!

14

Transformation in Buddhism

Transformation in Buddhism centers around the realization of death. The Buddhist notion of transformation cannot be legitimately grasped apart from the realization of death. This is true of the transformation of society as well as the transformation of the individual.

What, then, is the realization of death? Dōgen, a Japanese Zen master of the thirteenth century, said: 'It is a mistake to understand that one passes from life to death.'[1] In our daily life, we usually think that we are now alive, but that we may die sometime in the future. Dōgen insisted that this ordinary understanding of life and death is a mistake. In our usual way of thinking, life and death are distinguished from one another and their relationship is taken as a *process* that moves from life to death. Here we must pose a question to ourselves. When we consider the relationship between life and death in this way, *where* are we taking our stand – in life or in death? Or do we take a stand somewhere else? When we look upon the relation of life and death, as a *process* moving from the former to the latter, our 'existential' posture is *outside* of both. It is just like standing on an embankment and looking down the river of life flowing from its source to its lower reaches. Are we not, however, actually swimming right in the middle of this river? By taking our position outside of both life and death, we objectify our life as something 'present' and our death as something which will happen in the 'future.'

An objectified or conceptualized life, however, is no longer life as it is. In the same way, an objectified or conceptualized death is not actual death. An objectifying viewpoint makes no serious enquiry into the significance of life, and thus leads to no existential realization of the anxiety of death. Real life cannot be viewed objectively from the outside. It must be grasped subjectively from within, since we are living our lives existentially at every moment as though we are in the middle of a river. Even so, one is apt to reify or substantialize both the swimming self and the flow of the river as if they were two different entities. This static view misses the quality of living reality. One truly grasps his or her own existential living only when to use the present metaphor, the swimmer himself or herself at once seizes all – self, swimming, and the river – together at the same time. Here, the grasped and the grasper are dynamically one, not two. At this point, one comes to realize fully that one is swimming in a river which, having no bottom, cannot be made into a 'thing.'

The bottomless depths of life reach down into the realm of death itself. On the other hand, the undertow of death can be felt even in the ripples of the surface. Life and death touch one another at every moment. Death is not reached only at the end of life, but is continuously present and at work throughout. Just as we can swim forward only by overcoming sinking into the bottomless depths of the river, at every moment, we can live our lives only by overcoming death at each and every instant. To live our lives is no less than to continuously choose to live by rejecting the choice of death. (One can commit suicide by his or her free will.)

In the non-conceptualized, existential understanding of life and death, life and death are not two separate events but dynamically one. Being different principles, they are opposed to one another and negate each other and yet they are inseparably connected – an existential antinomy of life and death. Accordingly, it is not that we are moving from life to death, but that, at each and every moment, we are fully living and fully dying. Without dying, there is no living; without living, there is no dying. Living and dying are paradoxically one. Like the two sides of a single sheet of paper which are quite distinct and yet inseparable, 'living' and 'dying' are two different aspects of one and the same reality which are antithetical and yet inseparable. This is true throughout the spectrum of human life regardless of age. Even a new-born baby, fresh from its mother's womb, is beginning to die; and an old person on his or her death-bed can be said to be living – if life and death are grasped from within existentially, not from the outside objectively.

A rigid separation of life and death is abstract and unreal. It is only a conceptual understanding of life and death, and understanding which objectifies life and death by taking its stand beyond both – in an imaginary place established by thought alone. This is the reason

Dōgen said, 'It is a mistake to understand that one passes from life to death.' Accordingly, we should not speak of 'life *and* death' but 'living-dying.' One must overcome the dualistic view of life and death and must awaken to the non-dual reality of living-dying. In truth, at each and every moment we are 'living-dying.' And yet, this living-dying process is without beginning and without end. We are continuously involved in this beginningless and endless process of living-dying. Buddhism calls this beginningless and endless process of living-dying *saṃsāra*, often likening it to a great flowing ocean which is boundless and bottomless.

For Buddhists, this beginningless and endless process of living-dying in itself is regarded as 'death' in the true sense of the word. It is not death as a counterpart of life, or death in the relative sense, but death in the absolute sense. It is called 'Great Death' in Zen. Accordingly, what is problematic to Buddhists is not death as an event that counters life, but the endless process of living-dying, i.e., *saṃsāra*. And thus, the aim of Buddhism is not to overcome death and attain eternal life, but to be liberated from *saṃsāra* – the beginningless and endless process of living-dying – and thereby to awaken to *nirvāṇa*, the blissful freedom from transmigration. Transformation in Buddhism means transformation from an existence bound by *saṃsāra* to an existence liberated from *saṃsāra*, i.e., existence in *nirvāṇa*. To achieve this Buddhist transformation, it is crucial to realize the beginningless and endless process of living-dying as the true sense of absolute death. In Buddhism, transformation in the dimension of only life without the realization of absolute death or Great Death is not true transformation. And this is the case with the transformation of society as well as with the transformation of the individual.

II

It is not peculiar to Buddhism that transformation is grasped in relation to the realization of death. If we take Plato's idea of *kathársis* to indicate a kind of transformation, we can say that in his philosophy, transformation is grasped through the realization of death. To Plato, *kathársis* is purification of the soul from contamination by the body in order to prepare itself for a better life. For him, death is nothing but the purification of the soul through being released from the perished corporeal body. Death is not the body entering a tomb, but the releasing of the soul from the body (*sōma*) which is the tomb (*sēma*) of the soul.[2] Plato not only believes in the immortality of the soul after death but also encourages philosophers to 'practice dying' while living in this world. For Plato, to philosophize means to purify (*kathársis*) the soul from bodily corruption and to contemplate the world of ideas while the soul exists within the body.

In Plato, however, both the immortality of the soul and philosophy as the *kathársis* of the soul are based on a dualistic view of body and soul. Although the realization of death is essential for Platonic transformation, death is grasped as the separation of the soul from the body. There is no realization of Great Death in the Buddhist sense, which is the realization of the beginningless and endless process of living-dying as the absolute death, and in which body and soul, life and death, are grasped non-dualistically.

In this respect, Christianity is much closer to Buddhism than Platonism. In Christianity, both body and soul originate in the creation of God, and the body is not the prison of the soul as in Plato, but rather a 'temple of the Holy Spirit.'[3] What is essential to distinguish in Christianity is not the soul and body, but God and the human being. And, in Christianity, the human being must die not because of the perishability of the human body, but because of original sin. Death is grasped in Christianity not as natural death or as the separation of the imperishable soul from the perishable body, but as 'the wages of sin.'[4] Through faith in the resurrection of Jesus Christ, however, Christians can look forward to eternal life in the kingdom of God beyond sin and death. Paul says of baptism as a symbol of transformation:

> When we were baptized in Christ Jesus we were baptized in his death – we went into the tomb with him and joined him in death, so that as Christ was raised from the dead – we too might live a new life.[5]

Paul also says:

> Whereof we faint not: but though our outward man is decaying, yet our inward man is renewed day by day.[6]

In faith in Jesus as Christ, Christians die together with Christ day by day and revive together with Christ day by day. Everyday, therefore, indeed today, here and now, Christians die as the old person and resurrect as the new person with Christ Jesus. Thus, Christian transformation from the outward person to the inward person, from the old person to the new person, is realized through one's death and resurrection together with Christ. Apart from our death and resurrection day by day, together with Christ's death and resurrection, there can be no transformation in the Christian sense. This is strikingly similar to the Buddhist understanding of transformation.

Yet, we should not overlook an essential difference between Christianity and Buddhism in the understanding of death and transformation. Unlike Plato's philosophy, which regards body and soul dualistically, Christianity grasps body and soul as a unity, both in life and death. In Christianity, the body, *sarx* or *sōma*, and the soul, *pneūma* or *psyche* though somewhat antagonistic, are equally divine creations and are always to be grasped in relation to God. God, and a person as a unity of body and soul, are related not only vitally in terms of creation, but also personally in terms of an I–Thou relationship through the Word. Death is nothing other than 'the wages of sin' for rebelling against the word of God. Transformation from the old person to the new person is only possible through faith in the death and resurrection of Jesus as Christ, the only incarnation of the Word of God in history. In short, the unity of body and soul, life, death, and resurrection or transformation from the old to the new person are all grasped in relation to God as Lord. In Buddhism, however, this human relationship to one God is absent – at least in the fundamental form of Buddhism (historical and doctrinal). Instead of one God as the creator, judge, and redeemer, Buddhism puts forth the principle of *pratītya-samutpāda*, i.e., dependent origination, and an accompanying notion of the non-substantiality of everything in the universe. According to this Buddhist principle, everything co-arises and co-ceases with everything else; nothing exists independently. This is the reason why Gautama Buddha did not accept the age-old traditional notion of Brahman as the supreme creative principle of the universe. The notion of one God as the Lord of the universe is not found in early Buddhism.

The Buddhist principle of dependent origination is inseparably connected with the rejection of dualism and monism or monotheism. From the Buddhist point of view, dualism as a theory consisting of two basic and irreducible principles cannot be true because it presupposes two entities, such as body and soul, as the basic principles by objectifying and conceptualizing them from the outside.

Again, for Buddhism, both monism – the doctrine of one ultimate substance or principle – and monotheism – the doctrine or belief that there is but one God – cannot be true. In monism and monotheism, there must be a veiled person, other than one principle or one God, who speaks of the existence of that one principle or of that one God. The non-objectifiable, non-conceptual understanding of reality entails the principle of dependent origination, which is neither dualistic nor monistic.

Buddhism denies the notion of the soul as having an independent existence, and it insists upon the non-duality of the 'body' and the 'soul' on the basis of dependent origination. And, on the same basis, as mentioned earlier, life and death are grasped inseparably from one another in terms of living-dying which is without beginning and without end. In other words, Buddhism views human beings not as mortal in Plato's sense, nor as having to die because of original sin as in Christianity, but as engaged in a living-dying existence in terms of 'karma,' a concept soon to be discussed.

III

In the preceding sections, I have discussed the notion that transformation in both Christianity and Buddhism is inseparably connected with the realization of death, but that the realizations of death in these two religions are also significantly different. In Christianity, death is grasped as the 'wages of sin', i.e., as the result of sin committed by Adam rebelling against the word of God. On the other hand, in Buddhism, death, or living-dying is realized as *karma* committed by oneself from the far distant past. Just as the Christian transformation cannot be properly understood apart from the realization of sin, the Buddhist transformation cannot be adequately grasped apart from the recognition of *karma*.

Why is living-dying realized as *karma*? And, what is the religious significance of *karma* – an understanding of which is essential for Buddhist transformation? In order to answer these questions, the following four points must be clarified.

First, as I mentioned earlier, we usually think of life and death as two different entities by objectifying or conceptualizing them. In taking a dualistic view of life and death, we cling to life as a desirable state and dread death as an undesirable state. Thus, we are inevitably shackled by the opposition and conflict between life and death, not only conceptually, but also emotionally and volitionally – that is, with our whole existence. In this way, we are bound over to the endless process of a life–death conflict which is called *saṃsāra* in Buddhism. Accordingly, *saṃsāra* does not mean that living-dying is transmigration in a biological sense, but transmigration deeply rooted in human volition (thirst or craving) and ignorance. As the *Saṃyutta Nikāya*, one of the earliest Buddhist scriptures, states:

> No beginning is known of the eternal *saṃsāra* of beings, streaming and flowing to and fro [in the ocean of births and deaths], being covered by ignorance (*avijjā*, *avidyā*) and fettered in thrist (*taṇhā*).[7]

This is why the transmigration of living-dying is understood in Buddhism as *karma*, which means act or deed.[8] Our usual attachment to life and dread of death is deeply rooted in *bhāva taṇhā*, the thirst or craving to be, to live, to grow more and more – an unconscious, endless impulse in human existence which Schopenhauer called the *blinder Wille zum Leben* (blind will to live). It is also deeply rooted in *avidyā*, the fundamental ignorance of the non-duality of life and death, and of the beginninglessness and endlessness of transmigration. In Buddhism, our life and death struggle is grasped as *karma* because it is ultimately rooted in our blind craving to exist, and in our fundamental ignorance of the principle of dependent origination and the non-substantiality of everything in the universe.

Second, in order to achieve transformation in Buddhism – that is, transformation from an existence involved in *saṃsāra* to an existence living in *nirvāṇa*, we must clearly realize: (1) the non-duality of life and death; (2) the beginninglessness and endlessness of our living-dying; and (3) the total living-dying at this moment of the absolute present.

1. To grasp the essential of human life, we must reject the dualistic view of life and death and see this as a conceptualized view lacking true reality. We must awaken to the realization that we are living-dying at each and every moment. It is a realization that comes about when we existentially grasp our life from within.

2. We must also realize that the process of our living-dying is without beginning and without end. The process of our living-dying extends itself beyond our present life both in the direction of the remote past and in the direction of the distant future. This is the

reason, for example, why Zen raises the traditional question: 'What is your original face before your parents were born?'[9] It also asks: 'If you are free from life and death, you know where you will go. When the four elements [the physical human body] are decomposed, where do you go?'[10] Due to the absence of God as the creator and the ruler of the universe, in Buddhism, there is no beginning in terms of creation and no end in terms of last judgment. Accordingly, we must realize the beginninglessness and endlessness of *saṃsāra*; that is, the transmigration of living-dying. This realization is essential because it provides a way to overcome *saṃsāra* and to turn it into *nirvāṇa*.

3. The realization of the beginninglessness and endlessness of living-dying is inseparably linked with the realization of our living-dying at each and every moment. This is because if we clearly realize the beginningless*ness* and endless*ness* of the process of living-dying *at this moment*, the whole process of living-dying is concentrated *into this moment*. In other words, this moment embraces the whole process of living-dying by virtue of the clear realization of the beginningless*ness* and endless*ness* of the process of living-dying. Here, in this point, we can overcome *saṃsāra*, and realize *nirvāṇa* right in the midst of *saṃsāra*.

Third, the Buddhist notion of *karma* has both an individual and a universal aspect. Any *karma* is an act oriented by one's volition. Although it is affected by circumstances and external stimuli, fundamentally, *karma* is self-responsible action determined by one's will or thirst, consciously or unconsciously. Accordingly, *karma* is morally characterized and remains thoroughly the responsibility of each individual. At the same time, any *karma* affects not only the continuity of individual beings but also the solidarity of collective human existence. Due to this sympathetic or contagious character of *karma*, the whole universe is understood by Buddhism as the collective mass of *karmas* of all beings.

This twofold aspect of *karma* – the individual aspect and the universal aspect – are not exceptions to our living-dying. Rather, in Buddhism, the beginningless and endless process of our living-dying, that is, *saṃsāra*, is grasped as *karma* deeply rooted in our own blind will and ignorance and thus as *karma* for which each of us is thoroughly responsible. And yet, at the same time, the same *saṃsāra* is realized as universal *karma* firmly rooted in the craving and fundamental ignorance which are innate in human nature. Buddhist transformation is possible only when *saṃsāra* – the beginningless and endless process of living-dying – is realized as *karma* in the above double sense, is overcome, and *nirvāṇa* is realized. To be more specific, individual transformation is achieved on the basis of overcoming the individual aspect of *karma*, whereas the transformation of society can be realized on the basis of overcoming the universal aspect of human *karma* – although these two aspects are inseparably linked together.

Parenthetically speaking, the Christian notion of sin and the Buddhist notion of *karma* have a remarkable affinity in terms of their respective twofold aspects of individuality and universality. We have already seen that on the one hand, the Buddhist notion of *karma* is individual responsibility, and yet, on the other hand, it has a universality common to all humankind. In Christianity, the same is true of the notion of sin. As Paul says:

> Therefore, as sin came into the world through one man and death through sin, so death spread to all men because all men sinned.[11]

Sin and resultant death spread to all human beings through Adam's sin. However, as Kierkegaard rightly emphasizes in *The Concept of Dread*, each of us committed sin in Adam. If I am not mistaken, in Christianity, individual transformation is achieved through overcoming individual sin, whereas the transformation of society is possible on the basis of overcoming sin common to all human beings, although we should also clearly recognize the inseparability of these two aspects.

IV

Heretofore, I have tried to clarify how transformation takes place in Buddhism. Now, I would like to proceed to elucidate what happens in Buddhist transformation. In this regard, special attention will be given to the way the transformation of the individual is related to the transformation of society and to historical change.

As I mentioned earlier, Buddhist transformation is nothing but transformation from an existence living in *saṃsāra* to an existence living in *nirvāṇa*. This transformation is possible through overcoming *karma* in terms of the beginningless and endless process of living-dying. I also emphasized that this overcoming of *karma* is possible at each and every moment when we clearly realize the beginningless-*ness* and endless*ness* of the process of living-dying, and when thereby the whole process of living-dying *is concentrated into this present moment*. This means that in the midst of *saṃsāra*, *nirvāṇa* is fully realized.

In this connection it is important to note the following four points. First, Buddhist transformation takes place not in *nirvāṇa* apart from *saṃsāra*, but at the intersection of *saṃsāra*, and *nirvāṇa*. *Nirvāṇa* which is apart from *saṃsāra* is not true *nirvāṇa*. *Nirvāṇa* is realized when the beginninglessness and endlessness of *saṃsāra* is fully realized, i.e., when *saṃsāra* is fully realized as *saṃsāra*. A full realization of *saṃsāra* as it is is nothing but a full realization of *nirvāṇa*. This is the reason I stated that *nirvāṇa* is realized in the midst of *saṃsāra*. Again, this is the reason Mahāyāna Buddhist scriptures emphasize that *saṃsāra* is *nirvāṇa*; *nirvāṇa* is *saṃsāra*. Accordingly, Buddhist transformation takes place not somewhere off in the distance, past or future, but right here at this moment, right now in this actual immediate world.

Second, the statement '*saṃsāra* is *nirvāṇa*; *nirvāṇa* is *saṃsāra*' should not be understood to signify a static or immediate identity of *saṃsāra* and *nirvāṇa*. In one sense, they are essentially different and *saṃsāra* should be seen as *saṃsāra*; *nirvāṇa* should be seen as *nirvāṇa*. *Saṃsāra* is subjugated by *karma*, whereas *nirvāṇa* is free from *karma*. One must overcome attachment to *saṃsāra* and arrive at *nirvāṇa*. But if one stays in *nirvāṇa*, stays apart from *saṃsāra*, one is still selfish because abiding in *nirvāṇa*, one may enjoy one's own salvation while forgetting the suffering of one's fellow beings who are still involved in *saṃsāra*. To be completely unselfish, one should not stay in *nirvāṇa* but return to the realm of *saṃsāra* to save one's fellow beings who are suffering. This is the reason why Mahāyāna Buddhism emphasizes that: 'In order to attain wisdom one should not abide in *saṃsāra*: in order to fulfill compassion one should not abide in *nirvāṇa*.'[12] Not abiding either in *saṃsāra* or *nirvāṇa* – freely moving from *saṃsāra* to *nirvāṇa*, from *nirvāṇa* to *saṃsāra* without attaching to either – this dynamic movement is true *nirvāṇa* in Mahāyāna Buddhism. When I stated that Buddhist transformation takes place at the intersection of *saṃsāra* and *nirvāṇa*, I referred to this dynamism of true *nirvāṇa*. In Mahāyāna Buddhism, self-awakening in *nirvāṇa*, however important it may be, is not sufficient. Only when awakening others from *saṃsāra* is achieved is self-awakening also achieved. Here we see the basis for the transformation of society in Buddhism.

Third, the Four Great Vows, which all Mahāyāna Buddhists proclaim, are as follows:

However innumerable sentient beings are, I vow to save them;
However inexhaustible the passions are, I vow to extinguish them;
However immeasurable the Dharmas are, I vow to master them;
However incomparable the Buddha-truth is, I vow to attain it.

In these 'Four Great Vows,' the first vow is aimed at benefitting others, while the remaining three vows – to extinguish the passions, to master the Dharmas, and to attain the Buddha-truth – refer to self-benefits. It is worthy to note that the vow for benefitting others comes before the vows for self-benefit. This signifies the spirit of the Bodhisattva, the model of the Mahāyāna Buddhist who strives to save others before saving himself. One can attain true enlightenment only through helping others to attain enlightenment. Instead of becoming an enlightened being immediately, a Bodhisattva vows to save all other beings and works with compassion for the benefit of suffering beings. For the Bodhisattva, self-benefit and benefitting others are dynamically one. This is called *jiri-ritaenman*, the perfect fulfillment of self-benefit and benefitting others.

The vow of the Bodhisattva to save all beings and to attain Buddhahood is a single process involving both self and others, and it provides the basis for the transformation of society in Buddhism. Mahāyāna scriptures often talk about the construction of the Buddha Land. But, when Buddhism emphasizes the perfect fulfillment of self-benefit and benefitting others, the term 'others' actually indicates other persons and not necessarily society at large. Traditional Buddhism lacks a concrete program of social transformation. This is partly because Buddhism is more concerned with the ground or religious basis for social transformation rather than a practical program, and partly because in Buddhism, the ground or religious basis for social transformation is not limited to humans but includes all sentient beings. It is an urgent task for Buddhism to actualize the Bodhisattva idea in a concrete plan for social transformation in the contemporary human predicament.

Fourth, in connection with the transformation of society we must pay due attention to historical change as understood in Buddhism. Buddhism has a unique view of time. Time is understood to be entirely without beginning and without end. Since time is beginningless and endless, it is not considered to be linear as in Christianity or circular as in non-Buddhist Vedāntic philosophy. Being neither linear nor circular, time is completely reversible; and yet, time moves from moment to moment, each moment embracing the whole process of time. Because of this unique view of time. Buddhism is relatively weak in its view of history. Time is not directly history. Time becomes 'history' when the factor of spatiality (worldhood, *Weltlichkeit*) is added to it. History comes to have meaning when time is understood to be irreversible and each moment has an unrepeatable uniqueness or a once-and-for-all nature (*Einmalichkeit*). But, since in Buddhism time is understood to be entirely beginningless and endless and thus reversible, the uni-directionality of time and the uniqueness of each moment essential to the notion of history is not clearly expressed in Buddhism.

Buddhism, however, can develop its own view of history, if we take seriously the compassionate aspect of *nirvāṇa*. As I stated earlier, true *nirvāṇa* in Mahāyāna Buddhism is not *nirvāṇa* apart from *saṃsāra*. Just as one must overcome attachment to *saṃsāra* to attain *nirvāṇa*, one must overcome attachment to *nirvāṇa* to return to *saṃsāra*. 'In order to attain wisdom one should not abide in *saṃsāra*; in order to fulfill compassion one should not abide in *nirvāṇa*' is an important admonition for Mahāyāna Buddhists. In the wisdom aspect of *nirvāṇa*, in which *saṃsāra* is done away with, everything and everyone is freed from living-dying transmigration and thereby attains its original nature. Again, in this wisdom aspect of *nirvāṇa*, time ceases because the beginningless and endless process of time is totally concentrated in each moment which is realized as eternal now in the sense of absolute present. However, everything and everyone, though realized in its original nature in the light of wisdom, does not necessarily awaken to this basic reality. Many beings are still ignorant of this reality and are involved in the process of *saṃsāra*.

Accordingly, one who has attained *nirvāṇa* should not be abide in *nirvāṇa* but should return to the realm of *saṃsāra* to help these people equally awaken to their original nature by themselves. This is the compassionate aspect of *nirvāṇa* which can be actualized only by overcoming the attachment to one's own *nirvāṇa*. This process of actualizing the compassionate aspect of *nirvāṇa* is endless because people who do not awaken to their original nature are countless and appear to be endless. Here, the progress of history toward the future is necessary and comes to have a positive significance.

In the light of wisdom realized in *nirvāṇa* everything and everyone awakens to their original nature and time is overcome. In the light of compassion (also realized in *nirvāṇa*), however, time is religiously significant. Unidirectional history toward the future becomes essential. Here, we do have a Buddhist view of history.

It is not, however, an eschatological view of history nor a teleological view of history in the Christian or Western sense. If we use the term eschatology, the Buddhist view of history is a completely realized eschatology, because in the light of wisdom, everything and everyone without exception is realized in its original nature, and time is thereby overcome. If we use the term teleology, the Buddhist view of history is an open teleology, because in the light of compassion, the process of awakening others in history is endless. The completely realized eschatology and the entirely open teleology are dynamically united in this present moment, now. Buddhist transformation in history takes place dynamically at the intersection of the wisdom aspect and the compassionate aspect of *nirvāṇa*.

V

With regard to the relationship between the transformation of the individual and social and historical transformation, I would like to discuss Shin'ichi Hisamatsu's notion of FAS. Shin'ichi Hisamatsu (1889–1980) was the most outstanding Zen philosopher of contemporary Japan. He was Professor of Buddhism at Kyoto University during the period around World War II. But, far more than a scholar of Buddhism, Hisamatsu was a living personification of Zen, a man who lived his daily life and performed various activities deeply from the ground of his clear-cut Zen awakening. He was an excellent tea master, calligrapher, and poet, and yet a reformer of traditional Zen in Japan.[13] All aspects of his personality and activities stemmed from a single religious realization which he called 'awakening.'[14] His notion of FAS was not an exception to this realization. Rather, FAS represented Hisamatsu's basic understanding of human existence on which his philosophy, religion, art, and particularly his idea of reformation of traditional Zen were firmly established. (Hisamatsu used this English acronym, FAS, because there is no adequate Japanese abbreviation to express his threefold notion.)

What, then, is FAS? 'F' stands for 'Awakening to the Formless Self,' referring to the dimension of depth of human existence, i.e., the true

Self as the ground of human existence. 'A' stands for 'Standing within the standpoint of All Mankind,' referring to the breadth of human existence, i.e., human beings in all their entirety. And 'S' stands for 'Creating history Suprahistorically,' referring to the dimension of the chronological length of human existence, i.e., awakened human history. Accordingly, the three aspects of FAS indicate a threefold structure of human existence: depth, breadth, and length of human existence, or, speaking more concretely, self, world, and history. (This threefold notion may correspond to the traditional Western threefold notion of the soul, the world, and God. However, in Hisamatsu's threefold notion, God is absent.) In the notion of FAS, these three dimensions of human existence are grasped dynamically, and though different from each other, they are inseparably united with each other.

The first dimension, 'Awakening to the Formless Self,' signifies nothing other than *satori* in the Zen sense. Traditionally, it has been said that the primal concern of Zen is *koji-kyūmei*, 'investigation of self,' that is, to enquire and awaken to one's own true Self, or original face. Hisamatsu calls true Self the 'Formless Self'[15] because, being entirely unobjectifiable, true Self is without any form which can be objectified. True Self is realized to be really formless by going beyond both form (being) and formlessness (non-being). Traditional Zen greatly emphasizes the importance of investigating and seeing into the Self, but it also admonishes not to remain in silent illumination or fall into a nihilistic ghostly cave by attaching to the formlessness of the self. Zen thus stresses the necessity of great dynamism or the wondrous activity of helping others. Hisamatsu, however, criticizes this formulation of traditional Zen by saying that if the so-called 'wondrous activity' signifies only the process leading other individuals to awaken to their true Self, its activity remains limited to the problem of self without penetrating more widely beyond it even by one step. He says:

> If, as has been the case with traditional Zen, [wondrous] activity starts and ends only with the so-called practice of compassion involved in helping others to awaken, such activity will remain unrelated to the formation of the world or creation of history, isolated from the world and history, and in the end turn Zen into a forest Buddhism, temple Buddhism, at best, a Zen monastery Buddhism. Ultimately, this becomes 'Zen within a ghostly cave.'[16]

> In Zen, the all-out compassionate practice ought to be to have man awake to his original true Self, that is, to the solitarily emancipated, nondependent, Formless Self, who will form the true world and create true history self-abidingly, without being bound or fettered by anything.[17]

According to Hisamatsu, a formation of the true world necessitates the second dimension of human existence – that is, the 'A' which signifies 'Standing within the standpoint of All mankind,' because unless we grasp racial, national, and class problems from the perspective of all humankind, we cannot solve any of them adequately. Thus, in addition to the 'investigation of Self,' *sekai-kyūmei* (this author's term), an 'investigation of the world' is needed to find out the nature and structure of the world. Furthermore, a creation of true history requires the third dimension of human existence, the 'S', which stands for 'Creating history Suprahistorically,' because true history cannot be created by an approach immanent in history, such as class struggle in Marxism or social reform in humanism. Unless we take a suprahistorical religious standpoint, in Hisamatsu's case, the awakening to the formless Self as our basis, we cannot create true history. Thus, *rekishi-kyūmei* (again, this author's term), 'investigation of history' is necessary to understand the real meaning of history and its origin and purpose.[18]

Currently, we have different peace movements, human rights movements, and various other social reform movements. However, if these movements are pursued only from a political and social standpoint without a basis in our deep realization of the true Self, such approaches may not yield adequate solutions. Even though those who participate in such movements are full of much good will and possess a strong sense of justice, if they lack an awakening to the original nature of self and others, their actions are without real power, or worse, create more confusion. On the other hand, if only the internal religious aspect of human beings is emphasized, and priority is given to one's own salvation, thereby neglecting affairs of the world, however serious individuals may be in their religious quest, they cannot attain a profound religious solution. Mere concern with self-salvation is contrary to even the Bodhistattva's 'Four Great Vows,' but today's Buddhism is apt to be removed from social realities and confined to temples, engrossed only in the inner problems of the self.

Thus, together with his group of disciples, Hisamatsu formulated 'The Vow of Mankind' and proclaimed it in 1951, shortly after the Korean War. 'The Vow of Mankind' reads as follows:

Keeping calm and composed, let us awaken to our true Self, become fully compassionate humans, make full use of our gifts according to our respective vocations in life; discern the agony both individual and social and its source, recognize the right direction in which history should proceed, and join hands without distinction of race, nation, or class. Let us, with compassion, vow to bring to realization mankind's deep desire for self-emancipation and construct a world in which everyone can truly and fully live.

Koji-kyūmei, the 'investigation of self,' will necessarily become abstract and without reality if it is sought only for its own sake. Therefore, we should work upon *sekai-kyūmei*, the 'investigation of the world', that is, the problem of what is the true world, of what is the root and source of the world in which we live. Accordingly, the 'investigation of the world' is not separate from the 'investigation of self.' Further, to study and clarify what the world is also is inseparably linked with *rekishi-kyūmei*, the 'investigation of history', that is, studying and clarifying the origin and true meaning of history.[19]

In short, the question of what the self is, what the world is, and what history is, are all related to each other. The problem of what the self is cannot be resolved in its true sense if it is investigated independently of those problems of the nature of the world and the meaning of history. On the other hand, world peace, for example, cannot be established in the true sense, nor can history be truly created, unless one clarifies what the self is. These three problems are inseparably related and united at the root of our existence.

Hisamatsu thus emphasizes as follows:

Without the Self-Awakening of the Formless Self, world-formation and history-creation will miss their fundamental subject. Without true formation of the world and creation of history, the Formless Self cannot help ending in an imperfect practice of compassion.

Consequently, we may conclude that we should get rid of the imperfect narrow character of the former so-called 'Self-awakened, others-awakening' activity which disregards the world and history, and which satisfies itself at best by 'hammering out only a piece or half a piece.'[20] We should awake to the Formless Self ('F'), form the world on the standpoint of All mankind ('A'), and, without being fettered by created history, Suprahistorically create history at all times ('S'), that is to say, only the realization of FAS can be really called the ultimate Mahāyāna.[21]

Hisamatsu's notion of FAS is a remarkable example of a new understanding of transformation in contemporary Buddhism.

VI

In the preceding sections, I have discussed the 'transformation in Buddhism' mainly based upon the fundamental standpoint of Buddhism by referring to early Buddhism, to the typical form of Mahāyāna Buddhism, and to Zen. In Mahāyāna Buddhism as it developed in China and Japan, however, there are special forms which are significantly different from the forms of Buddhism discussed above in their understanding of the human being, death, *karma*, and salvation. The most important and conspicuous example of these types of Buddhism is Pure Land Buddhism, especially Jōdo Shinshū founded by Shinran (1173–1263). In order to clarify the issue of 'transformation in Buddhism' more comprehensively, I would now like to turn to Jōdo Shinshū and to the understanding of transformation which it puts forth.

Pure Land Buddhism developed out of the original Buddhism of India and finally reached the form known as Jōdo Shinshū. Shinran developed this reformed sect of Buddhism through a clear historical awareness of the degenerate age of the Dharma (Buddhist teaching) and a keen existential realization of sinfulness. A prevalent belief historically among Mahāyāna Buddhists is a gradual degeneration of the Buddhist Dharma in three periods. According to this belief, the first period, believed to last 500 or 1000 years after the Buddha's death, is called the period of the right Dharma, in which Buddhist doctrine, practices, and enlightenment all exist. The second period of 500 or 1000 years is the period of the semblance or imitative Dharma, in which doctrine and practices exist without enlightenment. The third and last period of 10 000 years is that of the latter or final Dharma (*mappō*), in which only the doctrine remains without practice and enlightenment. As the advent of *mappō* was approaching, many

Buddhists in China and Japan increasingly turned from original Buddhism (the right Dharma) to Pure Land Buddhism, which advocates the salvation of wretched people through faith in Amida Buddha, as the Buddhism most suitable for the *mappō* period. This historical awareness of the degeneration of Buddhist Dharma was very strong in the Kamakura Period (1185–1333) in Japan, a time in which Shinran and his teacher Hōnen were alive. Such historical awareness of the degeneration period is inseparably linked with the existential realization of one's helplessness and sinfulness. Shan-tao (613–681), a Chinese Pure Land patriarch, on whom both Hōnen and Shinran deeply depended in their understanding of Pure Land teaching, sincerely believed and confessed that 'Being a sinful, living-dying unenlightened being I have incessantly transmigrated for countless remote kalpas (aeons) without a single opportunity of emancipation.'[22]

For Pure Land Buddhists, the beginningless and endless process of living-dying is realized not only as *karma*, but also as *sinful karma* (*zaigō*). This is because: (1) it is only by the power of Amida's original vow to save all beings that wretched and powerless people living in the period of degenerated Dharma can be saved; and, (2) the beginningless and endless transmigration is the result of one's unbelief in the saving power of Amida's original vow – that is, the result of sin. Unlike original Buddhism, and some forms of Mahāyāna Buddhism, including Zen, in which a central, personal Buddha is absent, Pure Land Buddhism centers around Amida Buddha as the Buddha of infinite light and infinite life whose original vow to save all sentient beings is believed to be unconditional. Accordingly, transformation in Pure Land Buddhism is not conceivable without Amida's original vow and beneficence.

Transformation in Pure Land Buddhism is called *ōjō*, birth in the Pure Land. It implies going to and being reborn in the Pure Land after death in this present defiled world. To Pure Land Buddhists, it is impossible to attain *nirvāṇa* in the midst of *saṃsāra* right here, right now in this actual world as most forms of Mahāyāna Buddhism insist. One the basis of Pure Land scriptures, especially the *Larger Sukhāvatī-vyūha-sūtra*, Pure Land Buddhists believe that in an infinite time in the past, the Bodhisattva Dharmakāra observed the sufferings of mortal beings in the future, and from his great compassion, he vowed to establish a land of bliss wherein all beings could be emancipated from their sufferings. After labor and meditation for long aeons, Bodhisattva Dharmakāra accomplished his vow completely and became a Buddha named Amitābha or Amitāyus, residing in the Pure Land established by himself. It is a basic belief of Pure Land Buddhism that not by their own practice and meditation, but by reciting the name of Amida (*nembutsu*), and through pure faith in the saving power of Amida's vow, regardless of whether their activities are good or bad, all beings without exception can be saved and will be reborn in the Pure Land after death.

It is Shinran who radicalized this Pure Land faith and brought it to its final conclusion. Shinran's unique standpoint may be summarized in the following three points.

First, Shinran radicalized the Pure Land teaching of universal salvation by Amida's vow regardless of one's good or evil, and emphasized that evil persons were precisely appropriate candidates for Amida's salvation.

Hōnen, Shinran's direct teacher, stated:

> Even an evil person is born in the Pure Land, how much more so is a good person.[23]

Shinran declared:

> Even a good person is born in the Pure Land, how much more so is an evil person.[24]

To explain the reason for his position, Shinran says:

> The reason is that, as those who practice good by their self-power lack the mind to rely wholly on the Other-Power, they are not in accordance with the Original Vow of Amida ... Amida made His Vow out of compassion for us who are full of evil passions, and who are unable to set ourselves free from *saṃsāra* by any practice. Since the purpose of His Vow is to have evil persons attain Buddhahood, the evil person who trusts the Other-Power is especially the one who has the right cause for Birth in the Pure Land.[25]

Second, Pure Land teaching rejects various forms of Buddhist practice as invalid for one's salvation, and advocates as the way of salvation the *nembutsu*, that is, recitation of the name of Amida through faith. Shinran, however, radicalized this Pure Land teaching and rejected even the recitation of *nembutsu* as a remainder of human practice (self-power), emphasizing the single *nembutsu* in pure faith, or pure faith alone even before uttering *nembutsu,* as a necessary and sufficient requirement of one's salvation. While Hōnen stated his position as *Nembutsu ihon,* 'the *nembutsu* is the foundation of salvation,' Shinran advocated his position as *Shinjin ihon,* 'faith is the foundation of salvation.' For Shinran, one can be truly saved only through pure faith in the absolute other power of Amida's original vow, and the *nembutsu* is not a requirement of, but an expression of gratitude for, salvation through the unconditional mercy of Amida Buddha.

Third, Shinran emphasized *Sokutokuōjō,* 'the immediate attainment of rebirth' in this actual world rather than rebirth in the Pure Land after death.

In the *Yuishinshōmoni,* Shinran stated:

Sokutokuōjō means that since one attains faith, therefore he is reborn. 'Therefore he is reborn' means that he abides in the state of non-retrogression. To abide in the state of non-retrogression means, namely, that it is determined that one is in the rank of the company of the truly assured. It is also called *Jōtōshōkaku* 'to be in the state equivalent to right enlightenment.'[26]

Accordingly, as is often pointed out, we see a great affinity between Shinran's Jōdo Shinshū and Christianity, especially as represented by Paul and Luther. But, we must also pay due attention to the subtle difference between them.

First, both Jōdo Shinshū (Shinran) and Christianity (Paul and Luther) emphasize faith alone for salvation. But in Christianity, it is faith in the death and resurrection of Jesus Christ as the revelation of God's redemptive love which is definitely a historical event, while in Jōdo Shinshū it is faith in the original vow of Amida Buddha to save all beings, which is transhistorical reality.

Second, both Christianity and Jōdo Shinshū focus on one deity, that is, Jesus Christ and Amida Buddha respectively. But Jesus Christ is the incarnation through *kenosis* of the second person of the Trinity. His root and source is God the Father, who defines himself as 'I am that I am' ('*ehyeh 'asher 'ehyeh* – '*hayah*' as the root of '*ehyeh*' means to become, to work, and to happen). On the other hand, Amida Buddha is a personal manifestation of Dharmakāya (the Body of Truth or Buddha nature itself) which is without form and without color – a personal revelation of Śūnyatā (Emptiness) through its self-emptying nature.

Third, both Christianity and Jōdo Shinshū emphasize salvation in this actual world. Paul says: 'though our outward man is decaying, yet our inward man is renewed day by day,'[27] and Shinran emphasizes *Sokutokuōjō*, immediate attainment of rebirth. However, in Christianity, one's resurrection is ultimately an eschatological event which will happen at the end of history, but in Jōdo Shinshū, the fulfillment of one's rebirth is not an eschatological event but is realized after each one's death.

Although these three points would bear further discussion, in comparison with Christianity, Jōdo Shinshū is less future-oriented and more absolute present-oriented because of Amida's transhistorical character. This difference entails an important difference in the understanding of transformation in these two religions.

JAPANESE TERMS AND TITLES

jiri—rita — enman	自利利他円満	*rekishi — kyūmei*	歴史究明
jōtōshōkaku	成等正覚	*satori*	悟り
koji — kyūmei	己事究明	*sekai — kyūmei*	世界究明
mappō	末法	*shinjin ihon*	信心為本
nembutsu	念佛	*sokutokuōjō*	即得往生
nembutsu ihon	念佛為本	*Yuishinshōmoni*	唯信鈔文意
ōjō	往生	*zaigō*	罪業

15

Religious Tolerance and Human Rights: A Buddhist Perspective

In February 1985, I was asked by Professor Leonard Swidler to submit, from a Buddhist standpoint, a paper on the subject, 'Religious Tolerance and Human Rights,' and to present it at the Conference on Human Rights. Upon carefully reading the attached documents explaining the issues to be discussed at this conference and their implications, I felt I must attempt to make a response for two reasons. First, the issue of the relationship between human rights and religious freedom is one of the most urgent issues in contemporary human society; it is an issue that religious thinkers in particular can no longer ignore. Second, this issue derives fundamentally from the problematic innate in human existence and in the nature of 'religion' itself. Consequently, the problem of the relationship between religious tolerance and human rights cannot be easily resolved, however urgent the issue may be.

From a standpoint different from that of Semitic religions predominantly discussed in the United Nations documents sent to me, perhaps Buddhism may contribute something new to consideration of this dilemma. The Buddhist view of 'human rights' is significantly different from the views of its Western counterparts, as is the Buddhist attitude toward 'religious tolerance.' Since in most cases up to now both the notions of 'human rights' and 'religious tolerance' have been understood in terms of Western categories and have been discussed mainly from the Judeo-Christian-Islamic point of view, the Buddhist approach to these issues may help open up a new vista and may help provide an entirely new foundation to remedy serious conflicts in the contemporary world.

I

Before elucidating the Buddhist understanding of 'human rights' and 'religious tolerance,' let me try to clarify the differences between the two main types of world religions. Western scholars often discuss religion in terms of a contrast between ethical religion and natural religion (C. P. Tile), prophetic religion and mystical religion (F. Heiler), and monotheistic religion and pantheistic religion (W. F. Albright, A. Lang), the first in each pair referring to Judeo-Christian-Islamic religions and the second to most of the Oriental religions.

This kind of bifurcation has been set forth by Western scholars with such 'Western' religions as Judaism, Christianity, and Islam as the standard of judgment. Consequently, non-Semitic Oriental religions are often not only lumped together under a certain single category despite their rich variety but also grasped from the outside without any penetration into their inner religious core. Unlike the Semitic religions, which most Western scholars recognize as having a clear common character, such Oriental religions as Hinduism, Buddhism, Confucianism, Taoism, and Shintoism exhibit significant differences in their religious essences and, hence, cannot legitimately be classified into a single category. To bring this point into sharper focus, I will take up Buddhism alone from among the Oriental religions and contrast it with Judaism, Christianity, and Islam.

Most Western scholars correctly characterize Judaism, Christianity, and Islam not as natural, mystical, and pantheistic religions, but as ethical, prophetic, and monotheistic religions. All three religions are based on the One Absolute God: Yahweh in Judaism, God the Father in Christianity, and Allah in Islam. In each of these religions the One God is believed to be a personal God who is essentially transcendent to human beings but whose will is revealed to human beings through prophets and who commands people to observe certain ethico-religious principles. Although we should not overlook some conspicuous differences in emphasis among these three religions, we can say with justification that they are ethical, prophetic, and monotheistic religions.

In contrast, Buddhism does not talk about the One Absolute God who is essentially transcendent to human beings. Instead, it teaches the Dharma, which is *pratītya-samutpāda*, the law of 'dependent co-origination' or conditional co-production. This teaching emphasizes that everything *in* and *beyond* the universe is interdependent, co-arising, and co-ceasing (not only temporarily but also logically): nothing exists independently or can be said to be self-existing. Accordingly, in Buddhism everything without exception is relative, relational, non-substantial, and changeable. This is why Gautama Buddha, the founder of Buddhism, did not accept the age-old

Vedāntic notion of Brahman, which is believed to be the eternal, unchangeable reality underlying the universe. For a similar reason, Buddhism cannot accept the monotheistic notion of One Absolute God as the ultimate reality, but advocates *śūnyatā* (emptiness) and *tathatā* (suchness or as-it-is-ness) as the ultimate reality.

In Buddhism, even the divine or the holy does not exist by itself, independent of and transcendent to the human or the secular. Just as the human does not exist apart from the divine, the divine does not exist apart from the human. The divine and the human co-arise and co-cease and are entirely interrelated and interdependent. The divine which exists by itself, or the God who exists alone, is considered in Buddhism to be an unreal entity. Again, 'one' does not exist apart from 'many,' just as 'many' is inconceivable apart from 'one.' 'One' and 'many' always co-arise and co-cease. Accordingly, an absolute 'One' which is aloof from 'many' is just as much a conceptual construction as a 'many' which is unrelated to the 'One.' In Buddhism the ultimate reality is neither the divine God who is absolutely one nor human beings who are multitudinous but the relationality or 'dependent co-origination' of everything, including the relationality between one and many, God and humans.

From a Buddhist perspective, human conflicts and human-induced suffering derive from ignorance of this law of 'dependent co-origination' and the resultant self-centeredness. Accordingly, as the way of salvation from human suffering, Buddhism emphasizes the necessity of awakening to the law of 'dependent co-origination' by breaking through the ignorance innate in human existence, that is, self-centeredness and attachment to anything, divine or human. Above all, those forms of attachment which absolutize the divine or the holy as something substantial, self-existing, eternal, and unchangeable must be overcome. Further, awakening to the law of 'dependent co-origination' indicates awakening to the original nature of everything in the universe – and that awakening is simultaneously the awakening to one's own original nature or one's own true Self, for, without the awakening to one's own original nature, awakening to the original nature of everything in the universe is not possible.

In short, Buddhism fundamentally does not discuss a personal God, divine revelation, prophets, or salvation through faith; rather, it affirms the law of 'dependent co-origination,' self-awakening, the practice of meditation, and emancipation through non-attachment. Accordingly, I would like to characterize Judaism, Christianity, and Islam as 'religions of divine revelation' and Buddhism as a 'religion of

Self-Awakening.' Expressed differently, the former are 'religions of God,' whereas the latter is a 'religion of the true Self.'

II

To provide a basis for the discussion of the Buddhist view of 'human rights' and 'religious tolerance' we must clarify three points derived directly from the law of 'dependent co-origination.'

1. *Anātman or no-self.* Although the law of 'dependent co-origination' denies the self-existence and unchangeable substantiality of everything, including the divine or the holy, such interdependency and relationality are inconceivable without recognizing the particularity or individuality of the elements, human or non-human, which constitute that interdependency. Apart from the particularity or individuality of both sides of the relation, the very notion of relationality and 'dependent co-origination' are not possible. An emphasis on relationality without a recognition of the individuality of the constituent elements will entail relativism which finally culminates in a nihilistic anarchism. This kind of relationality is static and merely formal, and it thus loses the dynamism between individuality and interdependency. However, if the particularity or individuality of either of the sides of the relation is substantialized or absolutized, the relationality or 'dependent co-origination' will be destroyed. The law of 'dependent co-origination' is possible only when each element involved in the relationship has a distinguishable particularity which is, however, non-substantial. This means that, due to the absence of unchangeable substantiality or enduring selfhood, each entity is entirely interdependent without losing its own particularity. Accordingly, the key point of the law of 'dependent co-origination' lies in the realization of the absence of unchangeable substantiality or enduring selfhood, that is, the realization of no-self which is traditionally called *Anātman*.

2. *Tathatā or suchness (as-it-is-ness).* When everything is grasped in terms of 'dependent co-origination' and thus is understood to be without enduring selfhood, the situation is very different from that in monotheistic religion. In monotheistic religion, everything is understood, for instance, to be a creation of the One Absolute God, the creator. In this case, everything or everyone in the universe is equal before God, and, at least in Christianity, the resurrection after death is

a resurrection in the form of a spiritual body (*soma pneumatikon*) which is the transformation of the physical body without the loss of identity: 'Do you not know that your body is a temple of the Holy Spirit within you which you have from God?' (I Cor. 6:19).

The individual is not absorbed in the divine at death but continues to be the same individual preserving his or her identity in a different mode.[1] This is because Spirit is the principle of individualization. Unlike Judaism and Islam, Christianity has a unique doctrine of resurrection in which distinction and identity of an individual person go together. In Christianity, however, this togetherness of distinction and identity is supported by the Holy Spirit of the One God. Accordingly, however dialectical the relationship between distinction and identity may be, it is understood or believed in within the framework of the One God, who calls people into fellowship with God. This implies at least the following two points. First, since the relationship between distinction and identity is realized in terms of the One Absolute God, both distinction and identity, strictly speaking, are not fully or thoroughgoingly grasped as such. Both distinction and identity – and their dialectical relationship – can be thoroughgoingly realized only by breaking through the absolute Oneness of God. Second, in Christianity, the dialectical relationship between distinction and identity is applied only to a human being, not to individual things in the universe. This second point relates to the first point.

In this regard, Buddhism diverges from Christianity. In Buddhism, in which the One Absolute God is absent, not only all persons but also all things in the universe are thoroughly realized in such a way as to maintain their particularity or individuality without any transcendent, one absolute principle; yet, they are realized to be completely equal in the sense that regardless of their distinction all are equally and respectively grasped in their particularity or in their as-it-is-ness (suchness). For instance, an oak tree is thoroughly an oak tree and a pine tree thoroughly a pine tree in their distinctiveness; yet, an oak tree and a pine tree are equal in each one's being grasped in its own particularity or in its own suchness. A fish is thoroughly a fish and a bird thoroughly a bird in their distinctiveness; yet, a fish and a bird are equal in terms of each one's being grasped in its as-it-is-ness. Again, I am really I, and you are really you, with regard to our particular individuality; yet, you and I are equal in that each of us is realized in our own individuality and in our own personality. Exactly the same is true with the divine and the human. The divine is thoroughly the divine and the human absolutely the human; yet, the divine and the human are equal in the sense that both of them are equally apprehended in their essential characteristic or in their 'suchness.'

Accordingly, *tathatā* or suchness (as-it-is-ness) includes complete distinction and complete equality, full distinctiveness and full sameness, dynamically and without contradiction. This is the reason Mahāyāna Buddhism often states that *shabetsu-soku-byōdō: byōdō-soku-shabetsu*; that is, distinction as it is sameness; sameness as it is distinction (distinction *sive* equality; equality *sive* distinction). This dynamic relationship between distinction and equality extends not only to human persons but also more universally to nature and God as well. Such a dynamic relationship is possible because the One Absolute God is absent, and everything – including nature, humankind, and God – is realized without independent enduring selfhood or fixed unchanging substance.

3. *Madhyamā pratipad or the Middle Way*. Gautama Buddha rejected both extremes of sensual indulgence and asceticism and espoused the Middle Way as the true method of religious practice. To him, this meant the Noble Eightfold Path of right view, right thinking, right speech, right action, right livelihood, right effort, right mindfulness, and right concentration.

The 'middleness' of the Middle Way does not mean a mere compromise or a middle point between two extremes, as the Aristotelian notion of *to meson* might suggest. Instead, the Middle Way breaks through the two extremes by overcoming the dualistic standpoint as such, and it points to the non-dual ultimate reality which is realized by the Buddha and every other awakened self.

This point will become clearer when we consider the Eightfold Negation set forth by Nāgārjuna, a founder of Mahāyāna Buddhism. Interpreting Buddha's notion of Middle Way more radically than Gautama, Nāgārjuna advocated the Eightfold Negation: neither birth nor extinction; neither permanence nor impermanence; neither unity nor diversity; neither coming nor going. In this connection, as I have stated elsewhere:

> There is no primacy of one concept over the other in these four pairs. In Nāgārjuna, the real nature of existence (*tathatā*) manifests itself when fixed concepts such as birth and extinction are removed. Hence the Eightfold Negation is synonymous with the Middle Path.[2]

In the same book I stated further:

> Nāgārjuna not only repudiated the eternalist view, which takes phenomena to be real just as they are and essentially unchangeable: he also rejected as illusory the opposite nihilistic view which emphasizes emptiness and non-being as true Reality. This double negation in terms of 'neither–nor' is the pivotal point for the realization of Mahāyāna Emptiness which is never a sheer emptiness but rather Fullness.[3]

III

Next, I would like to discuss the Buddhist view of religious liberty and human rights. Some Western scholars say that Buddhism is a tolerant religion. Strictly speaking, however, this statement does not hit the mark of Buddhism. The term 'tolerance' is a counterconcept of 'intolerance,' which implies active (often violent) refusal to allow others to have or put into practice beliefs different from one's own. Since Buddhism is not a monotheistic religion – for it is based on the realization of the suchness or as-it-is-ness of everything in the universe – in Buddhism the active refusal of allowing others to have beliefs different from one's own is absent, while the positive recognition and approval of others' beliefs in their different modes is clearly present. Buddhism cannot be defined by the term 'tolerant' in the Western sense because it originally stands on a dimension transcending the duality of 'tolerant' and 'intolerant.' The 'tolerant' attitude of Buddhism is nothing other than an outcome of Buddhism's more fundamental attitude of 'suchness' or 'as-it-is-ness.' In this connection one may distinguish negative from positive tolerance, the former referring to tolerance in the Western sense, the latter to tolerance in the Buddhist sense. Since the realization of everything's suchness or as-it-is-ness is itself the Buddhist faith, the deeper the Buddhist faith becomes the more tolerant the attitude toward other faiths. In Buddhism, deep faith and true tolerance do not exclude one another but go together. This fundamental attitude is applied not only to different beliefs within Buddhism but also to different views and beliefs of non-Buddhist religions and ideologies.

The basic Buddhist attitude toward different beliefs within Buddhism is not to reject, denounce, or punish them as heresy, but rather to evaluate them critically as different views and to subsume them into its own doctrinal system.

In his essay 'Heresy,' T. O. Ling wrote:

> Heresy is primarily a Western religious concept: there is no exact Buddhist equivalent. The nearest approximation is *diṭṭhi* (Pali), *dṛṣṭi* (Skt), literally a view, usually a 'wrong' view, that is due not to reason but to craving or desire (*tanhā*). The most serious form of *diṭṭhi* is to assert the reality and permanence of the individual human ego, i.e., the assertion of *ātman*. Since the Western concept of heresy implies an orthodoxy capable of denouncing heresy and willing to do so, the approximation of Buddhist *diṭṭhi* to Western heresy here comes to an end, since Buddhism has no authoritative hierarchy, and no sacramental sanctions. Even the most serious form of *diṭṭhi*, assertion of reality of a permanent individual human 'self,' was maintained by certain Buddhists known as Pudgala-Vādins. They were regarded by all other Buddhist schools of thought as weaker brethren, and in error: but they maintained their existence and monastic institutions; as late as 7th cent. CE, Pudgala-Vādin monks amounted to about a quarter of the total number of Buddhist monks in India. On the whole, the attitude of other schools seem to have been that more prolonged meditation would eventually cause them to see error involved in this view, and its abandonment.[4]

In China and Japan, along with the establishment of various doctrinal systems and sectarian organizations, serious debates often took place among different Buddhist schools. Nichiren, a Japanese Buddhist leader of the thirteenth century, attacked Esoteric Buddhism, the Vinaya School, Zen, and particularly Pure Land Buddhism. His contemporary followers, who constitute the sect Nichiren-shōshū, are known for their aggressive attitude toward other Buddhist schools. On the whole, however, throughout the long history of Buddhism there has been no burning to death or any form of civil punishment due to different beliefs within Buddhism. Different views of the Dharma have been often regarded as *upāya*, skillful means to lead immature Buddhists to the ultimate truth of Buddha-dharma.

In regard to the Buddhist attitude toward others of different faiths, the early Buddhist scriptures often emphasize, 'Do not contend (*vivada*).' They also advocate non-controversy (*rana*). Gautama

Buddha is called 'One who cast aside contention' (*ranamjaha*). It is well known that Buddha answered with silence such metaphysical questions as whether the world is eternal or not eternal, whether the world is finite or infinite, and whether the sage exists or does not exist after death. Buddha's silence on these metaphysical questions is often regarded as a form of agnosticism. For Gautama, however, concern with such metaphysical theories was unprofitable and did not tend toward religious salvation. His radically practical reason for an avoidance of commitment to any of the alternative doctrines mentioned above was brought out by Buddha himself,[5] as can be seen, for instance, in his response to the monk Malunkyaputta in the *Majjhima Nikāya*, one of the earliest Buddhist writings. After emphasizing that the religious life did not depend on the dogma that the world is eternal or not eternal, Buddha said:

> Whether the dogma obtain, Malunkyaputta, that the world is eternal, or that the world is not eternal, there still remain birth, old age, death, sorrow, lamentation, misery, grief, and despair, for the extinction of which in the present life I am prescribing .... This [dogma] profits not, nor has to go with the fundamentals of religion, nor tends to aversion, absence of passion, cessation, quiescence, the supernatural faculties, supreme wisdom, and Nirvana: therefore have I not explained it.[6]

Further, as E. A. Burtt has rightly pointed out, in the Buddha's view:

> The assertion of any such theory naturally provokes the assertion of counter theories by others; this process generates heated and contentious argument, with its accompanying unresolved hostilities and mutual recriminations. It does not promote the humble self-searching and unity of understanding that are essential if the true spiritual goal is to be reached.[7]

Buddha's attitude toward sectarian dogmatism can be seen in the following exchanges with a monk extracted from the *Sutta-Nipata*, another early Buddhist scripture:

The Enquirer:	Fixed in their pet beliefs, these diverse wranglers bawl – 'Hold this, and truth is yours;' 'Reject it, and you're lost.'

	Thus they contend, and dub opponents 'dolts' and 'fools.' Which of the lot is right, when all as experts pose?
The Lord [Buddha]:	Well, if dissent denotes a 'fool' and stupid 'dolt,' then all are fools and dolts – since each has his own view.
	Or, if each rival creed proves love and brains and wit, no 'dolts' exist – since all alike are on a par.
	I count not that as true which those affirm, who call each other 'fools' – They call each other so, because each deems his own view 'Truth.'[8]

The Buddhist attitude toward other religions may best be clarified in terms of the Middle Way. The doctrine of the Middle Way advocates the avoidance of the extremes of religious imperialism and syncretism and the extremes of violent intolerance and universalism (all-is-one-ness). The tendency toward religious imperialism is somewhat unavoidable for any religion, for religion is precisely an existential and total commitment to that which is believed to be the ultimate truth. This tendency is evident in monotheistic religions which advance the One Absolute God as the ultimate reality. The tendency toward syncretism or universalism indicates an eclectic approach which attempts to incorporate all teachings into the fold of a given religion, thereby emphasizing the feelings of universality and humanhood. This tendency is evident in pantheistic or polytheistic religions. However, as Phra Khantipalo has stated, the first danger of syncretism is that it is idle to pretend that all religions lead to the same goal: 'To try to steamroller every religion into the concept of basic sameness or "all-is-one-ness" is to ignore facts in favor of a pre-conceived ideal.' The second danger of syncretism is that 'in trying to believe in everything, one does in fact neither believe anything sincerely nor understand anything thoroughly.'[9] Universalists thus lose the essence of both their own religion and that of others.

In Buddhism, which is based on the doctrine of the Middle Way, neither the Buddha nor the great Buddhist sages said, 'My teachings alone are true.' They did not encourage persecution by religious wars, burning at the stake, massacres, or forced conversions for the sake of their own Dharma, nor did they state that all teachings are the same. In the first Suttanta of the *Digha Nikāya*, the Buddha said: 'Make a trial, find out what leads to your happiness and freedom – and what does not, reject it. What leads on to greater happiness – follow it.'

This practical and sure way of distinguishing truth amid falsehood was meant by the Buddha to be applied to his own teachings as well, for he emphasized that one ought not to believe in the authority of any teachers and masters but should believe and practice the religious truth embodied by them. This the Middle Way in action – as something practiceable, by means of which one can steer a course between blind dogma and vague eclecticism.

Because of this 'Middle Way' approach to other religions, when Buddhism was introduced to South Asia, China, Tibet, Korea, and Japan it did not eliminate or drive out native religions but sought to co-exist with them. Of course, when Buddhism was introduced to China and Japan, for instance, there were conflicts between Indian-born Buddhism and such native religions as Confucianism and Taoism in China and Shintoism in Japan. Those conflicts were not necessarily purely religious but rather were caused by the nationalistic feelings of political leaders and their followers against the newly introduced foreign religion. In China, from the fifth to tenth centuries, Buddhism was seriously persecuted four times by pro-Confucian or pro-Taoist emperors. In those persecutions Buddhism was always passive; yet it survived serious damage to its temples and priesthood. There were even those who advocated the unity of Confucianism, Taoism, and Buddhism; thus, Buddhism came to be firmly rooted in Chinese soil. In Japan there was no serious Buddhist persecution except that of the Shogun Oda Nobunaga, who destroyed Buddhist centers at Mt Hiei and Negoro and the persecution during the early years of the Meiji Restoration in the mid-nineteenth century when the government tried both to revive Shintoism as the state religion and to destroy the affinity between Buddhism and Shintoism. Most of the fourteen-century history of Buddhism in Japan, however, proves the harmonious co-existence of Buddhism with the native Japanese religion of Shintoism. In short, in spite of its universal character and profound and systematic doctrine, Buddhism did not eliminate the native religions of the countries into which it was introduced.

The Buddhist attitude toward other religions stands in marked contrast with its counterpart in monotheistic religion. When Islam moved into India, it sought to destroy Hinduism and Buddhism. When Christianity entered into the Germanic world early in the medieval ages, it overwhelmed and absorbed the native religions of the Germanic peoples. Today, in Christian Europe and England, it is scarcely possible to find native religions or folklore beliefs in their living forms as they originally existed among the Teutonic and Anglo-Saxon races.

IV

The Buddhist view of 'human rights' is significantly different from that found in the Western tradition. Strictly speaking, the exact equivalent of the phrase 'human rights' in the Western sense cannot be found anywhere in Buddhist literature. In the Western notion of 'human rights,' 'rights' are understood as pertaining only to humans; non-human creatures are either excluded or at most regarded as peripheral and secondary. 'Human rights' are understood not from the non-human or wider-than-human point of view but only from the human point of view – an anthropocentric view of human rights. By marked contrast, in Buddhism a human being is not grasped only from the human point of view, that is, not simply on an anthropocentric basis, but on a much broader trans-anthropocentric, cosmological basis. More concretely, in Buddhism human beings are grasped as a part of all sentient beings or even as a part of all beings, sentient and non-sentient, because both human and non-human beings are equally subject to transiency or impermanency. (That nothing is permanent is a basic Buddhist principle.) If this universal impermanency that is common to both human and non-human beings is done away with, the problem of life and death peculiar to human existence cannot be properly resolved. Both the Buddhist understanding of human suffering and its way of salvation are rooted in this trans-anthropocentric, cosmological dimension.

This is in sharp contrast to Judaism, Christianity, and Islam, in which the understanding of human suffering and its way of salvation are based primarily on the personal relationship between the human being and God which Martin Buber rightly described in terms of the 'I–Thou relationship.' That the Buddhist understanding of human suffering and its way of salvation are based on the trans-anthropocentric, cosmological dimension, however, does not indicate that Buddhism disregards the special significance of human beings in the universe. On the contrary, Buddhism clearly esteems the special distinctiveness of human beings in the universe, as seen in the following verse, which is usually recited by Buddhists as a preamble to the Gatha, 'The Threefold Refuge':

Hard is it to be born into human life.
We now live it.
Difficult is it to hear the teaching of the Buddha.
We now hear it.
If we do not deliver ourselves in this present life,
No hope is there ever to cross the sea of birth and death,
Let us all together, with the truest heart,
Take refuge in the three treasures!

On this verse, I have made the following comments elsewhere:

The first and second lines express the joy of being born in human form during the infinite series of varied transmigrations. The third and fourth lines reveal gratitude for being blessed with the opportunity of meeting with the teaching of the Buddha – something which very rarely happens even among men. Finally the fifth and sixth lines confess to a realization that so long as one exists as a man one can and must awaken to one's own Buddha-nature by practicing the teachings of the Buddha; otherwise one may transmigrate on through *saṃsāra* endlessly. Herein it can be seen that Buddhism takes human existence in its positive and unique aspect most seriously into consideration.[10]

As a religion, Buddhism naturally is primarily concerned with human salvation. In this sense Buddhism is not different from Semitic religions. Both Buddhism and Semitic religions are anthropocentric in that they are equally concerned with human salvation. The difference between them lies in the fact that while the basis for human salvation in Semitic religions is the personalistic relationship between the human and God, that basis in Buddhism is the trans-personal, cosmological dimension common to the human and nature: the Dharma or suchness (as-it-is-ness) of everything in the universe. In Buddhism, the human problem is grasped not only from the human point of view within the human realm but also from the much wider trans-human, cosmological point of view far beyond the human dimension. Yet it is only human beings who, alone in the universe, have self-consciousness and can thus transcend their own realm and reach the universal, cosmological dimension.

In Buddhism, 'human rights' is to be understood in this trans-anthropocentric, universal dimension. If 'human rights' is understood to indicate human rights as grasped only from an anthropocentric point of view – as is the case in the West – we cannot find its counterpart in Buddhist literature. In order to understand the Buddhist view of 'human rights' properly we should return to the problem of 'self,' since in any religion, particularly in Buddhism, human rights and human freedom cannot by legitimately grasped without a proper understanding of the problem of self. Self is not an absolute but a relative entity. As soon as one talks about self one already presupposes the existence of the other. There can be no self apart from the other, and vice versa. Self and the other are entirely interdependent and relational.

Self is not an independent, self-existing, enduring, substantial entity. Nevertheless, because we human beings have self-consciousness and a strong disposition toward self-love and self-attachment, we often reify it as if it were an independent, enduring, substantial entity. Self-centeredness is simply an outcome of this reification or substantialization of the self. Buddhism emphasizes that this reification of the self and its resultant self-centeredness are the root-source of evil and human suffering. Accordingly, as a way of salvation, Buddhism teaches the necessity of realizing the non-substantiality of the self, that is, of realizing no-self or *anātman*.

The Buddhist notion of no-self, however, does not preclude human selfhood in the *relative* sense. It is undeniable that we come to a realization of the 'self-identity' of ourselves through memories from our childhood and through interaction with friends and other fellow beings. I am I and not you; you are you and not me. Hence, there is a clear distinction between self and other and, thereby, a clear realization of self-identity or selfhood. The question in this regard, however, is whether this self-identity or selfhood is *absolutely* independent, enduring, and substantial. The answer must be 'no.' For there is no 'I' apart from 'you,' just as there is no 'you' apart from 'I.' As soon as we talk about 'I,' we already and categorically presuppose the existence of 'you,' and vice versa. Accordingly, although we have self-identity in a relative sense, we do not have it in the absolute sense. I am I in the relative sense, but I am not I in the absolute sense. The notion of absolute self-identity or substantial, enduring selfhood is an unreal, conceptual construction created by human self-consciousness. Buddhism calls it *māyā*, or illusion, and emphasizes the importance of awakening to no-self by doing away with this illusory understanding of the self.

Once we awaken to our own no-selfhood, we also awaken to the no-selfhood of everything and everyone in the universe. In other words, we awaken to the fact that, just like ourselves, nothing in the universe has any fixed, substantial selfhood, even while maintaining relative selfhood. So, on the relative level, all have our own distinctive selfhood; yet, on the absolute level, we have no fixed, substantial selfhood but, rather, equality and solidarity in terms of the realization of no-self. Accordingly, from an absolute standpoint, we can say that, because of the absence of substantial selfhood, I am not I, and you are not you; thereby, I am you, and you are me. We are different relatively but equal absolutely, interfusing with one another, even while retaining our distinct identity. The same is true with the self and nature, and with the self and the divine. The self and nature are different from one another on the relative level, but on the absolute level they are equal and interfuse with one another because of the lack of any fixed, substantial selfhood. Consequently, nature is not merely a resource for the human self; it is grasped in sympathetic relationship with the self. Finally, and most importantly, the self and the divine – whether one calls it God, *das Heilige*, *Brahman*, or *Nirvāṇa* – are, relatively speaking, essentially different from one another; yet, absolutely speaking, the self and the divine are not different but equal, interfusing and interpenetrating with one another. This is the case because even the divine is understood here without independent, enduring, substantial selfhood.

Clearly, on this point Buddhism and monotheistic religions are radically different, and this difference has important ramifications when we come to the crucial point of the problem of religious tolerance. In Judaism, Christianity, and Islam the divine is the One Absolute God who, being the ruler of the universe, is free-willed and self-affirmative and essentially transcendent to human beings and nature. The self-affirmative character of Yahweh God is clearly seen when Yahweh's 'Self' is revealed to Moses on Mount Sinai by saying, 'I am that I am' (Ex. 24:12, 34) (the original Hebrew of this phrase, *'ehyeh 'asher 'ehyeh*, means 'I will be what I will be'). Further, in the Ten Commandments that Yahweh gave to Moses it was emphasized that, 'You shall have no other gods before me' (Ex. 20:3).

In Israelite religions this strongly monotheistic commandment comes first among the Ten Commandments. Buddhism has a Decalogue very similar to that of the Israelite religion, emphasizing that, 'You shall not kill, shall not steal, shall not lie, shall not commit adultery,' and so forth. In the Buddhist Ten Commandments, however, there is no equivalent to the first commandment of the Decalogue – 'You shall have no other gods before me.' Instead, the first of the Buddhist Ten Commandments is 'Not to destroy life,' and this commandment refers not only to human life but also to the life of all sentient beings. In the Judeo-Christian tradition the problem of human rights and human duty to other people must be considered in relation to the exclusive commandment of the supreme God, whereas in Buddhism the same problem should be grasped in relation to all living beings in the universe. This difference entails that in Buddhism conflict between human rights and religious freedom becomes much less serious than in Israelite religions. It also leads to a different attitude toward the problem of the environment, another burning issue of our time. Under the commandment 'Not to destroy any life,' the rights of animals and plants are as equally recognized as are human rights. Not only is nature subordinate to human beings, but human beings are also subordinate to nature.

V

How can Buddhism contribute to the issue of 'religious tolerance and human rights'? I would like to offer Buddhist solutions to this problem in three ways.

1. *Elimination of the attachment to doctrine and dogma.* No religion is without doctrine, but the attitudes toward doctrine are not the same. When doctrine is regarded as authoritative and binding upon all the faithful, it turns into 'dogma.' 'Dogma' is a fixed form of belief formulated in creeds and articles by religious institutional authority for acceptance by its followers. Within Christianity, the Roman Catholic Church still promulgates dogmas, while Protestant churches have 'confessions' in which the faithful confess what they believe from the heart rather than submit to an imposed, external doctrinal statement (dogma) – though the Protestant 'confessions' are also interpreted 'dogmatically' by some. When dogma is emphasized, schism often takes place within a religion, and opposition occurs among other religions. Conflict – even religious war – erupts. Religions which are based on divine revelation and which emphasize exclusive faith in the revealed truth are frequently liable to the intolerance generated by fixed forms of belief.

By contrast, Buddhism, which is not based on divine revelation but on self-awakening, has no dogma. Although Buddhism has various forms of doctrine – such as the Four Noble Truths, the Eightfold Path, and the twelve-link chain of causation – doctrines are not regarded in Buddhism as something essential. The Buddha himself said: 'My teaching is like a raft to cross the stream of life and death so as to reach the other shore of enlightenment. Once you reach the other shore there is no need to carry the raft.'[11] From the Buddhist standpoint, what is important for religion is not doctrine – to say nothing of dogma – but one's existential commitment to the religious truth underlying the doctrinal formulation. If we eliminate attachment to dogma and return to the religious truth as the root-source of doctrine, we can largely overcome schisms and religious wars and become more tolerant not only within our own religion but also toward other religions.

2. *Emphasis on wisdom rather than justice.* In the Judeo-Christian tradition, God is believed to have the attributes of justice or righteousness as the judge, as well as love or mercy as the forgiver. God is the fountain of justice, so everything God does may be relied upon as just. Since God's verdict is absolutely just, human righteousness may be defined in terms of God's judgment.

The notion of justice or righteousness is a double-edged sword. On the one hand it aids in keeping everything in the right order, but on the other hand it establishes clear-cut distinctions between the righteous and the unrighteous, promising the former eternal bliss but condemning the latter to eternal punishment. Accordingly, if justice or righteousness is the sole principle of judgment or is too strongly emphasized, it creates serious disunion and schism among people. This disunion is unrestorable because it is a result of divine judgment.

Although his religious background was Jewish, Jesus went beyond such a strong emphasis on divine justice and preached the indifference of God's love. Speaking of God the Father he said: 'He makes his sun rise on the evil and on the good, and sends rain on the just and on the unjust' (Mt. 5:45). Thus he emphasized, 'Love your enemies and pray for those who persecute you, so that you may be sons of your Father who is in heaven' (Mt. 5:44). Nevertheless, in the Judeo-Christian tradition the notion of divine election is persistently evident. The Old Testament preaches God's choice of Israel from among all the nations of the earth to be God's people in the possession of a covenant of privilege and blessing (Dt. 4:37, 7:6, 1 Kgs. 3:8; Is. 44:1–2). In the New Testament, divine election is a gracious and merciful election. Nevertheless, this election is rather restricted, for, as the New Testament clearly states, 'Many are called, but few are chosen' (Mt. 22:14). Thus 'the terms [election or elect] always imply differentiation whether viewed on God's part or as privilege on the part of men.'[12] In Christianity the notion of the 'Elect of God' often overshadows the 'indifference of God's love.' If I am not mistaken, this is largely related to the emphasis on justice or righteousness.

While Christianity talks much about love, Buddhism stresses compassion. In Christianity, however, love is accompanied by justice. Love without justice is not regarded as true love. In Buddhism, compassion always goes with wisdom. Compassion without wisdom is not understood to be true compassion. Like the Christian notion of righteousness, the Buddhist notion of wisdom indicates the clarification of the distinction or differentiation of things in the universe. Unlike the Christian notion of justice, however, the Buddhist notion of wisdom does not entail judgment or election. Buddhist wisdom implies the affirmation or recognition of everything and everyone in their distinctiveness or in their suchness. Further, as noted above, the notion of justice creates an irreparable split between the just and the unjust, the righteous and the unrighteous, whereas the notion of wisdom evokes the sense of equality and solidarity. Again, justice, when carried to its final conclusion, often results in punishment, conflict, revenge, and even war, whereas wisdom entails rapprochement, conciliation, harmony, and peace. Love and justice are like water and fire: although both are necessary, they go together with difficulty. Compassion and wisdom are like heat and light: although different, they work together complementarily.

The Judeo-Christian tradition does not lack the notion of wisdom. In the Hebrew Bible, wisdom literature such as Job, Proverbs, and Ecclesiastes occupies an important portion in which *hokma* (wisdom) frequently appears. This term refers to both human knowledge and divine wisdom. In the latter case, as a wisdom given by God it enables the human to lead a good, true, and satisfying life through keeping God's commandments. In the New Testament, *sophia* is understood to be an attribute of God (Lk. 11:49), the revelation of the divine will to people (1 Cor. 2:4–7). But, most remarkably, Jesus as the Christ is identified with the wisdom of God because he is believed in as the ultimate source of all Christian wisdom (1 Cor. 1:30). Nevertheless, in the Judeo-Christian tradition as a whole, the wisdom aspect of God has been neglected in favor of the justice aspect of God. Is it not important and terribly necessary now to emphasize the wisdom aspect of God rather than the justice aspect of God, in order to solve the conflict within a religion as well as among religions?

3. *A new understanding of monotheism.* Above, I criticized monotheistic religion in that, due to its strong emphasis on the One Absolute God, it is apt to be exclusive and intolerant. To any religion, however, the realization of the oneness of ultimate reality is important, because religion is expected to offer an integral and total – rather than fragmental or partial – salvation from human suffering. Even so-called polytheistic religion does not believe in various deities without order, but it often worships a certain supreme deity as a ruler over a hierarchy of innumerable gods. Further, the three major deities often constitute a trinity – as exemplified by the Hindu notion of *trimurti*, the threefold deity of Brahman, Visnu, and Siva. Such a notion of trinity in polytheism also implies a tendency toward a unity of diversity – a tendency toward oneness.

This means that in any religion, especially in higher religion, the realization of the Oneness of ultimate reality is crucial. Yet, the realization of Oneness necessarily entails exclusiveness, intolerance, and religious imperialism, which cause conflict and schism within a given religion and among the various religions. This is a very serious dilemma which no higher religion can escape. How can we believe in the Oneness of the ultimate reality in our own religion without falling into exclusive intolerance and religious imperialism toward other faiths? What kind of Oneness of ultimate reality can solve that dilemma and open up a dimension in which positive tolerance and peaceful coexistence are possible among religions, each of which is based on One Absolute reality?

In this connection I would like to distinguish two kinds of oneness: the first monistic, the second non-dualistic. It is my contention that not the former but the latter kind of oneness may solve this dilemma. How are monistic and non-dualistic oneness different from one another?

First, monistic oneness is realized by distinguishing itself and setting itself apart from dualistic twoness and pluralistic manyness; it is thus still dualistically related to dualistic twoness and pluralistic manyness. Monism excludes dualism and pluralism and, therefore, stands in opposition to them. Accordingly, monistic oneness is neither truly monistic nor true oneness. In order to realize true oneness we must go not only beyond dualism and pluralism but also beyond monistic oneness itself. *Then* we can realize non-dualistic oneness, because at that point we are completely free from any form of duality, including both the duality between monism and dualism and the duality between monism and pluralism. When we overcome monistic oneness we come to a point which is neither one nor two nor many but which is appropriately referred to as 'zero.' Since the 'zero' is free from any form of duality, true oneness can be realized through the realization of 'zero.' Monistic oneness is a kind of oneness which lacks the realization of 'zero,' whereas non-dualistic oneness is a kind of oneness which is based on the realization of 'zero.'

Though we should not confuse monism with monotheism, problems involved in monistic oneness in relation to dualistic twoness and pluralistic manyness may be applied to monotheism as well.

Buddhism often emphasizes the oneness of body and mind, the oneness of life and death, the oneness of good and evil, and the identity of *samsara* and *nirvāṇa*, Buddha and sentient beings. It also talks about *ekacitta* (one dharma Mind), *ekalapsana* (one Nature), *ekayāna* (one Vehicle), and the like. It appears to be quite monistic or 'mono-theistic' from a surface perspective. In view of the difference between monistic oneness and non-dualistic oneness as described above, however, it is clear that the Buddhist notion of oneness is not monistic, but non-dualistic. As stated before, Gautama Buddha rejected the age-old Vedāntic notion of Brahman as the sole and enduring reality underlying the universe. Instead, he advocated the law of 'dependent co-origination' and no-selfhood and the non-substantiality of everything in the universe, including the divine and the human. Even the notion of Buddha is non-substantial without enduring, fixed selfhood. Rather, one who awakens to the non-substantiality and no-selfhood of everything is called a Buddha.

Nirvāṇa, which is often regarded as the goal of Buddhist life, is not really the goal to be reached as the end of life. Mahāyāna Buddhism emphasizes, 'Do not abide in *samsāra* or *nirvāṇa*.' One should not abide in *samsāra*, the endless process of transmigration, but, through the realization of wisdom, should attain *nirvāṇa*, the blissful freedom from transmigration. However, if one remains in *nirvāṇa*, one may enjoy the bliss but forget the suffering of his or her fellow beings who are still involved in the process of *samsāra*. Thus it is necessary 'not to abide in *nirvāṇa*' by overcoming the attachment to *nirvāṇa*. *Nirvāṇa* should not be attached to as if it were a substantial, fixed, enduring entity. In order to fulfill compassion toward one's fellow beings, one should not abide in *nirvāṇa* but return to *samsāra*. This means that true *nirvāṇa* in Mahāyāna Buddhism does not lie either in *samsāra* or in *nirvāṇa* in a fixed sense of the terms but in a dynamic movement between *samsāra* and *nirvāṇa* without any attachment to either, without any reification of either. Accordingly, Mahāyāna sutras, particularly the *Prajñāpāramitā Sūtra*, emphasize detachment from the sacred realm. In a sense this sutra places greater emphasis on the harmfulness of attachment to the sacred realm than that of attachment to the secular realm. It stresses the necessity of detachment from the 'religious' life. This is simply because the attachment to the divine as something substantial is a hindrance for true salvation and because the divine which is substantialized and objectified cannot be the true divine. Yet, Buddhism talks about one Mind, one Nature, and one Dharma. This oneness, however, is not oneness before the realization of 'zero' but oneness beyond or through the realization of 'zero.' In short, it is not monistic oneness but non-dualistic oneness. In the long history of Buddhism we have had troubles from time to time when we deviated from this non-dualistic oneness in our faith.

When the divine, God or Buddha, is believed to be self-affirmative, self-existing, enduring, and substantial, the divine becomes author-itative, commanding, and intolerant. On the contrary, when the divine, God or Buddha, is believed to be self-negating, relational, and non-substantial, the divine becomes compassionate, all-loving, and tolerant. I believe all three monotheistic religions (Judaism, Christianity, and Islam) preach the love of God while emphasizing the Absolute Oneness of God. If our friends of these three religions place more emphasis on the self-negating, non-substantial aspect of their 'God' than on God's self-affirmative authoritative aspect, that is, if the Oneness of God in these monotheistic religions is grasped in terms of non-dualistic oneness rather than in terms of monotheistic oneness, or not as one before the realization of 'zero,' but as one beyond the realization of 'zero,' while thoroughly maintaining their faith in the One Absolute God, they may then overcome serious conflicts with other faiths. In this case, as a correlative attribute of God's love and mercy, the wisdom aspect of God must be more emphasized than the justice aspect of God.

This was my humble proposal to the conference as a Buddhist remedy to the problem of the religious intolerance and human rights. In conclusion, I quote the following words of Buddha:

> Not by hatred is hatred appeased:
> Hatred is appeased by the renouncing of hatred.
> It is so conquered only by love
> This is a law eternal.[13]

Part Four
Zen and Japanese Culture

16

Shinto and Buddhism: The Two Major Religions of Japan

It is inevitably necessary, for understanding Japanese culture, to have a sufficient understanding of Japanese religions, especially Shinto and Buddhism. This is somewhat similar to the case of Western culture, which can be understood well only with a good understanding of Hellenism and Judeo-Christian tradition. Western culture has developed like a rope closely interwoven with two strands – Hellenism and Judeo-Christian tradition. Similarly, Japanese culture has developed in such a way that Shinto and Buddhism have been closely interwoven, although Confucianism has also played an important part; and, after the Meiji Restoration (1868), the introduction of Western culture and civilization into Japan has been still another element. In Western culture, Hellenism and Judeo-Christian tradition, and in Japan, Shinto and Buddhism have been the two main sources upon which each culture has been built up. As for the comparison between Western and Japanese cultures, however, I will not say more than this. For the nature and mutual relationship between Hellenism and the Judeo-Christian tradition and that of Shinto and Buddhism have more differences than affinities.

While Shinto and Buddhism are the two main spiritual traditions out of which Japanese culture has been created, the origins of these two traditions are different. Shinto is the indigenous religion of Japan and is as old as Japanese people. By contrast, Buddhism was originally a foreign religion to the Japanese. Born in India about the fifth century BC, Buddhism was introduced to Japan by way of China and Korea early in the sixth century AD. The so-called Shinto around that time was not a formal 'religion' in the modern sense, but the very way of life for ancient Japanese people, which included their views of the world and of life, and which had no official scriptures, no institutional organization, nor a particular founder. It was a basic way of life in every sense, including spiritual and material aspects, that had been realized by Japanese people in their natural surroundings through the ages from remote antiquity.

The relationship of Shinto and the Japanese may be said to be like the relationship of Judaism and the Hebrews and of Hinduism and the Indians. These three religions and three nations are respectively so closely related to one another that even a contemporary Japanese, Jew or Indian who rejects his or her own religious tradition is not free from its ethos in the depths of his or her heart. These religions, however, are, by their nature, not widely applicable to a nation other than that of their original birthplace. Scholars call this type of religion a 'national religion', while they call Buddhism, Islam, and Christianity 'world religions', because of their super-national, universal character. This being so, Shinto is a national religion which originated in Japan and is peculiar to the Japanese people.

On the other hand, Buddhism is a religion which arose from ancient Hinduism, broke through its national framework and thereby obtained a super-national, universal character. In this respect Christianity is not different from Buddhism. Originating in Judaism, Christianity broke through its national framework and came to have a super-national, universal nature.

How could Christianity and Buddhism become 'world-religions' by breaking through the national character of their predecessors? This could be done by great religious personalities such as Jesus or Gautama Buddha, who were concerned, not necessarily with the nature and destiny of a particular nation but rather with the very nature and universal suffering of human existence. Their teachings, which contain their universal understandings concerning the origin of human suffering and the way towards salvation, were later formalized into systematic and metaphysical doctrines. At the same time, their religions evolved religious orders and institutional organizations, with Jesus or Gautama Buddha as their founders.

Buddhism, which was introduced into Japan early in the sixth century, was an Indian-born religion with a universal character in the above mentioned sense, that is, a religion with a metaphysical doctrine of man and his salvation, many holy scriptures and commentaries, and refined forms of ritual and worship. Although Buddhism was entirely foreign to the Japanese people, there was only a little conflict among the political leaders of those days until

Buddhism was officially accepted in Japan. Ever since then Buddhism has coexisted with Shinto, contributing deeply to Japanese culture and spiritual life.

When Christianity moved into the Germanic world early in the medieval age, it overwhelmed and absorbed the native religions of the Germanic peoples. Nowadays, in Europe and England, it is scarcely possible to find native religions or folklore beliefs in their living forms, as they originally existed among the Teutonic and Anglo-Saxon races, while Christianity is almost completely dominant in those areas. By contrast, in spite of its universal character and profound and systematic doctrine, Buddhism did not eliminate the native religions of the countries into which it was introduced. The different attitudes of Christianity and Buddhism toward other religions may be said to come from the very nature of their essential doctrines. Christianity is based on the only God who commands his people 'you shall have no other gods before me' (Ex. 20:3) and Jesus Christ who says, 'I am the Way, and the Truth and the Life: no man comes unto the Father but by me' (John 14:6). This monotheistic character of Christianity promoted a somewhat exclusive attitude towards other faiths and entailed an elimination of native religions in the countries into which it moved.

On the other hand, Buddhism does not preach the idea of the only God who is the exclusive creator, ruler, and judge of the universe, but the principle of dependent co-origination, or relationality, relational origination or dependent causation. This idea of dependent co-origination signifies that everything in and out of the universe, without exception, co-originates and co-ceases, and each is dependent on each other; nothing whatsoever exists independently. This means that there is no God who is self-existing. Even the divine and the human, the holy and the secular, nature and the supernatural, are completely mutually dependent. This is why, with its universal and elaborate doctrine, Buddhism did not eliminate Shinto on its introduction to Japan.

Another reason for the coexistence of Buddhism and Shinto may be said to come from the character of Shinto and the Japanese people. Shinto, in its original form, had no doctrinal system and no theoretical structure by which it could respond to foreign religions and thoughts. In addition, the essential nature of Shinto is not contradictory to that of Buddhism. The character of the Japanese people also was helpful in this respect. A Japanese appreciates synthesis rather than analysis, harmony more than logical consistency. This character of the Japanese people is also related to another of their characteristics. Whereas the Japanese are always eager to introduce foreign cultures, they carefully maintain the traditional one and gradually create a new form of culture through synthesis. We should not, however, overlook that in the characteristics just enumerated there exists an underlying laxity in critical thinking and an easy obedience to authority.

After some conflict among the political leaders of those days, Buddhism was accepted by the Japanese people, and developed rapidly among the upper classes, and then gradually among ordinary people, too. As I mentioned before, however, in spite of its universal nature and systematic doctrine, Buddhism did not drive Shinto away; but has always coexisted with it. The history of their coexistence, which has lasted for more than fourteen centuries, is, of course, not simple. In the course of this history, the syncretism of Shinto and Buddhism has been significant. There has been a deepening and dogmatization of Shinto, and the Japanization of Buddhism through their mutual contact. There have also been counter reactions to these developments, that is, attempts to purify Shinto's own essence from the influences of Buddhism and vice versa. In this process of mutual interaction, Confucianism has intermittently been a participant and, after the Meiji Restoration, Western culture as well. Consequently, the history of Shinto and Buddhism in Japan is indeed a complicated historical drama.

Nowadays there are more than eighty thousand Shinto shrines and many Shinto-orientated new religions with massive followings. Every New Year's Day, thousands and thousands of people visit shrines in urban and rural districts. At a ceremony for the commencement and the completion of an atomic nuclear study institute, Shinto priests are invited to perform a purification ritual. For instance, in front of a highly mechanized huge nuclear fusion reaction device a Shinto priest, dressed in traditional Shinto official robes, waves a branch of a holy tree to perform a purification ritual. A so-called 'progressive' critic may say that this is merely an anachronistic comedy. Before criticizing such phenomena cynically, we should try to understand the background of these social phenomena and the Japanese mentality which after all makes these practices possible. It may not be wrong to say that Japan is the only highly industrialized nation which still preserves its ancient native religious faith and ritual in their living forms. Such pluralism or multivalue system is one of the characteristics of Japanese society.

Now, I will clarify the nature of Shinto and Buddhism in a little more detail.

II

I said earlier that originally Shinto was the way of life for ancient Japanese people, and it included their views of the world and of life. To the ancient Japanese, nature was not something opposed to them and therefore not something to be overcome. Nature in Japan is not a bleak and severe desert but a mild natural environment covered with green. The ancient Japanese understood themselves as an intimate part of nature, realizing 'life' as a common element to man and nature. To the Japanese, animals and plants, and even stones and mountains, possessed the power of speech. They felt a mystical power in the 'life' of man and nature. Life and its mystical power was that which made everything exist as such, and the most existentially real entity.

The term 'Shinto', which was used to distinguish the ancient Japanese way of life from the newly introduced foreign religion, Buddhism, literally means 'Way of *kami*.' Although *kami* 神 is often translated as 'God,' I think this translation is misleading for Western minds. By *kami*, ancient Japanese referred not to the creator or ruler of the universe in the Christian sense, but to something unusual and superior in which they felt the remarkable mystical power of life. Thus, not only persons distinguished in their social status and abilities, but also large majestic rocks, old high trees, special mountains such as Mt Fuji, rivers, and oceans were called *kami* and reverenced as such. In this case, 'Something unusual and superior' includes something especially bad, awful, and harmful as well as something especially good, precious, and helpful. Thus thunder (*kami nari*), storms, dragons, wolves (*ō kami* (or *ōh kami*)) and so on were equally called *kami*. Accordingly, it has been said that there are *yao yorozu no kami*, 八百萬の神 eight million *kami*. Thus, it is not that we are surrounding the only *kami*, but that we are surrounded by many, many *kami*.

The ancient Japanese who had engaged in agriculture from long, long ago reverenced nature, praying to good entities for their beneficence and to bad entities to not harm their harvests. Among other things, water, wind, sun, storm, and so on were the most familiar *kami*. Besides nature, distinguished and superior personages such as the Emperor, the chief, or hero were regarded as *kami*.

What the ancient Japanese felt surprise and joy about more than anything else was the mystery of something being born or appearing, whatever it might be. It is for this reason that *Musubi no kami* 産霊の神, i.e. *kami* of generation, was regarded as the highest *kami*. Generation (the act or process of generating) is the most remarkable function of the mystical power of life. The theogony and cosmogony included in Japanese mythology show the story of *kami* bearing the world, countries, islands, and other *kami*. Not creation but generation is the basic principle of Japanese mythology.

The Judeo-Christian tradition emphasizes creation rather than generation. God created the world by his word, which is the expression of his will. According to Genesis, among the creatures, to man alone was ascribed the *imago dei* through which he can respond to the Word of God. Thus, man as a ruler of all creatures has a personal relationship with God, the Creator. Based upon the divine–human relationship in terms of 'word' or 'will,' all other doctrines such as original sin, incarnation, suffering, redemption, salvation, last judgment, and so on take place.

Shinto, which bases itself on the principle of generation, is quite different. First, when God's creation is emphasized, there is a clear distinction between creator and the created. The created cannot become creator. In the case of generation, however, that which was generated then becomes that which generates. There is no sharp contrast between them, but rather a continuity. Secondly, the fundamental factor of generation is not 'will' but 'life.' The emphasis of will leads to a distinction between man and nature, and thereby promulgates anthropocentrism in creatures. In contrast, the emphasis upon 'life' opens a common dimension for man and nature, and discourages anthropocentrism and any tension between creator and the created.

Western philosophy has two major philosophical currents: idealism and materialism. Idealism emphasizes idea, spirit, or human reason and intellect. Materialism reduces nature to lifeless matter and ultimately regards man as an impersonal mechanism. The conflict between the two 'isms' is very serious in that their views are diametrically opposed to each other and thus lead people to a disintegrity.

Shinto, though naive in a certain sense, offers neither idea nor matter as fundamental to reality, but rather a third principle – life. It is a vital force which can provide a synthesis of idea and matter. Ancient Shinto understood birth as appearance from the invisible world to the visible world by the mystical power of life, while it regarded death as disappearance or hiding from the visible world in the invisible world. Death is abominated and is regarded as something defiled that must be purified. There is no concept of death as 'the wages of sin.' Birth and this visible world are positive realities, while death and the other world are merely negative aspects of the former. The standard for beings is this actual world. And this world is understood to be based on a mystical power of life which manifests the function of generation and development. Mankind is also understood to be rooted in this mystical power of life and to communicate with nature through the power of life.

Further, ancient Shinto understood evil and sin as defilement or pollution. Thus, evil and sin are not innate or original to man but are something added to man which should be and can be purified. So purification is an important ritual of Shinto. There is no idea of absolute evil and eternal punishment in Shinto.

Neither good nor truth, but purity, is the highest value for Shinto, and neither evil nor falsity, but defilement, is the most remarkable anti-value. And the sense of purity and defilement is somewhat aesthetic rather than moralistic. Shinto's idea of purity, however, may be said to include good, truth, and beauty within itself. This can be seen through Shinto's use of the mirror as a symbol of the value of purity, and its emphasis upon *seimei-shin*, 清明心 , pure and bright mind, and *shōjiki*, 正直 , honesty.

The song of Motoori Norinaga (1730–1801), an outstanding scholar of 'national learning' of the Tokugawa era, well expressed the spirit of Shinto and the Japanese mind:

Shikishima no yamato gokoro o hitotowaba
敷島の大和心を人とはば
Asahi ni niou yamazakurabana
朝日に匂ふ山櫻花

If one asks me
what the Japanese mind is,
let me answer,
'Cherry blossoms of mountains, fragrant in the rising sun.'

The way of life realized in ancient Shinto is the fundamental driving force of the Japanese people, and has been consistently working at the basis of Japanese history. Today it still, consciously or unconsciously, exists in the depth of the Japanese mind.

III

Now let me outline what Buddhism is. Buddhism understands that the fundamental problem of human existence is life-and-death, and shows a way to free ourselves from this problem. The way is to awaken to Buddhahood and to become a Buddha. The term Buddha, unlike the term God, does not refer to something supernatural or transcendental, but to one who awakens to the truth of the universe, i.e., the truth of dependent co-origination. The historical Buddha is the first Buddha who awakened to the truth, but he is *not the only* Buddha. Anyone can become a Buddha if he or she awakens to the truth of dependent co-origination. There are no exceptions to this potential for awakening. Indeed, Buddhism ultimately teaches the necessity of awakening to our being originally enlightened. It also emphasizes that 'All living beings without exception have Buddhahood.' Thus, denying anthropocentrism, Buddhism opens up a common dimension for human beings and other living beings, i.e., the dimension of 'life.' Buddhism furthermore says 'Mountains, rivers, and the earth attain Buddhahood.' This means not only the living beings but everything in nature, living or non-living, has Buddhahood. Thus you may see that both Shinto and Buddhism understand human beings as a part of nature, and, denying anthropocentrism, put human beings on a common basis with nature. For this reason I mentioned before that Shinto and Buddhism are not contradictory to one another.

There is, however, an important difference between Shinto and Buddhism. As I mentioned, Shinto finds 'life' as the real entity in everything in nature, including mountains, rivers, and the earth, but Buddhism does not necessarily do so. The common basis of man and nature, for Shinto, is 'life' whereas that for Buddhism is *suchness* (*tathatā*) which is another term for Buddhahood. *Suchness* means that everything is realized as it is in its own particularity or in its original nature. Shinto understands life with a mystical power as the most real entity and death as something defiled that must be purified. Buddhism, however, takes death much more deeply and emphasizes that life and death are inseparable and that it is essential not to overcome death, but to be liberated from *life-and-death itself*. Are we moving from life to death? No! At any moment of our life we are living and at the same time we are dying. If we grasp our life not from without, but from within, we must say that without dying there is no living, and without living there is no dying. Living and dying are like the two sides of a sheet of paper which cannot be separated from each other. A rigid separation of life and death is an abstract and unreal conceptualization.

Then why does Buddhism ground human beings in a dimension common to human beings and nature? In Buddhism, the life–death transmigration, as the fundamental problem of man, is understood to be fully eliminated only when it is taken as a problem of more universal nature than that of man's life and death. In other words, man's life–death transmigration is fully eliminated only when it is understood as the more universal problem of generation and extinction common to all living beings or, more basically, as the most universal problem of being and non-being, which is common to all beings, including living and non-living. This means that in Buddhism the problem of life–death for human beings, though fundamental to them, is wrestled with and eliminated as the problem of being–non-being in a dimension of trans-human, universal nature. Unless the impermanence or mutability which is common to all beings is overcome at the root of a person's existence, this problem of life and death cannot be properly and definitely resolved. In this way, Buddhism opens up a dimension common to human beings and nature.

But, how can the problem of being and non-being be eliminated? We usually are attached to life and try to avoid death; we appreciate being, and dread non-being. In so doing, however, we limit ourselves by adhering to an opposition and conflict between life and death, or between being and non-being. To resolve the problem of being and non-being it is necessary to go beyond the very opposition between being and non-being. And to go beyond the conflict between being and non-being is to realize the dependent co-origination of being and non-being, of life and death. In the Western spiritual tradition, being has taken priority over non-being. In contrast, in the Eastern spiritual tradition, particularly in Buddhism, neither being nor non-being is given priority over one another. They are dependent upon and inseparable from each other. This realization is essential to overcome the seeming conflict between them and to awaken oneself to absolute Emptiness and real freedom. However, absolute Emptiness is not merely empty in the ordinary sense. Since it is beyond being and non-being, absolute Emptiness includes both being and non-being. In this sense absolute Emptiness is at the same time absolute Fullness. In the realization of absolute Emptiness, both being and non-being coexist, and one can freely put being and non-being, life and death to practical use, without being involved in their conflicts.

In this connection, let me quote a discourse by a Chinese Zen master of the T'ang dynasty:

> When I did not yet practice Zen Buddhism, to me a mountain was a mountain, and water was water; after I got an insight into the truth of Zen, I thought that a mountain was not a mountain and water was not water; but now that I have really attained the abode of final rest, to me a mountain is really a mountain and water is really water.

The symbol of Buddhism is a lotus flower. In spite of rising out of dirty mud, a lotus flower is pure and beautiful. Its purity is the purity realized through mud; likewise human passions can be regarded as 'mud' in terms of attachment to life or being and dread of death or non-being. And yet, it is in and through human passions that Buddhahood can often be awakened. The cherry blossom and lotus flower are equally pure. While cherry blossoms are most fragrant when they are in the rising sun, a lotus flower is especially beautiful because it rises out of mud.

IV

Let me conclude this chapter with a few remarks concerning comparative religion. Western scholars often mention such distinctions as monotheism versus polytheism, personal God versus impersonal Dharma, prophetic religion versus natural religion, presupposing that the former, that is monotheism, personal God, and prophetic religion are higher than the latter, that is polytheism, impersonal Dharma, and natural religion. What is the basis of this evaluation?

I do not begrudge an appreciation of the religious significance of monotheistic, prophetic religion, and of a personal God. At the same time, however, I wonder whether it is the *only* basis for evaluating the religions of human beings. Is creation higher than generation in its religious significance? Is life-principle lower than will-principle in our religious life? Does not Christian personalism lead to anthropocentrism among creatures, and thereby promote man's estrangement from nature? Cannot the value of purity open up a significant value-dimension as a synthesis of good, truth, and beauty? Does not the idea of mountains and rivers attaining to Buddhahood suggest something inspirational to the Western mind?

As you know, however, Japan is changing, and the West is also changing. Now East and West have come together in a dialogue on a scale and depth never experienced before. Japan has eagerly studied Western culture for more than one hundred years. Recently, Japan has advanced economically and technologically to a degree well comparable with Western countries, but her understanding of Western religion and philosophy is still insufficient. On the other hand, in the West people have become somewhat acquainted with certain aspects of Japanese culture and literature, but their understanding of Japanese religion and thought is still quite limited. It is now urgently necessary to deepen our mutual understanding in the deeper dimension of religion and thought without which the truly harmonious one world cannot be built.

17

Zen in Japan

In this chapter I will clarify several characteristics of Zen in Japan which differ somewhat from those of Chinese Zen. I will also consider the character of Zen culture, culture inspired by Zen, which was created in the Muromachi period (1393–1573) and flourished until the early part of the Tokugawa period (1603–1867).

In writing this chapter, I have drawn heavily from D. T. Suzuki's writings, especially *Zen and Japanese Culture*. I am also indebted to Father Heinrich Dumoulin's book, *A History of Zen Buddhism*, which includes an excellent account of the history of Zen in Japan.

The characteristics of Zen in Japan I shall examine are: (1) the close relationship between Zen and the warrior class; (2) the congeniality between the Buddha Dharma and the Dharma (law) of the state; (3) the spread of Zen amongst the populace; and (4) the development of cultural forms based on Zen.

THE CLOSE RELATIONSHIP BETWEEN ZEN AND THE WARRIOR CLASS

When Zen was introduced to Japan in the Kamakura period (1185–1333), the warrior class readily supported it. As described in the following, Zen and the warrior class had a close relationship in Japan, a phenomenon which did not arise in China.

Eisai (1141–1215) is the actual founder of Zen in Japan. He went to Sung China twice, and on his second journey (1187–1191) received the seal of enlightenment in the Huang-lung line of transmission of the Lin-chi sect. When he returned to Japan and tried to spread Zen in his home country, he met with the opposition of the monks of Mt Hiei, the powerful headquarters of the Tendai Buddhist sect, which was closely connected with the imperial court and the nobility. Eisai, however, was supported by the Shogun Minamoto Yoriie, and became the first abbot of the newly built Kenninji Temple in Kyoto, and later the abbot of another temple, Jūfukuji in Kamakura. The Hōjō family, which succeeded the Minamotos, also supported Zen and invited eminent Chinese Zen masters to Kamakura, including Lan-ch'i Tao-lung (Rankei Dōryū) and Tsu-yüan Wu-hsüe (Sōgen Mugaku). They introduced the strict and severe Zen practice of Sung China, and their way of Zen had much appeal for the warrior class. The Shogun Hōjō Tokiyori (1227–1263) himself was most eager in his rigorous practice of Zen under the guidance of Lan-ch'i. The second Shogun, Hōjō Tokimune (1251–1284), received spiritual instruction from Tsu-yüan during the national crisis of the Mongolian invasion of Japan.

There are several reasons for Zen's attractiveness to the warrior class. Whereas in Kyoto the imperial house and the nobility had a refined cultural tradition and close ties with Shingon and Tendai Buddhism, in Kamakura the newly rising warrior class lacked such a cultural tradition and religious affiliation. Hence they looked for their cultural and religious resources in Zen, the newly introduced form of Buddhism. But how was Zen able to give the warrior class spiritual guidance and influence their fighting spirit? In this regard D. T. Suzuki's following comments are helpful:

Although it has never actively incited them to carry on their violent profession, it has passively sustained them when they have for whatever reason once entered into it. Zen has sustained them in two ways, morally and philosophically. Morally, because Zen is a religion which teaches us not to look backward once the course is decided upon; philosophically, because it treats life and death indifferently. This not turning backward ultimately comes from the philosophical conviction; but, being a religion of the will, Zen appeals to the samurai spirit morally rather than philosophically. From the philosophical point of view, Zen upholds intuition against intellection, for intuition is the more direct way of reaching the Truth. Therefore, morally and philosophically, there is in Zen a great deal of attraction for the military classes. The military mind, being – and this is one of the essential qualities of the fighter – comparatively simple and not at all addicted to philosophizing finds a congenial spirit in Zen. This is probably one of the main reasons for the close relationship between Zen and the samurai.[1]

Another reason D. T. Suzuki offers is as follows:

> Zen discipline is simple, direct, self-reliant, self-denying; its
> ascetic tendency goes well with the fighting spirit. The fighter is
> to be always single-minded with one object in view: to fight,
> looking neither backward nor sidewise. To go straight forward in
> order to crush the enemy is all that is necessary for him. He is
> therefore not to be encumbered in any possible way, be it
> physical, emotional, or intellectual. Intellectual doubts, if they are
> cherished at all in the mind of the fighter, are great obstructions
> to his onward movement, while emotionalities and physical
> possessions are the heaviest of encumbrances if he wants to
> conduct himself most efficiently in his vocation. A good fighter is
> generally an ascetic or stoic, which means he has an iron will.
> This, when needed, Zen can supply.[2]

The ascetic discipline of Zen and its straightforwardness not only
guided the fighting spirit of the warriors but also deepened their
spiritual life.

This relationship between Zen and the warrior continued into the
Tokugawa era. For instance, Takuan Sōhō (1573–1645), a spiritual
teacher of the Shogun Tokugawa Iemitsu, emphasized *Fudōchi*, Prajñā
Immovable, as essential for swordsmanship. According to Takuan,
'Prajñā (wisdom) remains immovable, though this does not mean the
immovability or insensibility of such objects as a piece of wood or
rock. It is the mind itself endowed with infinite mobilities: it moves
forward and backward, to the left and to the right, to every one of ten
quarters, and known no hindrances in any direction. Prajñā
Immovable is this mind capable of infinite movements.'[3]

In the above book Suzuki summarizes the ideas of Takuan as
follows:

> The mind must be left to itself, utterly free to move about
> according to its own nature. Not to localize or partialize it is the
> end of spiritual training. When it is nowhere it is everywhere.
> When it occupies one tenth, it is absent in the other nine tenths.
> Let the swordsman discipline himself to have the mind go on its
> own way, instead of trying deliberately to confine it somewhere.[4]

Takuan's so called Prajñā Immovable does not exclude the movability
of the mind. Rather, it preserves the fluidity of the mind and yet is

immovable in the depths of one's being. But, how is this possible? On this point Suzuki comments as follows:

> The fluidity of mind and Prajñā Immovable may appear contradictory, but in actual life they are identical. When you have one, you have the other, for the Mind in its suchness is at once movable and immovable, it is constantly flowing, never 'stopping' at any point, and yet there is in it a center never subject to any kind of movement, remaining forever one and the same. The difficulty is how to identify this center of immovability with its never-stopping movements themselves. Takuan advises the swordsman to solve the difficulty in his use of the sword as he actually stands against the opponent.[5]

Motion in stillness, stillness in motion – this is a practice common to Zen and swordsmanship. In this way, unlike in China, Japanese Zen and the warrior class maintained a close relationship through which swordsmanship became deeply spiritual.

THE CONGENIALITY BETWEEN THE BUDDHA DHARMA AND THE DHARMA OF THE STATE

In Japan the Buddha Dharma (*buppō*) and the Dharma of the state (*ōbō*) are not antagonistic to one another, but rather harmonious or even congenial.

When Eisai was persecuted by the monks of Mt Hiei, he issued a treatise entitled *Kōzen gokokuron* (The Spread of Zen for the Protection of the Nation). In this treatise, he emphasizes that Zen is the heart of Buddhism and the Ultimate Truth of many religions, and that the propagation and permanent rooting of Zen in the country is nothing other than the protection of the nation. In contrast, Dōgen (1200–1253), another founder of Zen in Japan and the initiator of Japanese Sōtō Zen, strongly insisted that a monk should not involve himself in political power or civil authority. Accordingly, when he met the opposition of the monks of Mt Hiei, Dōgen moved to a secluded area deep in the mountains of Echizen and concentrated on training his disciples. 'Even when he was given the purple robe by the ex-Emperor Go-saga, who evidently was deeply impressed by his spirituality, Dōgen refused the honor. When a messenger came for the third time from the court, Dōgen accepted but never wore the garment.'[6] With Dōgen as a notable exception, many Zen masters in the Kamakura and the Muromachi period were open to royal authority or the Dharma of the state. Although they clearly realized that the Buddha Dharma transcends the Dharma of the state, they did not take the two Dharmas as mutually exclusive. Rather, they held that the Buddha Dharma gives a spiritual foundation to the Dharma of the state.

In China, there was the idea that Buddhists should not pay homage to rulers. In the case of a great man like Hui-chung (Echū Kokushi, d. 769), Emperor Su-tsung (r. 756–762) grew more and more eager to have him come, and when he went to the palace in a carriage the Emperor himself helped draw it to welcome him … And Hui-chung nonchalantly let himself be pulled. Such scenes often occurred in China. To take another example, there was Lau-tsan (Ransan Oshō, n.d.) who – however many times the T'ang Emperor Te-tsung (r. 779–805) summoned him – would not leave his mountain cave. In China there was this way of thinking where one did not consider keeping a person's company simply because he happened to be emperor.[7]

In Japan, the situation is somewhat different. Musō Soseki (1275–1351) was one of the most outstanding Zen figures in the early Muromachi period. After receiving the seal of enlightenment from Kennichi (Bukkoku Kokushi, d. 1314), Musō lived an austere life in seclusion. However, upon the urgent invitation of Emperor Go-daigo, he could not help but accept the position of abbot of Nanzenji, at one time the most prestigious Zen temple in Kyoto. After Go-daigo passed away in despair in Yoshino following a struggle with the Shogun Ashikaga Takauji, Musō urged the latter to build a temple for the repose of the spirit of the deceased emperor. In this way, Tenryūji was built in the western outskirts of Kyoto in 1339, with Musō as the first abbot.

In addition to his great achievements in literature and art, Musō exerted himself to mediate between the two imperial dynasties which were then divided. He became the spiritual teacher of seven emperors and was bestowed the title Kokushi (National Teacher) by each of the seven. It was Musō's desire that both the Buddha Dharma and the Dharma of the state should prosper.

Another Zen master of the early Muromachi era, Shūhō Myōchō (Daitō Kokushi, 1282–1337), further illustrates the relation between the Buddha Dharma and the Dharma of the state. Myōchō rigorously practiced Zen under his master, Nampō Jōmyō (Daiō Kokushi, 1235–1309), who had gone to China and become a dharma heir of the Chinese master Hsü-t'ang Chih-yü. After attaining enlightenment, Myōchō secluded himself as a beggar under the Gojō Bridge in Kyoto. In 1326, when the Emperor Go-daigo erected Daitokuji Temple in the northern part of Kyoto, Myōchō became the first abbot of the temple. His manner of Zen was pure and strict. Unlike Musō, Myōchō did not move beyond religion into literature, art, or politics. He strictly confined himself to Zen practice. However, when the Emperor Hanazono, who had great admiration for Myōchō's spirituality, invited him to give talks on Buddhism, Myōchō agreed to such interviews with the Emperor. On one occasion, Myōchō, while properly attired in a robe, appeared before the Emperor and seated himself, at which point the Emperor remarked, 'Is it not a matter of unthinkability that the Buddha Dharma should face the Royal Dharma (the Dharma of the state) on the same level?'

Myōchō replied, 'Is it not a matter of unthinkability that the Royal Dharma (the Dharma of the state) should face the Buddha Dharma on the same level?'

The Emperor was pleased with the reply.[8]

In this *mondō* (question and answer), both the Emperor and Myōchō used the same term, 'unthinkability.' However, the Emperor used it in a relative sense, whereas Myōchō uttered it in the absolute sense. When the Emperor said, 'Is it not a matter of unthinkability that the Buddha Dharma should face the royal Dharma on the same level?' he was still limited by the notion that the Emperor is superior to all of his subjects, including Myōchō. The Emperor was asking how it was possible for the Buddha Dharma to come face-to-face with the Royal Dharma, and it was in connection with this questioning that he used the term 'unthinkability.' He thus took 'the matter of unthinkability' as something outside of himself. At first glance, Myōchō's reply, 'Is it not a matter of unthinkability that the Royal Dharma should face the Buddha Dharma on the same level?' looks like a mere response to the Emperor's words. It indicates more than that, though – Myōchō was beyond all distinctions. He did not take the matter of unthinkability as something outside of himself, Rather, he was an embodiment of the unthinkable Reality. He was not talking *about* it, but was talking *out of* it. In his response, he took the Royal Dharma (the Dharma of the state) as a manifestation of the unthinkable Reality, and identified it with the Buddha Dharma. He was not questioning, but rather affirming that the Royal Dharma (the Dharma of the state) as a manifestation of the unthinkable Reality is in no way different from the Buddha Dharma.

And so, relatively speaking, the Buddha Dharma and the Dharma of the state are different in their form and function. However, absolutely speaking, that is, speaking from Reality which itself is beyond thinking, they are not two, but one.[9]

This is the implication of the above *mondō* between Myōchō and the Emperor Hanazono. As we see in this *mondō*, the Buddha Dharma and the Dharma of the state are not mutually exclusive, but rather congenial. This is one salient characteristic of Zen in Japan.

THE SPREAD OF ZEN AMONGST THE POPULACE[10]

In the Kamakura period, Zen was first supported by Shoguns and the warrior class. It later appealed to the imperial court and the nobility. Yet from the outset Zen was concerned with all of the people in Japanese society. Eisai proclaimed the ideal behind this concern: 'To possess in one's heart the great compassion of the Bodhisattva and to become the kindly father of all sentient beings.'[11] He was ready to help the poor whenever necessary. Similarly, Dōgen emphasized that in the Buddha Dharma there is no distinction between high and low, rich and poor, man and woman, priest and layman.[12] In fact, his followers included many lay men and women.

One factor which contributed to the spread of Zen amongst the populace was the development of *kana-hōgo* (Dharma words in a completely Japanese style). Up until the Kamakura period, Buddhist leaders in Japan wrote their treatise and discourses in Chinese. In the Kamakura period, some of them began to write in Japanese so as to reach the general population. This development of *kana-hōgo* also indicates the Japanization of Zen. The Zen of Sung China was introduced to Japan in the Chinese language, but for it to be indigenized, it had to be expressed in Japanese. The popularization of Zen and the Japanization of Zen went hand in hand in the development of *kana-hōgo*. The *kana-hōgo* of such National Teachers as Shōichi, Daiō, and Daitō appeared successively. This tendency was more and more pronounced in the Muromachi period. The National Teachers Musō, being gifted in literature and language, explained Buddhist doctrine and Zen teaching in simple Japanese terms close to daily life. Among his many writings, *Muchū-mondō* is a collection of his Dharma talks given in answering the questions raised by Ashikaga Tadayoshi, brother of Shogun Ashikaga Takauji. In *Muchū-mondō*, Musō shows a way from popular folk belief to authentic Buddhist faith. The work is unique in dealing directly with concrete problems of secular life in relation to Zen. Musō takes up such problems as craving, secular happiness, social fame, and political ethics. *Muchū-mondō* was printed during Musō's lifetime – a rare case in those days – and, through many reprints, was widely read among the people in subsequent centuries.

Following Musō, two Rinzai masters, Bassui Tokushō (1327–1387) and Gettan Sōkō (1326–1389), were particularly popular among the people by virtue of their excellent *kana-hōgo*. Bassui attached importance to the things of this world by saying: 'All of the things of this world and the things of the Buddha-world without exception are the beneficial power for enlightenment.'[13] And yet he stressed, 'When the things of this world approach, they must be severed. When the things of the Buddha-world approach, these likewise must be severed. When the delusions approach, they must be severed. Enlightenment must be severed. The Buddha must be severed, The Mara (devil) must be severed.'[14] In this way, he tried to show the people a higher point of Zen which is beyond both the things of this world and the things of the Buddha-world.

Gettan preached that 'There is no special way for *zazen* and Zen practice. The point lies in just seeing and just doing. Beginners do not know this. They ask a teacher to give a *kōan* whatever it may be. If they think to be able to grasp the Buddha Dharma in this way it is like trying to beat the sun with a stick. Which day or which time can he successfully beat it?'[15] Gettan thus emphasized that the point of Zen practice is 'just seeing and just doing' rather than 'asking a teacher to give a *kōan*.' This way of practices is accessible to all lay people. Gettan also emphasized that in order to realize this way of practice in the true sense, 'you should be like a baby who knows neither being nor non-being, neither the law of the world nor the Law of Buddha'; in other words, 'without any calculation, you should not have even an expectation of enlightenment. Just believe that only the truth-seeking mind is the true awakening.'[16] In this way Gettan tried to lead laymen to a way of authentic Zen.

Ikkyū (1394–1481) was the most popular Zen master of the latter half of the Muromachi period. He was pure-hearted and anti-authoritarian. He severely criticized the degeneracy of the established Buddhist orders and the hypocrisy of the monks. In so doing, he identified himself with the laity. However, Ikkyū was extreme in his identification with the people. He was closely associated with the people of all levels of society. He behaved freely like a depraved priest. Going beyond precepts, Ikkyū mingled with the general population. His contribution to making Zen familiar to the people was remarkable. And in this action, he never lost the pure heart and insight into genuine Zen through which he was highly appreciated and loved by the populace.

Two of the many notable Zen masters active in the renewal of Zen during the Tokugawa period were Bankei Yōtaku (1622–1693) and Hakuin Ekaku (1685–1768).

Bankei rejected kōan practice and never used the staff or shouting in his teaching. If someone came to him for instruction, he just talked to the person intimately, using the common language of everyday life, and asked the person to examine his personal affairs by himself. Throughout his life he emphasized awakening to and living as the unborn Buddha-heart:

> If you live in accordance with the Buddha-heart and do not become confused, you need seek no further enlightenment. Only sit with the Buddha-heart, be only with the Buddha-heart, sleep and arise only with the Buddha-heart, and dwell only with the Buddha-heart! If your normal walking and standing, your sitting and standing, your sitting and reclining, are the work of a living Buddha, nothing further remains to be done. To sit contentedly in the consciousness of the Buddha-heart is *zazen*. It is *zazen* perpetually, and not merely during the time of practice called *zazen*.[17]

Bankei was eloquent and tireless in teaching the Way, and he helped many people overcome the difficulties of daily life. He did so by speaking from his profound religious realization of the unborn Buddha-heart in language anyone could understand. Thus his 'unborn Zen' spread widely amongst the people of the various classes of Japanese society.

Hakuin was born several years before the death of Bankei. Unlike the latter, Hakuin strongly emphasized the importance of kōan practice on the basis of his won *satori* experience, which he attained only after serious kōan practice lasting for many years. He reformed the traditional form of kōan practice and established a new kōan system. He also invented an entirely new kōan, that of 'the sound of a single hand'. In his treatise, *Yabukoji*, Hakuin says, 'When you clap together both hands, a sharp sound is heard; when you raise the one hand, there is neither sound nor smell – Listen now to the sound of a single hand!'[18] Hakuin was convinced that through grappling with this kōan one comes more easily across the Great Doubt which is the necessary accompaniment of Great Enlightenment.

In addition to the reformation of kōan practice, Hakuin was extremely active in developing Zen among the people. Being highly learned in Buddhist doctrine and Chinese classics, Hakuin addressed himself in simple daily language without distinctions of rich and poor, high and low, or male and female. Further, he presented his teachings in a folk-song style so that even the illiterate could understand them without reading.

In Ming China, Zen became popular amongst the populace. However, that Zen mixed with the *nembutsu*, the recitation of the name of Amida Buddha. This type of alloyed Zen was practiced in Tokugawa Japan as well. But through the enormous activities of Zen masters such as Bankei and Hakuin, The unadulterated, genuine form of Zen became popular in Japan to a degree unparalleled in the history of Chinese Zen.

THE DEVELOPMENT OF CULTURAL FORMS BASED ON ZEN

As we saw before, in the Muromachi period, Zen developed greatly and came to flourish with the capital, Kyoto, as its center. Such names as Musō Soseki, Nampō Jōmyō, Shūhō Myōchō and Kanzan Egen mark the high points of Zen in those days. Zen inspired people to create particular forms of culture. This Zen-inspired culture includes the art of tea, flower arrangement, Noh theater, Zen painting, Zen calligraphy, and Zen gardening. Zen was able to create such cultural forms because it has no particular form of religious dogma and thus can freely enter into various aspects of non-religious mundane life. In his book *Zen and Japanese Culture*, D. T. Suzuki says, 'It is a significant fact that the other schools of Buddhism have limited their sphere of influence almost entirely to the spiritual life of the Japanese people; Zen has gone beyond it. Zen has entered internally into every phase of the cultural life of the people.'[19]

In this connection, we must have a closer look at the difference between Zen and the other schools of Buddhism. Certain other schools of Buddhism have created their own painting, sculpture, and literature, too. For instance, Pure Land Buddhism has its own style of painting. However, its subject matter is usually limited to something sublime and peculiar to its religion, such as Amida Buddha, his attendants, or visions of the Pure Land. Non-religious, mundane subjects cannot become the subject matter of Pure Land paintings. On the other hand, in Zen painting, the subject matter is not limited to religious objects such as Śākyamuni Buddha or Bodhidharma. Even a monkey, pine tree, or natural landscape can become the subject matter of a Zen painting. Zen can express itself freely, whether the subject matter is 'religious' or not, for in reality Zen is not limited by the idea of the 'religious,' the idea of the 'holy,' or the idea of the 'sacred.' It is well known that when Emperor Wu asked Bodhidharma 'What is the first principle of the holy truth?' Bodhidharma answered, 'Vast emptiness, and nothing in it to be called holy.' In the 'Verses of the Ten Ox-Herding Pictures,' Kuo-an Chi-yüan (Kakuan Shion), a Zen master of the Sung dynasty, said:

> Worldly passions fallen away,
> Empty of all holy intent.
> I linger not where Buddha is, and
> Hasten by where there is no Buddha.

As these examples show, Zen is neither profane nor holy, secular nor sacred, mundane nor religious. It is vast emptiness: śūnyatā. However, this does not mean that Zen is a mere empty void. Rather, this means that Zen is free from the distinction or duality between the profane and the holy and can freely enter into these two realms to express itself. Hence Liang K'ai's Śākyamuni and Mu-ch'i's persimmons are equally appreciated in the sense that both of them are expressions of the spirit of Zen which is the realization of śūnyatā. This is again why Zen could enter into the mundane life and create various forms of culture. Precisely the realization of śūnyatā is the root and source of the freedom and creativity in Zen.

In the following I would like to talk about two matters in the hope that I may further clarify the character of Zen culture. The first is Kakuzō Okakura's *The Book of Tea* and his explanation of the tea-room, and the second is Paul Tillich's observation of the stone garden of Ryōanji Temple in Kyoto.

In his well-known book, *The Book of Tea*, Okakura explains that the tea-room (the *sukiya*) means the Abode of Fancy, the Abode of Vacancy, or the Abode of the Unsymmetrical. As for the third meaning, that is, the Abode of the Unsymmetrical, he says 'It (the *sukiya*) is an Abode of the Unsymmetrical in as much as it is consecrated to the worship of the Imperfect, purposely leaving something unfinished for the play of the imagination to complete.'[20] He also says:

> The dynamic nature of their (the Taoist and Zen) philosophy laid more stress upon the process through which perfection was sought than upon perfection itself. True beauty could be discovered only by one who mentally completed the incomplete. ... In the tea-room it is left for each guest in imagination to complete the total effect in relation to himself.[21]

From the above-quoted words we see that Okakura understands the dissymmetry of the *sukiya* (1) as the imperfect in the process toward perfection and (2) as something unfinished for the play of the imagination to complete. This understanding I do not agree with. In this understanding, Okakura presupposes a duality of perfection and imperfection, and on that presupposition he understands the dissymmetry of the *sukiya* as something imperfect which is in a process toward perfection. 'Perfection' is grasped as an ideal end to arrive at, whereas the dissymmetry is understood as something which, being imperfect, has not yet arrived at the end and which is halfway to being completed by one's imagination. However, the Zen working behind the art of tea is beyond the duality of perfection and imperfection. It does not take the perfection as an ideal end to arrive at. Being a realization of *śūnyatā*, Zen is free from both perfection and imperfection, and expresses itself freely in both ways. The dissymmetry of the *sukiya*, for instance, is a self-expression of *śūnyatā*. It is not something imperfect that has yet to arrive at the perfection. On the contrary, it is beyond perfection.[22]

Accordingly, it is not that in the face of Zen art one should employ imagination to complete something unfinished. Instead, one may realize the *śūnyatā* which is working through the dissymmetry.

Next, I would like to discuss Paul Tillich's observations of the rock garden of Ryōanji Temple. Paul Tillich, one of the most outstanding theologians of our time, came to Japan in 1960 and stayed there for several months. In his book *Christianity and the Encounter of the World Religions,* Tillich described as follows a statement he heard concerning the rock garden: 'These expressively arranged rocks are both here and, at the same time, everywhere in the universe in a kind of mystical omnipresence, and their particular existence here and now is not significant.'[23] Tillich calls this statement 'a quite conspicuous expression of the principle of identity'[24] which is characteristic to Buddhism.

However, Buddhists would say more exactly that 'these expressively arranged rocks are both here and, at the same time, everywhere in the universe' not in a kind of mystical omnipresence but in *śūnyatā*. The empty garden covered by white sand expresses *śūnyatā*. True *śūnyatā*, however, is by no means mere emptiness, i.e., emptiness as the privation or negation of things which are. True *śūnyatā* is neither emptiness nor fullness in the relative sense. It is an active and creative Emptiness which, precisely in being empty, allows everything and everyone to be and work in their particularity. It may be helpful here to mention that *śūnyatā* is not a state which is objectively observable, but a realization which is subjectively or existentially realized. In Zen *śūnyatā* is the subjective realization of true Self. The several rocks with different shapes and characters which are placed here and there on the white sand are nothing but the self-expression of the true *śūnyatā* which makes everything stand as it is and function freely. It can properly be said that 'these expressively arranged rocks are both here and, at the same time, everywhere in the universe' because they are just here and now in the empty garden both as they are and, at the same time, as the self-expression of true *śūnyatā* which is beyond time and space. If 'their particular existence here and now (were) not significant' the white sand garden would express a dead emptiness, which Mahāyāna Buddhism, especially Zen, severely rejects as a false equality or annihilatory nothingness. The very existence of these rocks in the empty garden equally and uniquely shows the real profoundness, the creative profoundness, of true Self which embraces everything and everyone in their identity and individualization.

In short, the Buddhist rock garden is the product of the creative expression of the realization of *śūnyatā* as one's true Self. A visitor may be strongly impressed by it because he, in looking at it, is drawn into that *śūnyatā* which is expressed in, and as, a rock garden, a *śūnyatā* which, even through not yet consciously realized by the visitor, is nevertheless the root-source of his existence, i.e., his true Self.[25]

In the above, as the characteristics of Zen in Japan, I discussed the close relationship between Zen and the warrior class, the congeniality between the Buddha Dharma and the Dharma of the state, the development of Zen among the populace, and Zen-inspired cultural forms. There are, of course, other distinctive characteristics of Japanese Zen. Here I have touched upon a few. Since Zen itself is without form, it can penetrate into any form of human culture, yet one cannot clearly grasp the various forms of Zen culture without realizing *śūnyatā*, which is working as the creative force in them.

18

The Japanese View of Truth

In order to clarify the basic character of Japanese people and culture this chapter tries to elucidate the Japanese view of truth and a few other key notions appearing in the intellectual history of Japan.

In the *Manyōshū*, the ancient collection of Japanese poetry, Japan is called 'a country where people, following implicitly the way of the gods, are not argumentative.' Regarding this, the eminent modern Japanese philosopher Nishida Kitarō (1870–1945) had made the following comment:

This means only that argument is not indulged in for argument's sake and concepts are not bandied about for their own sake. As Motoori Norinaga explained in *Naobi no Mitama*,[1] 'It [the way of the gods] is nothing but the way of going to things,' which should be taken in the sense of going straight to the true facts of things. Going to the true facts, however, does not mean following tradition out of mere force of custom or acting in direct response to subjective emotions. Going to the true facts of things must also involve what we call a scientific spirit. It should mean following the true facts of things at the expense of self. 'Not being argumentative' should be understood as not being self-assertive, but bending one's head low before the true facts. It ought not to be a mere cessation of thinking or readiness to compromise: to penetrate to the very source of things is to exhaust one's own self.[2]

This well expresses the Japanese view of truth. Japanese have traditionally esteemed the individual fact rather than the universal principle, and have found reality in unification with things attained by 'emptying' themselves. This involves a sharp contrast to the Western way of thinking.

From the time of ancient Greece the Western mind is generally rationalistic. This bent is conspicuous in Greek philosophy, Roman law, and modern European natural science. It emphasizes idea, *logos*, *ratio*, reason, law, and so forth. The rational is always universal, essential, necessary, eternal, absolute, and is thus regarded as the prototype of phenomenal things because the latter are taken to be merely particular, non-essential, contingent, temporal, relative, and are thus regarded as copies of the former. However, the traditional Japanese view, rooted in 'not being argumentative,' does not regard phenomenal things merely as particular, non-essential, and contingent. They are something deeper than that; not copies of the universal, but rather in themselves prototypes for the universal. In other words, individual things or facts have a profound meaning which cannot be exhausted by rational thinking: it is the individual thing that makes the universal possible. The characteristic Japanese way of life sees in an individual fact something essential and absolute which cannot be measured by a universal law, and takes it as the norm for life and behavior.

This esteeming of the individual fact rather than the universal principle is not mere irrationalism or mysticism, for it does not altogether exclude the rational: it penetrates the depth of a fact by breaking through the rational framework. It is beyond both relative rationality and relative factualness, beyond both rationalism and irrationalism.

The ancient Japanese view of life regarded 'facts' not as objects of intellectual cognition but as something realized through one's subjective activity. A fact is established inseparably by the active and not by the conscious self. That an individual fact is regarded as essential, eternal, and absolute is not therefore based on cognition or contemplation, but on action. One realizes truth by devoting oneself to practice in and through facts. Only in concentrative, egoless practice does the reality of a fact reveal itself.

In the West, cognition and action are first clearly separated, and are subsequently to be connected. Cognition of an objective truth precedes an action to realize it. For the ancient Japanese, action rather precedes cognition. For just as an individual fact does not follow a universal principle, action does not follow cognition. More strictly speaking, in realization of truth, action and cognition as well as subject and object are not separated from one another, but go together as one.

This is why the Japanese term *makoto*, which means 'truth,' also indicates 'sincerity' or 'faithfulness.' Literally, *ma* means 'true' and *koto* 'fact' and 'word.' Therefore, *makoto* signifies 'true fact' as distinguished from a fiction, and at the same time 'true word,' which in turn stands for 'sincerity' or 'faithfulness.'

In other words, *makoto* may be said to denote a fact as it is without modification by human intellect, and at the same time a spirit to express it as it is, at the expense of ego-self. This is not unrelated to the fact that *makoto* has also been regarded historically as one of the fundamental ideas of Japanese aesthetics. In short, *makoto* involves cognitive, moral, and aesthetic truth because in *makoto* god and man, man and nature, man (self) and man (other) are understood to be completely fused.

Buddhism, which has nourished Japanese spirituality since the sixth century, deepened this original view of truth. Buddhism clearly denies the existence of something universal, rational, or transcendental behind facts. It realizes the 'no-thingness' behind facts. This means an individual fact is completely and definitely realized as it is – irreducible to anything – through the realization of 'no-thingness.' This as-it-is-ness[3] backed up by the realization of 'no-thingness' stands for truth in the Buddhist sense. And as-it-is-ness is realized respectively in and through every individual fact. Accordingly, although all individual facts are different from each other in their individuality, they are equal in their as-it-is-ness. The Buddhist expression, 'Differentiation as it is is equality; equality as it is is differentiation' indicates this.[4]

As-it-is-ness as truth is most clearly formulated in the fourfold world view in Kegon (Hua-yen) doctrine. The first three levels are: (1) the world of phenomena, (2) the world of noumena, and (3) the world of unhindered mutual interpenetration of noumena and phenomena as the higher unity of (1) and (2). Kegon philosophy, however, goes beyond (3) and takes as ultimate reality (4) the world of unhindered mutual interpenetration of phenomena and phenomena. This is simply another way of expressing 'as-it-is-ness' in which all individual facts, being different from each other in their individuality, are equal and undifferentiated in their as-it-is-ness. This is the basis for wisdom and compassion in Mahāyāna Buddhism which took deep root in the Japanese soil.

The truth in this sense is not an object of contemplation, but the ground of existence and action. It should not be taken as a goal of cognition but as a point of departure for a life of truth.

'As-it-is-ness' is not contradictory to the modern scientific view of truth. In fact there is a similarity between them in the sense that both are realized at the expense of the subjective self. This is why, referring to the Japanese tendency to go to the true facts of things, Nishida stated that it 'involves what we call a scientific spirit.' However, we should not overlook their essential difference.

Modern science presupposes nature as an objective entity and investigates the objective law functioning in natural phenomena through an emptying of subjectivity on the part of the scientist. In this case, emptying of subjectivity means to objectify and rationalize natural phenomena. Therefore modern science accepts and follows phenomena as they are, and at the same time reconstructs them through a process of rationalization. Here the human intellect is the law-giver of nature. In modern science, human subjectivity is not altogether negated but rather strengthened through a partial self-negation. Contrary to this, emptying of subjectivity in the case of 'as-it-is-ness' indicates a return to and realization of the ground prior to any subject–object duality by an emptying of the corresponding objectivity as well. This is not an objectification or rationalization of nature but a total realization of the ground or the groundless ground (*Ungrund*) from which the very opposition of man and nature, subject and object emerges. Realization of as-it-is-ness is nothing but the realization of this ground which is neither subjective nor objective and yet really both subjective and objective.

This may be exemplified by the Japanese garden. Unlike the typical European garden which is designed by a geometrical arranging of flowers, trees, stones, and so forth, the Japanese garden looks somehow natural and non-artificial. Nevertheless, it is man-made, and in this sense it is not different from the European garden. But Japanese gardeners build a garden so that not the slightest trace of human artifice is left behind, thereby allowing nature to manifest itself in its essential form. They do not arrange rocks and plants merely from an artificial human point of view or try to copy wild nature. Theirs is an artificiality leaving no trace of itself, i.e., in a form more 'natural' than is found in wild nature. In Japanese gardens the highest reach of artificiality is rather the deepest reach of nature, with both being brought into oneness beyond their relativity.

This is true not only with Japanese gardens but also with most traditional Japanese disciplines in which the view of truth in terms of 'as-it-is-ness' is consistent. However, this view of truth includes the danger of falling into mere anti-rationalism, shallow intuitionism, or sheer behaviorism. At least, it does not intellectually analyze, synthesize, and reconstruct objects. This is the reason rationalistic philosophy, experimental natural science, and technology by which man can overcome nature did not develop in Japan until after the Meiji Restoration in 1868.

Intuitionism excluding rationality is poor, whereas rationalism excluding intuition is abstract. By overcoming the dangers inherent in it, the Japanese view of truth in terms of *makoto* and 'as-it-is-ness' must be developed and deepened to include Western forms of rationalism, which have produced science, logic, law, technology, and the like. This is a future task for Japanese and may be their contribution to the coming one world, the establishment of which will necessitate a critical, constructive synthesis of East and West.

Notes

Chapter 2 The Core of Zen: The Ordinary Mind is Tao

1. Zenkei Shibayama, *Zen Comments on the Mumonkan* (New York: Harper & Row, 1974), p. 141.
2. Ibid., p. 141.
3. Ibid., p. 142 (adapted at points).
4. Ibid., p. 143.

Chapter 3 'Life and Death' and 'Good and Evil' in Zen

1. Paul Tillich, *The Courage to Be* (New Haven: Yale University Press, 1952), p. 34.
2. Paul Tillich, *Systemic Theology*, Vol. I (Chicago: University of Chicago Press, 1951), p. 189.
3. II Cor. 4:10.
4. See Heb. 2:14f.
5. In the *Lin-chi Lu*, one of the most important Zen records of China, we read as follows:

   > Encountering a Buddha, killing the Buddha;
   > Encountering a Patriarch, killing the Patriarch;
   > Encountering an Arhat, killing the Arhat;
   > Only thus does one attain liberation and disentanglement from all things, thereby becoming completely unfettered and free.

6. When Emperor Wu of the Liang dynasty asked Bodhidharma, 'What is the ultimate principle of the holy truth?', the First Patriarch replied: 'Emptiness, no holiness.'
7. Paul Tillich, *The Courage to Be*, p. 186.
8. See D. T. Suzuki, *Essays in Zen Buddhism*, Second Series (London: Rider, 1933), p. 219 ff.

Chapter 4 Emptiness

1. Garma C. C. Chang, *The Buddhist Teaching of Totality: The Philosophy of Hwa Yen Buddhism* (University Park: Pennsylvania State University Press, 1971), p. 60.
2. Frederick J. Streng, *Emptiness: A Study in Religious Meaning* (Nashville: Abingdon Press, 1967), pp. 199–200.
3. Ibid., p. 204.
4. *The Tannishō*, trans. by Ryukoku Translation Center, Kyoto, 1966, p. 22.
5. John Cobb and Christopher Ives (eds), *The Emptying God: A Buddhist–Jewish–Christian Conversation* (New York: Orbis Press, 1990), pp. 162–169.

6. *Mūlamadhyamakakārikā* (24:11). See Streng, *Emptiness: A Study in Religious Meaning*, p. 213.
7. *The Emptying God*, p. 9.
8. Ibid., p. 14. See also Hans Küng, *Does God Exist? An Answer for Today* (New York: Random House, 1981), pp. 684–865.
9. The author is indebted to Gadjin Nagao, *Chūkan to Yuishiki* (Tokyo: Iwanami, 1978), pp. 6–21; *The Fundamental Standpoint of Mādhyamika Philosophy*, trans. John Keenan (Albany: SUNY Press, 1989); and Yuuichi Kajiyama, *Kū no Ronri* (Tokyo: Kadokawa, 1980).
10. Streng, *Emptiness*, p. 213.
11. Ibid., p. 183.
12. Nagao, *The Fundamental Standpoint of Mādhyamika Philosophy*, p. 23.
13. Ibid., p. 31 (with adaptation).
14. Masao Abe, *Zen and Western Thought*, ed. William R. LaFleur (Honolulu: University of Hawaii Press, 1985), p. 178 (with adaptation).
15. Ibid., p. 49 (with adaptation).
16. Ibid., p. 178 (with adaptation).
17. See also *The Emptying God*, pp. 29–33.

Chapter 5   God, Emptiness, and the True Self

1. Elmer O'Brien, *Varieties of Mystical Experience* (New York: Holt, Rinehart & Winston, 1964), pp. 86–88.
2. William Johnston, 'Zen and Christian Mysticism,' *The Japanese Missionary Bulletin*, Vol. XX (1966), pp. 612–613.
3. D. T. Suzuki, *An Introduction to Zen Buddhism* (London: Rider, 1969), pp. 54–55.
4. Ibid., pp. 52–53.

Chapter 7   Education in Zen

1. 'Gakudō-yōjinshū,' *Dōgen Zenji Zenshū*, ed. Ōkubo Dōshū (Tokyo: Chikuma Shobō, 1970), p. 255.
2. Ibid., p. 256.
3. Ibid.
4. A. H. Armstrong, *An Introduction to Ancient Philosophy* (London: Methuen, 1965), p. 31.
5. Ibid.
6. D. T. Suzuki, *An Introduction to Zen Buddhism* (London: Rider, 1960), p. 49.
7. *The Record of Lin-chi*, trans. by Ruth Fuller Sasaki (Kyoto: Institute for Zen Studies, 1975), p. 4.
8. *Tsung-men wu-k'u* by Ta-hui P'u-chüeh (Daie Sōkō).
9. *The Record of Lin-chi*, p. 51.
10. A term coined by Takeuchi Yoshinori.
11. Donald Keene, *Landscapes and Portraits* (Tokyo: Kōdansha International, 1971).

Chapter 8 Substance, Process, and Emptiness: Aristotle, Whitehead, and Zen

1. *Metaphysics*, 1028, b2, tr. by W. D. Ross.
2. *Categories*, 4 a 10.
3. Alfred North Whitehead, *Process and Reality* (New York: Free Press, 1969) (hereafter *PR*), p. 122. As for the discussion of Whitehead's philosophy in this chapter the author owes a debt to John B. Cobb and David Ray Griffin, *Process Theology: An Introductory Exposition* (Philadelphia: Westminster, 1976) and the following two papers: Ivor Leclerc, 'Whitehead's Transformation of the Concept of Substance,' *Philosophical Quarterly*, 3 (1953) and D. Bidney, 'The Problem of Substance on Spinoza and Whitehead,' *Philosophical Review*, Vol. 45 (1936).
4. *PR*, p. 28.
5. *PR*, p. 45.
6. *PR*, p. 45; also see p. 209.
7. *PR*, p. 208.
8. *PR*, p. 78.
9. *PR*, p. 241.
10. *PR*, p. 71.
11. *PR*, p. 339.
12. *PR*, p. 81. It is noteworthy that although Whitehead strongly attacks the subject–predicate habits of thought as something 'which had been impressed on the European mind by the overemphasis on Aristotle's logic during the long medieval period' he seems to attribute that habit not to Aristotle himself but to his followers.
13. *PR*, p. 65.
14. *PR*, pp. 34/35.
15. *PR*, p. ix.
16. *PR*, p. 320.
17. *PR*, p. 135.
18. *PR*, p. 528.
19. *PR*, p. 32.
20. *Pratītya-samutpāda* is a combination of the terms *pratītya*, that is, 'Having come on account of', and *samutpāda*, that is, 'arising.' *Pratītya-samutpāda* is often translated as 'dependent origination' or 'dependent co-origination.' These translations may indicate that origination or co-origination is dependent on something else. To avoid this misunderstanding 'co-dependent origination' may be a better one because it indicates the origination takes place co-dependently.
21. Masao Abe, 'Zen and Western Thought,' *International Philosophical Quarterly*, Vol. X, No. 4, December 1970, p. 506.
22. *Lakṣaṇa* has at least two meanings: (1) sign, mark, or form in distinction from *dhātu* (nature or essence); (2) essential nature as synonym of *dhātu*, *prakṛti* or *svabhava*. Here in this chapter the term *lakṣaṇa* is taken in the first sense.
23. Frederick J. Streng, *Emptiness, A Study in Religious Meaning* (Nashville: Abingdon Press, 1967) p. 63.

Chapter 9 The Problem of Death in East and West: Immortality, Eternal Life, Unbornness

1. The Greek word corresponding to *nephesh* is *psyche*. In the Bible, *nephesh* expresses the life which is in creatures, that is, soul, and it is often translated into Japanese as *inochi* (life). In contrast, the Greek term corresponding to *rûah* is *pneúma*; *rûah* indicates life which has been given by God that is spirit. The Greek term corresponding to *bāsār* is *sarx*, besides which in the New Testament, the word *sōma* is used to express the body.

    Since these terms are not necessarily used in a single sense throughout the Bible, we must be careful in interpreting them. Yet in the Bible, body (*sōma*) and soul (*psyche*) are not understood as dualistically opposed, as in the case of Greek philosophy (again, meanings implied in these terms are not the same as in the case of Greek philosophy). A conspicuous feature of Hebraism is that the body is the expression of the soul and both are understood as a unity.

    However, Paul saw in man a duality of what is corruptible namely flesh (*sarx*), and what is incorruptible, namely spirit (*pneúma*); the former he calls 'the outer man,' and the latter 'the inner man' (2 Cor. 4:16, Rom. 7:22). In this way he establishes a dualism of body and soul (*sōma* and *psyche*), the body belonging to the outer man, as things pertaining to natural life in general, and the soul to the inner man namely the spirit (*pneúma*), that is linked to God. Thus, he says, 'For the mind that is set on the flesh is hostile to God' (Rom. 8:7), so the flesh that is the power of sin and death wars in man with the spirit, and 'For those who live according to the flesh set their minds on the things of the flesh, but those who live according to the Spirit set their minds on the things of the Spirit' (Rom. 8:5). It must be fully borne in mind, however, that this Pauline teaching of the dualistic complication of spirit and flesh is one in which man still lives in relation to God, even as man, having both inner and outer natures, feels the tension of whether to entrust to himself to and follow the Holy Spirit that is the creative power of God; the Pauline teaching remains essentially different from Plato's philosophy where we find an opposition of soul and body without the relation to a transcendent personal God.

    Thus in Paul, in contrast to the fact that for one who lives following the flesh, as neither the body (*sōma*) nor the soul (*psyche*) as things that are 'perishable' (1 Cor. 15:42), namely as comprising the animate body (*sōma psychikon*), death can be avoided, it is promised that for one who follows the Spirit of God, and in whom dwells the spirit of Christ, the body (*sōma*) will become 'the temple of the Holy Spirit' and 'member of Christ' (1 Cor. 6:15), and after death will rise again as a spiritual body (*sōma pneumatikon*).

2. Oscar Cullman, *Immortality of the Soul or Resurrection of the Dead?* (New York: Macmillan, 1958), p. 22.

3. Karl Barth, *Credo: Die Hauptprobleme der Dogmatik dargestellt im auschluss an das Apostolische glaubeskenntnis*, 3rd edn (München: C. Kaiser, 1935), p. 75.

4. Ibid., p. 78.
5. Norbert Luyten, Paul Portmann, Karl Jaspers and Karl Barth, *Unsterblichkeit* (Basel: F. Reinhardt, 1957), p. 50.
6. K. Rahner, *Foundations of Christian Faith: An Introduction to the Idea of Christianity* (New York: Crossroad, 1982), p. 221.
7. Ibid., p. 220.
8. Emil Brunner, *Eternal Hope*, trans. Harold Knight (Philadelphia: Westminster Press, 1954), p. 106.
9. Ibid., p. 111.
10. Alan Richardson (ed.), *A Theological Word Book of the Bible* (London: SCM Press, 1950), p. 60, cf. Heb. 2:14 ff.
11. There is a kind of resurrection story in Buddhism, too, about the appearance of Śākyamuni from the golden casket. But this story is hardly essential to Buddhist teaching, unlike the resurrection of Jesus Christ which is essential to the Christian teaching, and actually constitutes the core of its faith. This story may be interpreted merely as a kind of legend customarily attached to the biography of a great religious personality.
12. The eightfold negation is 'neither birth nor extinction, neither interruption nor permanence, neither sameness nor difference, neither coming in nor going out.'
13. Norman Waddell (trans.), *Unborn: The Life and Teachings of Zen Master Bankei* (San Francisco: North Point Press, 1984).
14. Dōgen's *Shōbōgenzō Shōji* (Birth and Death), trans. Norman Waddell and Masao Abe, *Eastern Buddhist*, Vol. V, No. 1 (Spring 1972), p. 79.
15. The doctrine of right, semblance, and final (*shōzōmatsu* 正像末) Dharma refers to the three periods of the Buddhist teaching after the Buddha's decease. It was especially influential during the Sui and T'ang dynasties in China and during the Heian and Kamakura periods in Japan. There are different views as to the duration of these periods. According to the one prevalent in the Kamakura period, the first period, believed to last 1000 years, is called the right Dharma (*shōbō* 正法), in which Buddhist doctrine, practice, and enlightenment all exist; the second period of 1000 years is the period of the semblance, 'imitative' Dharma (*zōhō* 像法), in which doctrine and practices exist without enlightenment; the third and last period of 10 000 years is that of the latter or final Dharma (*mappō* 末法), in which only the doctrine remains.
16. I consider it crucial to clarify the difference between the 'instant' (*Augenblick*) in Christianity such as used by Kierkegaard, and the Buddhist notion of 'moment' (*kṣaṇa*) in order to clarify the differences between the theory of time and history of each religion.
17. Tao-wu 道吾, a Zen master of the late T'ang dynasty, went one day with his disciple Chien-yüan 漸源 to visit a family in mourning. Chien-yüan was a young monk seeking for truth, and was especially concerned with the problem of life and death. To learn what was in his master's mind, Chien-yüan knocked on the coffin and said, 'Living or dead?' Tao-wu instantly responded, 'Living? I tell you not! Dead? I tell you not!' 'Why not?' asked the disciple. To this the master replied, 'I won't tell! I won't tell!' (*Iwaji, iwaji* 道じ道い). Chien-yüan, however,

had not yet come to the point of realization for himself. When they were halfway on their homeward walk, he again accosted his master, saying, 'Master, please tell me about it. If you don't I will strike you down.' The master responded, 'As for striking, it is up to you. As for talking, I have nothing to tell you.' Thereupon the disciple struck him. Had Tao-wu at that time proclaimed the immortality of soul or eternal life to Chien-yüan, the disciple might have been satisfied. But the master had repeated the same negative answer, and Chien-yüan was quietly sent away. Later, he went to Shih-shuang 石霜 , one of Tao-wu's disciples, and telling him his story, he asked the monk to enlighten him on the matter. Shih-shuang also said, 'Living? I tell you not! Dead? I tell you not!' 'Why won't you tell me?' demanded Chien-yüan. 'I won't tell! I won't tell!' repeated Shih-shuang. This instantly opened up Chien-yüan's mind. See *Pi-yen-lu* (Blue Cliff Record), Case 55. See also D. T. Suzuki, *Essays in Zen Buddhism*, Second Series (London: Rider, 1933), p. 219 ff. and Masao Abe, '"Life and Death" and "Good and Evil" in Zen,' *Criterion*, Vol. 9, No. 1 (1969), p. 10 (Chapter 3 in this volume).

Chapter 10   Śūnyatā as Formless Form: Plato and Mahāyāna Buddhism

1. Arthur H. Armstrong, *An Introduction to Ancient Philosophy* (London: Methuen, 1949), p. 37.
2. Ibid.
3. Timaeus 51, Dic.
4. Armstrong, op. cit., p. 41.
5. Edvard Zeller, *Philosophie der Grieschen*, 6th edn. (Leipzig O. R. Reisland: 1920), Vol. 1, p. 149.
6. Armstrong, op. cit., p. 38.
7. Parmenides, 132 a; Zeller, op. cit., pp. 149–150.

Chapter 11   The Self in Jung and Zen

1. Walpola Rahula, *What The Buddha Taught* (New York: Grove Press, 1959), p. 51.
2. Ibid., p. 56.
3. Ibid., pp. 52 and 57.
4. D. T. Suzuki, Erich Fromm, and Richard DeMartino, *Zen Buddhism and Psychoanalysis* (London: George Allen & Unwin, 1960), p. 32.
5. On Hisamatsu's life and thought, see my articles, 'A Buddhism of Self-Awakening, Not a Buddhism of Faith' in *Añjali: A Felicitation Volume Presented to Oliver Hector de Alwis Wijesekera on his Sixtieth Birthday* (Peradeniya, Ceylon, 1970), pp. 33–39; and 'Hisamatsu's Philosophy of Awakening,' *The Eastern Buddhist*, Vol. XIV, No. 1 (Spring 1981), pp. 26–42; for his obituary, see pp. 142–147 of the latter.
6. The dialogue was subsequently published in Carl G. Jung and Shin'ichi Hisamatsu, 'On the Unconscious, the Self and the Therapy,' *Psychologia*, Vol. 11 (1968), pp. 25–32. In 1960, when Satō Kōji, the editor of *Psychologia*, first asked Jung for permission to publish a transcript of the dialogue, Jung refused. This was partly because Jung was already seriously ill and could not see to its revision, and partly because he felt

that a satisfactory mutual understanding had not been reached in the course of that brief encounter. Several years after Jung's death, a transcript of the dialogue in German was sent to Hisamatsu by Jung's secretary Frau Aniela Jaffé, which later appeared as the English translation cited here.

7. Page numbers from *Psychologia* dialogue are given in parentheses.
8. C. G. Jung, *Aion: Contributions to the Symbolism of the Self*, Collected Works, Volume 9.2 (New York: Pantheon Books, 1959), pp. 3, 5.
9. C. G. Jung, *Archetypes and the Collective Unconscious*, Collected Works, Vol. 9.1 (New York: Pantheon Books, 1959), p. 43.
10. D. T. Suzuki, *Essays in Zen Buddhism*, First Series (London, Rider, 1949; reprinted 1973), p. 190; adapted.
11. The eighteenth-century Zen master Hakuin was an exception; his disciple Tōrei discusses some of the psychological problems that may occur in the process of Zen practice in his *Shūmon mujintō ron* (The Inexhaustible Lamp of Zen), Taishō 81: 581a–605b.
12. Jung, *Aion*, p. 6.

Chapter 12   Time in Buddhism

1. Oscar Cullmann, Christ and Time: *The Primitive Christian Conception of Time and History* (Philadelphia: Westminster, 1964).
2. The other two of the three fundamental doctrines of Buddhism are 'all elements are non-substantial' and '*nirvāṇa* is quiescence.'
3. Dōgen, *Shōbōgenzō*, Uji, trans. Norman Waddell (1979) *Eastern Buddhist*, Vol. XII, No. 1 (1972), p. 126.
4. An exception to this is Sarvāstivāda in Abhidharma Buddhism which holds the reality of the three time periods (past, present, future). Nāgārjuna, however, criticizes Sarvāstivāda by emphasizing that everything including time is non-substantial and empty.
5. *Aṣṭasāhasrikā Prajñāpāramitā*, ed. by P. L. Vaidya (Darbhanga, 1960), p. 8.
6. For example, *Millindapañha*, ed. by V. Trenckner, p. 49–52.
7. The twelve links of causation are as follows: Because of ignorance (*avidyā*), mental constituents (*saṃskāras*) arise; because of mental constituents, consciousness (*vijñāna*) arises; because of consciousness, name and form (*nāmarūpa*) arise; because of name and form, the six sense organs (*sadāyatana*) arise; because of the six sense organs, contact (*sparśa*) arises; because of contact, feeling (*vendanā*) arises; because of feeling, craving (*tṛṣṇa*) arises; because of craving, grasping (*upādāna*) arises; because of grasping, becoming (*bhava*) arises; because of becoming, birth (*jati*) arises; because of birth, old age and death (*jaramarana*) arise. Due to old age and death, ignorance arises and thus the wheel begins again. *Buddhism*, ed. by Charles S. Prebish (University Park: Pennsylvania State University Press, 1978), pp. 33–34.

Chapter 14   Transformation in Buddhism

1. Dōgen, *Shōbōgenzō*, 'Zenki' and 'Shōji,' trans. Norman Waddell and Masao Abe, *Eastern Buddhist*, Vol. 5, No. 1 (1972), pp. 70–80.
2. Gorgias, 493A.

3. I Cor. 6:19.
4. Rom. 6:23.
5. Rom. 6:3–7.
6. II Cor. 4:16.
7. *Saṃyutta Nikāya*, ii: 178f.
8. Masao Abe, 'Kenotic God and Dynamic Śūnyatā,' in John Cobb and Christopher Ives (eds), *The Emptying God: A Buddhist–Jewish–Christian Conversation* (New York: Orbis, 1990).
9. *Deshinhōyō*: Taishō 48, no. 2012.
10. *Mumonkan*, Case 47: Taishō 48, no. 2005.
11. Rom. 5:12.
12. *Shōdaijōron (Mahāyāna-saṃgraha)*: Taishō 31, no. 1594.
13. Masao Abe, 'Hisamatsu Shin'ichi: 1889–1980,' *Eastern Buddhist*, Vol. 14, No. 1 (1981), pp. 142–149.
14. Masao Abe, 'Hisamatsu's Philosophy of Awakening,' *Eastern Buddhist*, Vol. 14, No. 1 (1981), pp. 26–42.
15. Shin'ichi Hisamatsu, *Zen and the Fine Arts* (Tokyo: Kodansha International, 1975), pp. 45–52; Hisamatsu Shin'ichi, 'Ultimate Crisis and Resurrection, Part II: Redemption,' *Eastern Buddhist*, Vol. 8, No. 2 (1975), pp. 37–65.
16. Hisamatsu, 'Ultimate Crisis and Resurrection,' op. cit., p. 64.
17. Ibid., pp. 64–65.
18. Masao Abe, 'A History of FAS Zen Society,' *FAS Newsletter*, Autumn (1984) pp. 1–12.
19. *Sekai-kyūmei* and *rekishi-kyūmei* are the author's terms. See ibid.
20. A Zen set phrase often indicating the role of the Zen master who should train at least a small number of enlightened disciples throughout his life.
21. Hisamatsu, 'Ultimate Crisis and Resurrection,' op. cit., p. 65.
22. Honpa Hongwanji Mission of Hawaii, *The Shinshu Seiten* (Tokyo: Kenkyusha, 1955), p. 150.
23. *Tannishō*, trans. under the general supervision of Kenju Masuyama, Ryukoku Translation Center (Kyoto: Ryukoku University, 1966), p. 22.
24. Ibid.
25. Ibid., pp. 22–23.
26. *Shinshū Shōgyō Zenshō*, Vol. II (Kyoto: Kokyo Shoin, 1953), p. 625.
27. II Cor. 4:16.

Chapter 15   Religious Tolerance and Human Rights: A Buddhist Perspective

1. Lynn A. deSilva, *The Problem of the Self in Buddhism and Christianity* (New York: Barnes & Noble Imports, 1979; repr. of 1975 original). p. 111.
2. Masao Abe, *Zen and Western Thought*, ed. William R. LaFleur (Honolulu: University of Hawaii Press, 1985), p. 284.
3. Ibid., p. 159.
4. T. O. Ling, 'Heresy,' in S. G. F. Brandon (ed.), *A Dictionary of Comparative Religion* (New York: Scribner, 1970), pp. 324–325.
5. E. A. Burtt (ed.), *The Teachings of the Compassionate Buddha* (New York: New American Library, 1955), p. 32.
6. *The Majjhima Nikāya*, Sutta 63. See Burtt, op. cit., p. 36.

7. Burtt, op. cit., pp. 36–37.
8. Ibid., p. 37.
9. Phra Khantipolo, *Tolerance: A Study from Buddhist Sources* (London: Rider, 1964), pp. 35–37. The author is indebted to this book, especially for the discussion of the Middle Way.
10. Masao Abe, 'Man and Nature in Christianity and Buddhism,' in Frederick Franck (ed.), *The Buddha Eye: An Anthology of the Kyoto School* (New York: Crossroad, 1982), p. 152.
11. *The Dhammapada: The Path of Perfection*, trans. Juan Mascaro (Harmondsworth: Penguin, 1973).
12. 'Elect, Election,' in Everett F. Harrison (ed. in-chief), *Baker's Dictionary of Theology* (Grand Rapids, Mich.: Baker Book House, 1960), p. 179.
13. *Maha-Vagga*. See Burtt, op. cit., p. 40.

Chapter 17   Zen in Japan

1. D. T. Suzuki, *Zen and Japanese Culture* (New York, Pantheon Books: 1959), pp. 61, 62.
2. Ibid., p. 62.
3. Ibid., p. 97.
4. Ibid., p. 108.
5. Ibid.
6. J. M. Kitagawa, *Religion in Japanese History* (New York, Columbia University Press: 1966), p. 127.
7. Osaka Kōryū in 'Symposium: Japanese Zen', *The Eastern Buddhist*, Vol. 10 (1977), No. 2, pp. 82, 83.
8. Adaptation of D. T. Suzuki, *The Essence of Buddhism* (Kyoto: Hōzōkan 1968), p. 15.
9. 'Symposium: Japanese Zen', *The Eastern Buddhist*, Vol. 10 (1977), No. 2, p. 85.
10. In this section I drew from Heinrich Dumoulin, *A History of Zen Buddhism* (New York: Pantheon Books 1965), pp. 179–186, 232, 233, 267.
11. *Kōzen gokokuron*, Section 8.
12. Dōgen, *Bendōwa*, trans. by Norman Waddell and Masao Abe, *The Eastern Buddhist*, Vol. 4 (1971), No. 1, p. 148.
13. *Enzan Wadeigasuishu*, cf. Shōkin Furuta, *Zen shisōshiron* (Tokyo: 1966), p. 30.
14. *Bassui kana-hōgo*, cf. Furuta, ibid., p. 30.
15. *Gettan kana-hōgo*, cf. Furuta, ibid., pp. 30, 31.
16. Ibid.
17. Cf. Heinrich Dumoulin, *A History of Zen Buddhism*, p. 233.
18. Cf. *The Zen Master Hakuin*, trans. Philip B. Yampolsky (New York: Columbia University Press, 1971), p. 163.
19. D. T. Suzuki, *Zen and Japanese Culture*, p. 21.
20. Kakuzō Okakura, *The Book of Tea* (New York: Kodansha, 1989), p. 76.
21. Ibid., p. 40.
22. See Shin'ichi Hisamatsu, *Zen and the Fine Arts* (Tokyo: Kodansha, 1975), p. 28.
23. Paul Tillich, *Christianity and the Encounter of the World Religions* (New York: Columbia University Press, 1961), p. 70.

24. Ibid.
25. Cf. Masao Abe, 'Review Article: Christianity and the Encounter of the World Religions', *The Eastern Buddhist*, Vol. 1 (1965), No. 1, pp. 118, 119.

Chapter 18   The Japanese View of Truth

1. Motoori Norinaga (1730–1801) is the founder of *kokugaku* (National Learning). Counteracting the exaggerated attention then given to Chinese literature he studied the ancient Japanese literature philologically and interpreted from a purely Japanese point of view. *Naobi no Mitama* is one of his important works.
2. Nishida Kitarō, *Nihonbunka no mondai* (The Problem of Japanese Culture) in *Nishida Kitarō zenshū* (The Collected Work of Nishida Kitarō) (Tokyo: Iwanami, 1966), Vol. XII, pp. 279–280. See also *Sources of the Japanese Tradition*, eds W. Theodore de Bary *et al.* (New York: Columbia University Press, 1963), Vol. II, p. 352.
3. Masao Abe, *Zen and Western Thought*, ed. William R. LaFleur (London: Macmillan, and Honolulu: University of Hawaii Press, 1985), pp. 103, 208, 224.
4. Ibid., pp. 177–178, 184, 209, 213.

Index